D0099736

THE ILLUSTRATED ENCYCLOPEDIA OF CAT BREEDS

THE ILLUSTRATED
ENCYCLOPEDIA OF
CAT BREEDS

Angela Rixon

THE WELLFLEET PRESS
WELLFLEET

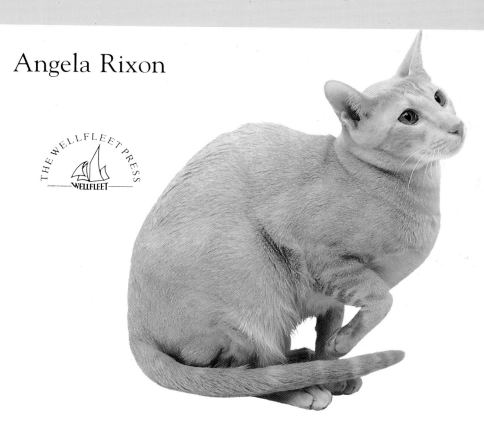

A QUARTO BOOK

Published by Wellfleet Press
114 Northfield Avenue
Edison, New Jersey 08837

This edition produced for sale
in the U.S.A., its territories
and dependencies only.

Reprinted 1997, 1998, 1999,

ISBN 0-7858-0364-5

This book was designed and produced by
Quarto Inc
The Old Brewery
6 Blundell Street
London N7 9BH

Art Director: Moira Clinch
Senior Art Editor: Penny Cobb
Designer: Karin Skånberg
Senior Editor: Sian Parkhouse
Copy Editor: Sandy Ransford
Editorial Director: Mark Dartford
Photographer: Paul Forrester
Picture Researcher: Jo Carlill
Picture Manager: Giulia Hetherington

Typeset in Great Britain by Genesis Typesetters, Rochester
Manufactured in Singapore by Eray Scan Pte Ltd
Printed in Singapore by Star Standard Industries Pte. Ltd.

INTRODUCTION

8
The Cat

11
Origins

16
Body shape

26
Behavior

32
Sexual behavior

35
Maternity

38
Breeding pedigree cats

42
Showing

46
Cat care

CONTENTS

LONGHAIRED BREEDS

58
Longhair
60 White
61 Black
62 Red
63 Cream
64 Blue
65 Blue-cream
66 Smoke
69 Cameo
70 Bicolor
72 Tabby
75 Tortoiseshell
76 Silver and Golden

78
Colorpoint
80 Solid points
82 Tabby points
84 Chocolate and lilac

SHORTHAIRED BREEDS

120
British Shorthair
122 Solid varieties
125 Bicolor varieties
126 Tortoiseshell varieties
128 Tabby varieties
132 Other varieties

134
Chartreux

136
Manx
138 Manx varieties
139 Cymric

140
Scottish Fold

142
European Shorthair
144 European Shorthair varieties

146
American Shorthair
148 American Shorthair varieties
149 Tabby varieties

154
American Wirehair

156
Exotic Shorthair
158 Solid varieties
159 Tabby and Bicolor varieties
160 Other varieties

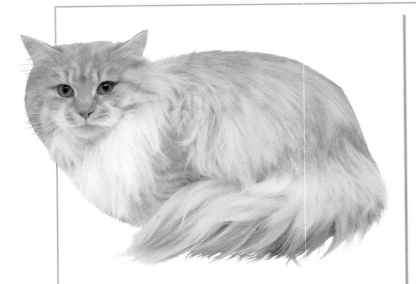

SEMI LONGHAIRED BREEDS

88
Birman
90 Solid points
92 Tortoiseshell and tabby points

94
Maine Coon
96 Solid varieties
96 Tortoiseshell and Particolor varieties
97 Smoke and shaded varieties
98 Tabby varieties

100
Ragdoll
102 Mitted
103 Bicolor
104 Colorpoint

105
Snowshoe

106
Norwegian Forest Cat
108 Solid varieties
109 Tabby varieties
110 Particolor varieties
111 Smoke and cameo varieties

112
Angora
114 Angora varieties

116
Turkish

FOREIGN SHORTHAIRED BREEDS

164
Abyssinian
166 Abyssinian varieties

168
Somali
170 Somali varieties

174
Russian Blue

176
Korat

178
Havana Brown

180
Egyptian Mau

182
Ocicat

184
Bengal
186 Bengal varieties

188
Cornish Rex
190 Cornish Rex varieties

192
Devon Rex
194 Devon Rex varieties

196
Sphynx

198
Japanese Bobtail

200
Burmese
202 Solid varieties
205 Tortoiseshell varieties

206
Tiffanie

207
Singapura

208
Tonkinese
210 Mink varieties
212 New varieties

214
Bombay

216
Burmilla
218 Burmilla varieties
221 Asian

ORIENTAL BREEDS

224
Siamese
226 Siamese varieties

230
Colorpoint Shorthair
232 Colorpoint varieties

234
Balinese
236 Balinese varieties

238
Oriental
240 Solid varieties
243 Tortoiseshell varieties
244 Tabby varieties
246 Smoked, shaded, and tipped varieties

249
Seychellois

250
Javanese

252
Index

256
Acknowledgements

INTRODUCTION

The domestic cat enjoys a special niche in human society. There are anthologies of poems and prose, encyclopedias of breeds, manuals on care, breeding and showing. Cats appear on greeting cards, stationery, and fabrics; glass and china ornaments abound – whether in natural or cartoon form, the cat is the most enduringly popular animal portrayed throughout the world.

CATS HAVE BEEN valued and protected and their history recorded since the days of the ancient Egyptians, and although their fortunes have fluctuated from time to time, they have managed to remain virtually unchanged in overall size and basic character. Today's domestic cat tolerates its relationship with humans and takes advantage of the comforts of a good home environment while retaining its independent nature.

The innate behavior patterns of the cat's wild ancestors still exist, even in a highly bred pedigree cat whose coat and conformation bear little resemblance to them. Even the most pampered of today's pet cats reacts to the thrill of hunting and retains all the physical skills and abilities of its ancestors.

Having a pet cat in the home can be therapeutic, as well as rewarding. No other pet is as clean and fastidious in its habits, or as easy to care for. Every cat is beautiful in its own way, but the very wide range of breeds, colors, and varieties of pedigree cats existing today means every cat lover can indulge his or her particular preference.

The cat is probably the most common domestic animal in most parts of the world. Wherever there are concentrated populations of people, there are groups of cats, either living as free-ranging feral animals or kept as pets to keep down rodents, insects, or snakes. Yet despite its familiarity with humans, the domestic cat manages to retain its air of mysterious independence.

A paradoxical animal, the cat can be both loving and bold. It combines caution with courage, and alternates periods of total relaxation with those of remarkable agility. It is often easy to imagine, in watching one's pet cat, its successful little mammalian ancestor *miacis*, which first evolved during the age of the dinosaurs. Small in build, the cat has always had to rely on skill and speed to escape from predators and to catch its own prey. Its specialized dentition and retractile claws helped to guarantee its survival as a

A resting ginger adorns the lid of a small tin (top left), a nursery rhyme feline family make a simple jigsaw puzzle (top), while a trio of stylized nesting cats make an unusual keepsake (left).

Even the most sophisticated of today's pedigree cats, like this Abyssinian (right), retains all of its natural hunting instincts.

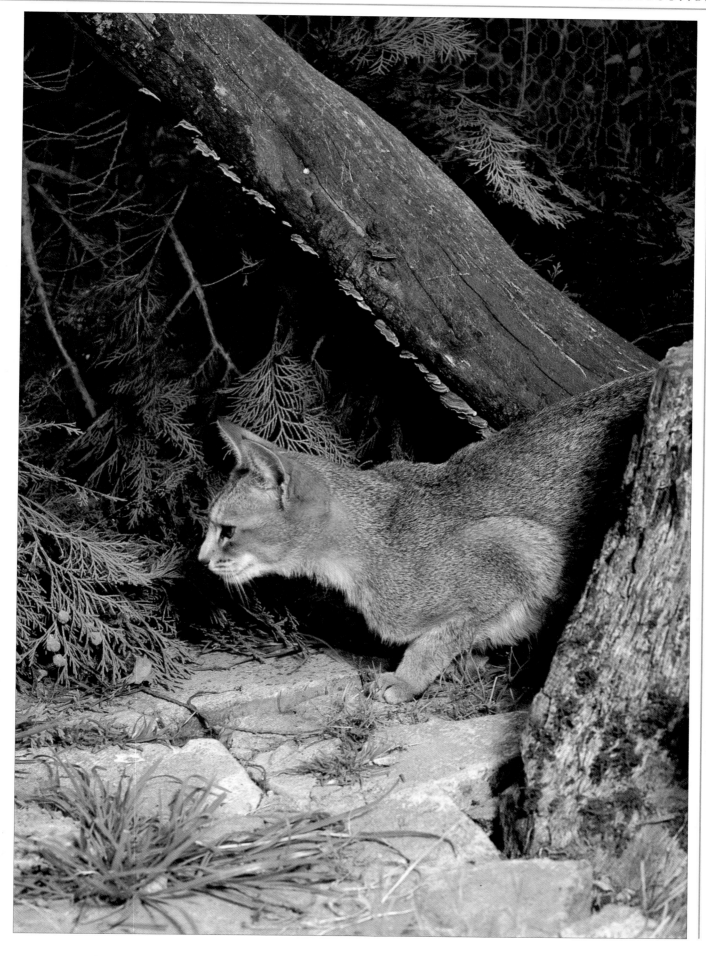

THE EVOLUTION OF THE CAT

Dinictis About 50 million years ago, this carnivorous cat-like mammal, ancestor of the cats, inhabited the earth.

Pseudaelurus Until about 25 million years ago, this relatively long-legged mammal had evolved with more cat-like features.

Felis lunensis Among several species of wild cat that evolved and lived until about 12 million years ago was Martelli's wildcat.

Felidae Today's cats, large and small. Highly developed and efficient carnivores, designed for hunting and killing.

SELECTIVE BREEDING

Over the years, cats have been selectively bred to conform to standards of points laid down by various cat associations. Here we see the extremes in type between the svelte, long-headed Oriental (left) and the heavy, round-headed Persian (below).

carnivore during its evolution, and these qualities stand the cat in good stead.

Today, the genetic make-up of the domestic cat has been so manipulated by selective breeding that some felines bear very little resemblance to those of ancient Egypt's homes and granaries. The noses of Persian cats have been reduced in size, those of the Orientals have been lengthened. Breeders have selected for heavy bone in some breeds, for light bone in others. Despite all the efforts to thwart nature, however, the basic structure of the domestic cat has been undefiled by human intervention, and the biology of the animal is the same whether it is a champion Chinchilla or a stray tabby. The great cat goddess Bast continues to watch over *Felis domesticus*, making sure that all cats remain virtually the same in size and character; affectionate, fastidious felines who are willing companions, but who will never be subordinate or subservient to humans.

The aim of this book is to show the diverse and interesting range of domestic felines throughout the world, exploring conformation, coat types, and patterns. It also examines the breeds' varying care requirements and their special characteristics, and acts as an introduction to the world of showing.

ORIGINS

A weasel-like creature called Miacis lived on Earth in the Eocene period of 50 million years ago. From this fierce, successful creature evolved countless generations of carnivores. We can recognize in those early creatures the ancestors of our domestic cats, and identify the same survival skills.

ANCIENT EGYPT
The cat was deified in ancient Egypt and, also used for the protection of the granaries and for wildfowling.

BAST, PASHT, or OUBASTED
The Cat-goddess Bast, with a sistrum, used as a sacred rattle to frighten evil gods, and a small, lion-headed aegis or shield. Both objects serve to protect the litter of kittens sitting at her feet.

As any pair of domestic cats, from anywhere in the world, will readily interbreed, it means that they are of a single species, descended from a common ancestor.

Domestication of the cat probably first took place in the Middle East, and the cats encouraged to approach people were almost certainly *Felis lybica*, the African wild cat. This is a lithe animal, very similar to a domestic tabby in color. Many of the skulls from ancient Egyptian cat cemeteries resemble *Felis lybica*, while a small proportion are of cats resembling the jungle cat, *Felis chaus*. It would appear that the ancient Egyptians tamed both types, but the African wild cat was easily the more popular, and probably more amenable to domestication.

Egypt was the greatest grain-growing area of the ancient world, and huge granaries were constructed to store the grain from good harvests for use in leaner years. As rodent controllers, cats must have been vital to the economy of those times. The ancient Egyptians also appreciated the natural link between the cat and the lion, and worshipped the goddess Bast, also called Pasht or Oubasted, who first appeared with the head of a lion, and later with the head of a cat. Bast was seen as a goddess of love, and of the moon. The cat was connected with her as love-goddess because of the animal's natural fecundity, and as moon-goddess because of the varying shape of the pupils of the cat's eyes, which were thought to enlarge and contract with

DESCENT OF THE MODERN CAT

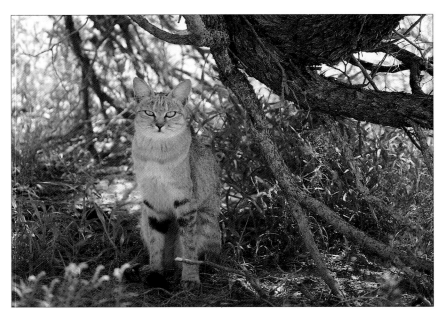

SMALL CATS
Felis

DOMESTIC CATS *F. Catus*

AFRICAN GOLDEN CAT *F. aurata*

ASIATIC GOLDEN CAT *F. temmincki*

BAY CAT *F. badia*

BLACK-FOOTED CAT *F. negripes*

BOBCAT *F. rufus*

CARACAL *F. caracal*

CHINESE DESERT CAT *F. bieti*

FISHING CAT *F. viverrina*

CARNIVORES
Carnivora

CATS
Felidae

FLAT-HEADED CAT *F. planiceps*

GEOFFROY'S CAT *F. geoffroyi*

JAGUARUNDI *F. yagouaroundi*

IRIOMOTE CAT *F. iriomotensis*

JUNGLE CAT *F. chaus*

CHEETAH *Aciononyx*

KODKOD *F. guigna*

MAMMALS

LEOPARD CAT *F. bengalensis*

LYNX *F. lynx (F. pardina)*

MARBLED CAT *F. marmorata*

LION *P. leo*

MARGAY *F. wiedi*

HERBIVORES
Herbivora

MOUNTAIN CAT *F. jacobita*

TIGER *P. tigris*

OCELOT *F. pardalis*

PALLAS'S CAT *F. manul*

LEOPARD *P. pardus*

PAMPAS CAT *F. colocolo*

PUMA *F. concolor*

**ROARING
CATS**
Panthera

CLOUDED LEOPARD
P. nebulosa*

RUSTY-SPOTTED CAT *F. rubiginosus*

SAND CAT *F. margarita*

JAGUAR *P. onca*

SERVAL *F. serval*

TIGER CAT *F. tigrinus*

SNOW LEOPARD
P. uncia

WILD CAT *F. silvestris*

*sometimes classed as a separate genera

A Roman mosaic found in the ruins of Pompeii, dating from the first century B.C., depicts a bright-eyed cat pouncing on its prey.

the waxing and waning of the moon. Egyptian statues of Bast show her connection with fertility and pleasure. In several statues, she stands upright, an alert cat's head surmounting a figure holding a sistrum in one hand and a rattle in the other. The rattle symbolized both phallus and womb, and the symbolic fertility of the goddess was further reinforced by several kittens, usually five, sitting at her feet. Women of the period often wore fertility amulets depicting Bast and her feline family.

The original Egyptian name of the cat was *mau*, perhaps from its call of "meow," which also meant "to see." The Egyptians considered that the cat's unblinking gaze gave it powers to seek out truth and to see into the afterlife. Bast was sometimes called the Lady of Truth, and was used in mummification ceremonies to ensure life after death.

Cats played such a complex and important part in the lives of the ancient Egyptians that the living animals were pampered and in some cases worshipped. After the death of a cat, whole families would go into mourning, and the cat's body was embalmed and placed in a sacred vault. Thousands of mummified cats have been discovered in Egypt, some so well-preserved that they have added to our store of knowledge of the earliest domesticated cats.

The custom of keeping cats spread slowly throughout the Middle Eastern countries. A Sanskrit document of 1000 B.C. mentions a pet cat, and the Indian epics *Ramayana* and *Mahabharata*, of about 500 B.C., both contain stories about cats. The Indians at that time worshipped a feline goddess of maternity called Sasti, and for decades Hindus were obliged to take responsibility for feeding at least one cat. Cats reached China around A.D. 400, and in A.D. 595 an empress was recorded as having been bewitched by a cat spirit. By the twelfth century A.D. rich Chinese families kept yellow and white cats known as "lion-cats," which

were highly valued as pets. Vermin control was undertaken by longhaired cats, and cats were traded in street markets. Pet cats were introduced into Japan from China in the reign of Emperor Ichi-Jo, who lived from A.D. 986 to 1011. It is recorded that on the tenth day of the fifth moon, the emperor's white cat gave birth to five white kittens, and a nurse was appointed to see that they were brought up as carefully as royal princes. Many legends and stories of cats survive in Japanese literature, the most enduring image being that of the *Maneki-neko*, the listening or beckoning cat, which can still be found in ornaments and amulets today.

The beckoning cat provides an example of the dual role of charms and amulets to attract good fortune and to ward off evil.

13

Throughout the world, prior to the witch hunts of the Middle Ages, cats were treated with affection and respect. Their greatest attribute was their efficiency in controlling vermin.

Gods of one religion may become the demons of its successor, and in the case of the cat, its nocturnal habits, independence, sense of self-preservation, and often erotic behavior accelerated the process during the sixteenth and seventeenth centuries. Witch hunting then reached its climax, and cats figured prominently in most witch trials throughout Europe. Even as late as the nineteenth century, Basque farmers claimed that witches appeared as black cats, which made such animals greatly feared.

Eventually the cat's fortunes turned once more. They became prized possessions, and those with unusual colors and markings were favored as pets. They were carried between the world's continents as precious gifts, and gave rise to the many breeds and varieties that we know today.

In the Middle Ages, the art of witchcraft was rife. A witch would often have as her "familiar" a black cat. The witch was said to be able to transform herself into her familiar's form.

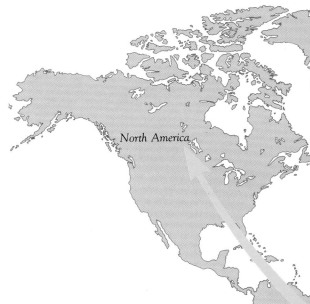

North America

The fact that domestic cats have been systematically bred for only about one hundred years makes it difficult to ascertain the origins of certain key factors in their makeup. The stocky body type found in the Persians and the various Shorthairs points to the possible influence of the European wild cat in their ancestry, whereas the lightboned and slender "foreign" cats, such as the Abyssinian, have bodies similar to that exhibited by the African wild cat. In Asia, lightboned cats have been known for centuries, and isolated gene pools aided the standardization of specific colors and coat patterns. Very few mutations affecting the original wild type conformation, coat length, color and pattern have been necessary to provide the ingredients from which all of today, cats have been bred.

MAPS

The country of origin of the cat is given for each breed. This is shown on the small map at the top of the entry in every case.

REX
The first Cornish Rex, its curled coat caused by the action of a mutant gene, was discovered in a litter of kittens in 1950.

MANX
The Isle of Man, midway between England and Ireland, is generally agreed to be the homeland and birthplace of the Manx.

SPREAD OF THE DOMESTIC CAT

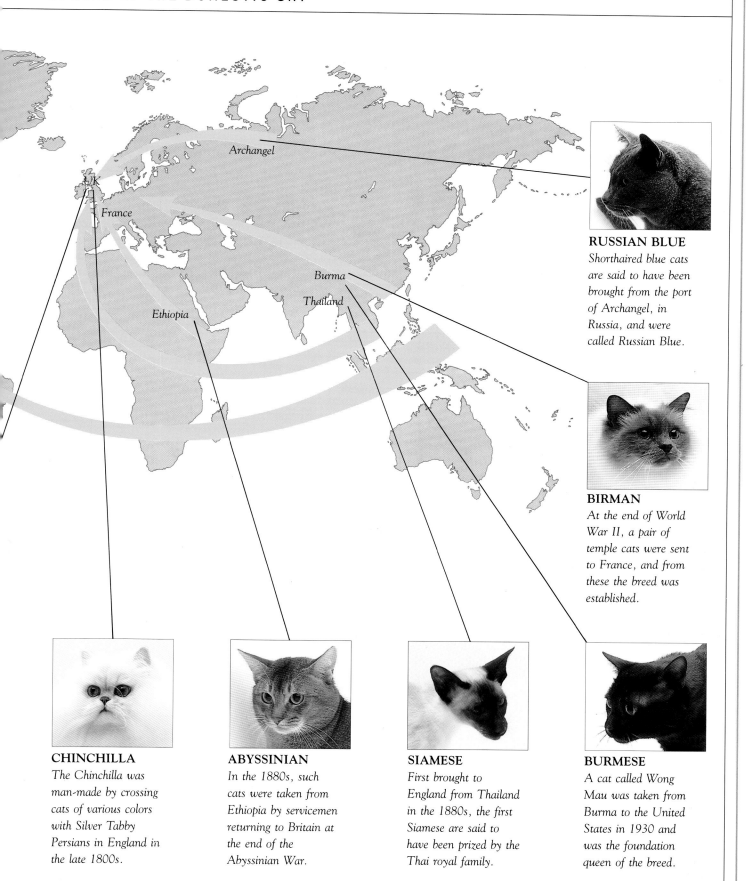

Archangel

UK

France

Burma

Thailand

Ethiopia

RUSSIAN BLUE
Shorthaired blue cats are said to have been brought from the port of Archangel, in Russia, and were called Russian Blue.

BIRMAN
At the end of World War II, a pair of temple cats were sent to France, and from these the breed was established.

CHINCHILLA
The Chinchilla was man-made by crossing cats of various colors with Silver Tabby Persians in England in the late 1800s.

ABYSSINIAN
In the 1880s, such cats were taken from Ethiopia by servicemen returning to Britain at the end of the Abyssinian War.

SIAMESE
First brought to England from Thailand in the 1880s, the first Siamese are said to have been prized by the Thai royal family.

BURMESE
A cat called Wong Mau was taken from Burma to the United States in 1930 and was the foundation queen of the breed.

BODY SHAPE

For over a century, cat fanciers have tried, using various techniques, to manipulate the conformation, coat colors, and patterns of their favorite varieties of the domestic cat. By carefully controlled selective breeding, they have endeavored to create new varieties, and even entirely new breeds.

IN GENERAL SHAPE and overall size, all breeds of domestic cats have retained the same basic structure as their ancestors, unlike dogs, which have been selectively bred to produce very wide variations of shape and height. Cats are therefore free from many of the skeletal abnormalities that can affect dogs. Some defects are occasionally encountered: these include shortened, bent or kinked tails, cleft palates, flattened chests, and polydactylism (extra toes). In the main, evolution seems to have been particularly kind in designing the cat, proceeding along such a well-ordered path of natural selection that it remains an efficient and perfect carnivore of convenient size, still well capable of hunting and killing small animals and birds. The cat's frame permits fluid, coordinated, and graceful movements at all speeds. Its taut-muscled body and legs enable it to make impressive leaps and bounds. The retractile nature of the sharp claws allows fast sprinting over short distances, holding and gripping of prey, and fast climbing of convenient trees

when danger threatens. The cat's brain is large and well-developed, enabling it to assimilate facts rapidly and react quickly. Its adaptable eyes can cope with extremes of lighting conditions, allowing perfect vision in both bright sunlight and dim twilight. The mobile ears work to catch the faintest sound, and the sensitive nose, allied to the perceptive Jacobson's organ in the mouth, can identify the faintest of scents imperceptible to humans.

Pedigree breeds of domestic cats have been developed to fit certain standards of conformation, color and coat pattern. This has been done over many generations, with dedicated breeders working out exactly what the desired feline end-product would look like, and setting out to achieve it with careful and selective breeding. Today there are two main types of pedigree cat: those with chunky, heavyweight bodies and large round heads, and a lighter, finer type with lighter bone and a longer head.

Cats of the heavier type come in a wide variety of

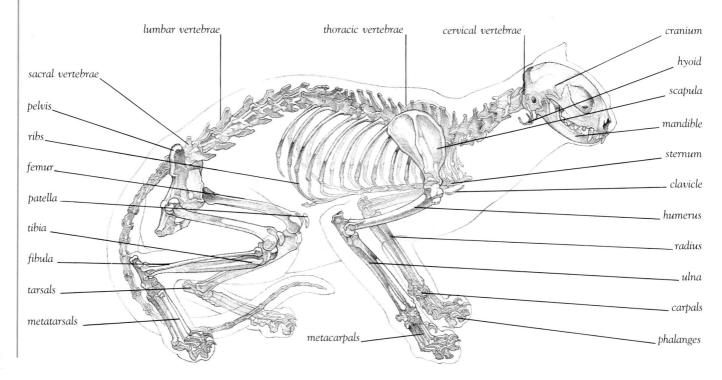

lumbar vertebrae

thoracic vertebrae

cervical vertebrae

cranium

hyoid

scapula

mandible

sternum

clavicle

humerus

radius

ulna

carpals

phalanges

sacral vertebrae

pelvis

ribs

femur

patella

tibia

fibula

tarsals

metatarsals

metacarpals

The cat is the perfect predator, built for a combination of speed and coordination. Its skeleton consists of a highly evolved framework of efficient levers, connected by powerful muscles. Massive muscles in the hindquarters enable the cat to propel itself forward in short bursts of speed.

colors and coat patterns, and may be longhaired or shorthaired. The former include Persians and similar breeds; while the shorthairs cover cats such as the British, American, European, and Exotic shorthairs. Lightweight cats are more variable in their characteristics. The Orientals, including the distinctive Siamese, are at the furthest extreme from the heavier types, with very fine bone; very long bodies, legs, and tails; long, wedge-shaped heads and large ears. Less extreme are the Foreign Shorthairs and Rex cats, each variety having its own very recognizable features. Some breeds have arisen from mixtures of heavy and lightweight types; these have intermediate features.

Cats keep their muscles in trim at all times. The awakening cat yawns and stretches, first the spine, tail and forelegs, then the hips and the hindlegs.

The famous feline attribute of always being able to land on its feet is not wholly accurate, but a falling cat is often able to reposition its body during falling to avoid serious injury on landing. A set of information which reaches the brain from the eyes is combined with impulses from the vestibular apparatus in the ears to transmit an orienting signal to the animal's neck muscles. The head is twisted into an upright and horizontal position, and the rest of the body twists and lines itself up accordingly before landing.

SIGHT

A cat's eyes differ from ours in several ways. They observe less of the color spectrum, having fewer cones, but more rod sensors allow the perception of more brightness in dim light. The iris of the cat's eye opens and closes to a greater extent, and the eyeball is more spherical and, in relation to body size, very much larger than in the human.

Although it is said that cats can see in the dark, this is not true, though the feline pupils are able to expand widely, giving excellent vision in very dim light conditions. The pupil is contracted and expanded by an intricate web of muscles set in a figure-eight configuration in the iris. Within the eye, light is reflected off the *tapetum lucidium*, which has a photomultiplying effect on the light admitted.

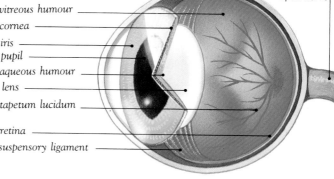

The cat's eye is set in a bony socket in the skull, cushioned by pads of fat and connected by muscles, enabling it to move in various directions. Lacrimal glands provide tears to wash the eye.

VISION

Humans may have better daylight vision than cats, but as dusk falls, the cat scores, for although it cannot see in total darkness, its unusual pupils are able to expand to give excellent vision in very dim conditions.

1 Changes in the size and shape of the pupil generally relate to the amount of light entering the eye. In darkness the pupil dilates.
2 In natural diffused daylight, the pupil is seen a normal vertical oval shape.
3 In very natural light, when the cat is relaxed, the pupil closes down to a narrow slit.

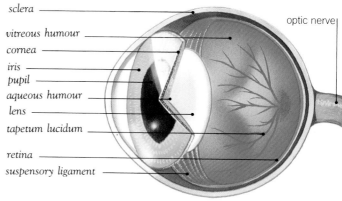

The slightly egg-shaped eye is surrounded by the tough schlera, replaced at the front by the transparent cornea, behind which the aqueous humour protects the iris and pupil. Jellylike vitreous humour fills the cavity behind the lens, and at the back of the eye is the light sensitive retina and the reflective tapetum lucidum. The optic nerve transmits signals from the eye to the brain.

Both eyes face forward, allowing the fields of vision to overlap. This produces stereoscopic sight and allows the hunting cat to assess distance and prey location accurately.

TASTE AND SMELL

Smell is the most important of its senses to the cat. Smell is closely linked to taste, since the nasal passage opens into the mouth. In addition to assisting its hunting pursuits, smell is an essential part of the cat's sexual life. The vomeronasal or Jacobson's organ in the roof of its mouth allows the cat to identify minute particles of scent.

olfactory lobe
olfactory mucosa
hypothalmus
nasal passage
Jacobson's organ
mouth
tongue

The cat exhibiting the flehmen reaction stretches its neck, opens its mouth, and curls back its upper lips in a snarl. It may be so affected by a smell that it also starts salivating.

Flehmen Reaction This is exhibited when the cat is confronted by chemicals in smells, either of sexual origin or from musky odors. Airborne molecules are trapped on the tongue, which is flicked back to press on the opening of the Jacobson's organ. Information is relayed to the brain's hypothalamus, which dictates the cat's response.

HEARING

This sense is highly developed in the cat and registers two octaves higher than the human ear. The comparatively large and mobile ears of the ordinary domestic cat enable it to flex them sideways and backward in order to pinpoint the source of very slight sounds – important to a natural crepuscular predator.

Even when apparently occupied, cats are alert to sounds around them.

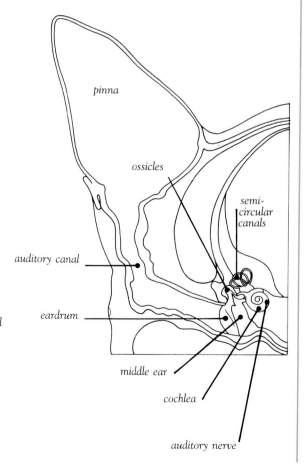

pinna
ossicles
semi-circular canals
auditory canal
eardrum
middle ear
cochlea
auditory nerve

ANATOMY OF AN EAR
Sound waves are funneled down the external auditory canal to the eardrum. In the middle ear, weak vibrations are turned into stronger vibrations. Nerve signals are then sent along the auditory nerve to the brain.

CLAWS

The domestic cat has retractile claws which are normally sheathed, allowing the animal silent footfalls. When needed for grasping prey, defensive measures, or climbing, the claws are extended by muscles tightening the tendons.

terminal bone _____

germinal cells _____

claw tip _____

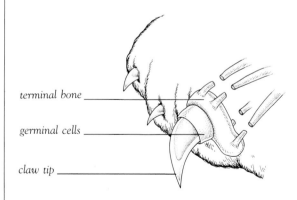

DECLAWING Onychectomy is an operation involving the surgical removal of a cat's claws, normally performed only on the forepaws. Illegal in Britain and not generally advised by the US veterinary profession, the declawing process removes the claw and the germinal cells responsible for its regrowth, as well as all or part of the terminal bone of the toe. Declawed cats are deprived of their prime form of defense and therefore should never be allowed outside.

BODY TYPES

The Longhaired or Persian body type is large-boned and stocky.

The Shorthair breeds are similar in structure to Persians.

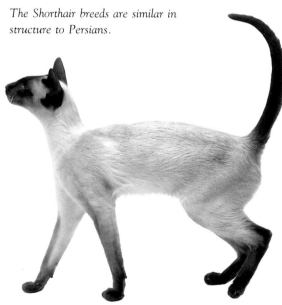

Foreign and Oriental cats are fine-boned and dainty.

HEADS AND EYES

Most cat breeds with heavy conformation, such as the Persian and the Shorthair, have large round heads, with large round eyes set wide apart above a short snub nose on a broad face. The ears are small but have a wide base, and are placed far apart on the head, complementing the rounded appearance of the skull.

Cats of light conformation, such as the Oriental and Foreign Shorthairs, have longer heads of various shapes, and the eye shape varies for each specific breed. Long-coated cats with light conformation have various head and eye shapes, according to the standards laid down by their breed associations.

The head of the Longhair or Persian is typically round, with round eyes and full cheeks. The tiny ears set wide apart.

The head of the Shorthair is similar in shape to that of the Persian when viewed from the front only.

Foreign and oriental cats have long, narrow heads and large ears. Head shape varies in the individual breeds.

In profile, the Persian's head is rather flat. The short snub nose shows a definite "break" at eye level.

The profile of a typical Shorthair breed is less flat than that of the Persian with its short, broad nose.

Oriental cats have long, almost Roman noses with no "break" at eye level and a flat forehead.

EYES

ROUND

Longhaired or Persian cats as well as most of the Shorthairs have large, round, lustrous eyes.

OVAL/ALMOND

Some breed standards call for oval or almond-shaped eyes, often tilted at the outer edge toward the ears.

ORIENTAL

Siamese and similar related breeds have eyes of Oriental shape, set slanting toward the outer edge of the ear.

COAT TYPES

Pedigree cats have diverse variations of coat types, ranging from the full and profuse pelt of the Persian to the very fine sleek and close-lying coats of the Siamese and Orientals. Between the two extremes are the long, soft and silky coats of the longhaired foreign breeds and the thick, dense coats of some of the shorthaired varieties. Some breeds should have "double" coats, with a thick wooly undercoat and a longer, sleeker top coat. The Cornish Rex has a coat devoid of guard hairs, and naturally curled awn and down hairs. The Devon Rex has modified guard, awn, and down hairs, which produce a waxy effect. The Sphynx or Canadian Hairless cat is at the extreme end of the coat-type range, being covered in some parts merely with a fine down.

PERSIAN

Long, soft coat with profuse down hairs nearly as long as the guard hairs, producing a typically long and full coat.

MAINE COON

Long silky coat, heavier and less uniform than that of the Persian due to less uniform and denser down hairs.

SHORTHAIR

Shorthair coats are very variable, ranging from the British and American breeds to the foreigns.

SPHYNX

Apparently hairless, the Sphynx does have a light covering of down hairs on some areas of the body.

CORNISH REX

The tightly curled coat of the Cornish Rex is caused by the absence of guard hairs and short awn hairs.

DEVON REX

Genetically modified guard and awn hairs in this breed closely resemble down hairs.

AMERICAN WIREHAIR

Quite different to the two rex coats, the wirehair has crimped awn hairs and waved guard hairs.

ORIENTAL

In the Siamese and Oriental cats, the coat is short, fine, and close-lying, quite different from other cats.

TYPES OF TIPPING

In the unusually colored tipped, shaded, and smoke breeds, each effect is produced by a proportion of each hair having a colored tip while the rest of the hair is of a paler color.

1 *Tipped cats such as the British Tipped or Chinchilla have tipping at the very ends of the hairs, producing a sparkling effect.*
2 *Tipping extending further down the hair shaft produces the more strongly colored shaded varieties.*
3 *Variable bands of color in different areas of the coat give rise to tabby effects.*
4 *Tipping extending almost to the white hair roots produces the smoke coat in many breeds.*
5 *In golden varieties, the white base coat of the silver varieties is replaced by a tawny yellow color.*

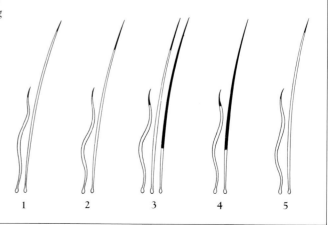

COAT COLORS AND PATTERNS

The natural color of the domestic cat is tabby, which may be one of four basic patterns. The wild type is ticked tabby or agouti, and the other tabby patterns are mackerel (striped), spotted, and classic (marbled or blotched). The pigment melanin produces black hairs, and most of the self-colored coats seen in cats are produced by modification of this pigment, or by the way in which it is distributed in the individual hair fibers.

Solids
Cats of self- or solid-colored breeds must be of a single, solid color throughout with no pattern, shading, ticking, or other variation in color. These are the most common solid colors.

BLACK

BLUE

CHOCOLATE

LILAC

RED

CREAM

CINNAMON

WHITE

Tabby Markings
There are four varieties of tabby patterns, each of which can be found in any of the tabby colors.

TICKED

MACKEREL

SPOTTED

CLASSIC

Tabby Colors
Tabbies are found in a wide variety of colors. Here we show a selection.

BROWN

BLUE

CHOCOLATE

BROWN PATCHED

BLUE PATCHED

RED

Abyssinian
Abyssinian cats have coats which are gently shaded, because each hair is lighter at the root and darker at the tip.

USUAL BLUE SORREL FAWN

Colored Tips
Coats of this sort, with the hairs darkening in varying degrees toward the roots, are found in a number of colors, some of which are shown here.

BLACK SMOKE BLUE SMOKE CHOCOLATE SMOKE LILAC SMOKE

CHINCHILLA SILVER CHINCHILLA GOLDEN BLACK TIPPED SILVER BLUE TIPPED SILVER

Himalayan
Cats with the Himalayan coat pattern, such as the Siamese, have pale coats with the main color restricted to the head and extremeties.

SEAL POINT BLUE POINT RED POINT

CREAM POINT LILAC POINT

CHOCOLATE POINT SEAL TABBY RED TABBY POINT

Tonkinese
Tonkinese cats, which are light-phase Burmese cats, show a modified "pointed" effect. The coats are darker than those of cats with true Himalayan coloring, so the "points" are not so dramatic.

BROWN

LILAC

CHOCOLATE

RED

CREAM

LILAC TORTIE

BLUE TORTIE

TABBY

Multiple Colors
As every cat lover knows, cats come in coats of many colors in addition to those already described, most of which are recognized for show purposes in one breed or another. The tortoiseshells are the most common, but there are endless varieties, including the unusual Mi-ke pattern of the Japanese Bobtail.

TORTOISESHELL

CHOCOLATE
TORTOISESHELL

LILAC
TORTOISESHELL

BLUE
TORTOISESHELL

MI-KE

TORTOISESHELL
AND WHITE

BLUE
TORTOISESHELL
AND WHITE

BEHAVIOR

An insight into feline behavior can enhance the cat owner's enjoyment of the pet cat, and a basic understanding of the animal's complex psychology assists in simple training and in providing the very best of care. Cats are intuitive and highly sensitive creatures who respond and react to the sort of treatment they receive from humans.

CATS ARE OFTEN considered less intelligent than dogs, possibly because they do not respond to training to sit on command and will rarely perform tricks. It is questionable whether the performance of unnatural actions necessarily equates with a high intelligence quotient. It may be that the cat is better equipped to channel its brain power into different behavior, such as survival techniques and adapting to environmental change. And could cats perhaps be considered more intelligent than dogs for questioning the reason behind performing tricks, or being obedient to commands?

Young kittens begin to exhibit predatory behavior at about six weeks old. In the wild, the mother cat would bring prey to the kittens. In the domestic situation, a mother cat brings small pieces of meat to the maternity box, making a special encouraging sound to attract her kittens' attention. Mother cats often pat the meat, teaching the kittens to pounce upon it. At

Though cats and dogs get along well together as family pets, it is sometimes difficult for them to understand one another's body language and play behavior.

this stage of their development, kittens begin to practice hunting movements, crouching down, pouncing, and making mock attacks on their litter mates. Their mother waves her tail, enticing her youngsters to pounce and grasp it.

Adult cats prefer to hunt alone within the confines of their own established territory. Some cats roam long distances from home to visit favorite hunting grounds, and very occasionally, cats from the same family learn to hunt cooperatively. Acute hearing and excellent vision in dim light enable cats to become efficient, silent hunters. A cat often lies in ambush, waiting with infinite patience for its victim to emerge from its place of refuge. The cat attacks in a swift bounding leap, grasping its prey with extended claws and killing with a lethal bite to the creature's neck. Hungry cats dispatch their prey quite quickly, but well-fed cats, highly stimulated by the excitement of stalking and capture, often play with the prey for some time before finally dispatching it. Playing with prey gives the cats the opportunity to practice their trapping techniques.

Throughout a cat's lifetime, its behavior is governed by the innate patterns inherited from its wild ancestors. Here we see a Burmilla hunting (left), a Persian playing at killing prey, and a pair of Oriental kittens play-fighting (below).

Despite centuries of domestication, most cats will hunt, given the chance. If you keep pet cats entirely indoors, you should compensate for their loss of hunting opportunities by providing lots of toys, and encouraging them to play chasing, pouncing, and catching games. Such stimulation and exercise keeps them fit, stops them from getting too fat, and may help to guarantee their survival if they get lost.

TERRITORIAL MARKING

Cats identify their property and places by scent marking. They employ various glands for this purpose. Scent glands on the head, called temporal glands, are situated above the eyes on each side of the forehead. The perioral glands are along the lips, and both sets of glands are used for marking when the cat rubs its head against a friend or a chosen object – behavior which appears to give the cat extreme pleasure. Some cats, usually full males, mark their territory by urine-spraying on various boundaries (below). Head rubbing (middle) is used for identifying objects rather than as boundary marking. Some stropping behavior is used to scratch at a cat's boundary marker after spray marking (top).

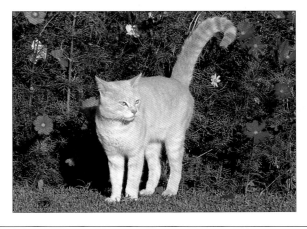

Sleeping

Cats have two distinct types of sleep – light sleep and deep sleep. During light sleep, the blood pressure remains normal, the body temperature drops slightly, and the muscles are mildly tensed. In deep or paradoxical sleep, the blood pressure falls, the body temperature rises, and the muscles relax completely. The hearing, however, remains extremely acute, and any sudden sound will wake the cat instantly. Cats seem able to sleep at any time, in any temperature, and in all manner of seemingly uncomfortable situations.

Newborn kittens spend most of the time in periods of deep sleep, secure in the nest area chosen by their mother.

Cats like to sleep in unusual places and enjoy curling up in confined spaces which make them feel protected and secure.

Small kittens sleep most of the time, and this is an important part of their development process. Newborn kittens spend most of their first week of life in deep sleep, and during the next three weeks have gradually increasing periods of wakefulness.

Dreaming takes place during deep sleep, and cats often twitch their muscles, growl, or purr. They may make sucking sounds and twitch the tail. It is probably during dreaming that the cat's brain sorts and sifts data for storage in its long-term memory. At least one-third of the cat's sleeping time is spent in deep sleep mode, and this seems to be essential for its well-being.

SLEEP PATTERNS

As a cat becomes drowsy and falls into a light sleep, it may remain sitting or lying with its head up but relaxed, and its paws tucked into its body. It may remain in this condition for 10 to 30 minutes, and at this stage it is easy to awaken with any slight noise.

In deep sleep, the cat is completely relaxed and usually curled on its side. Deep sleep is characterized by rapid eye movements, and the cat may also twitch its whiskers and paws, or quiver the ears, and tail. It may even growl or emit little muttering sounds. Deep sleep normally lasts for about 6 to 10 minutes before the cat resumes a period of light sleep.

WASHING

The cat thoroughly cleans each shoulder and flank.

It washes its underside and inside each hindleg in turn.

The paws are licked, and any dirt is bitten from between the paws.

Each forepaw is licked in turn and used to wash the corresponding side of the face and head.

Most cats wash themselves frequently. Family cats often indulge in mutual washing sessions, and mother cats spend a great deal of time washing their young kittens. Pet cats will often attempt to wash their humans, and many cats wash meticulously after being touched or stroked by humans, probably in an attempt to remove an unacceptable scent from their coats.

The cat uses its tongue and paws to groom itself. The tongue, covered with tiny hooked projections called papillae, acts as both brush and comb. Front paws are used to clean the places the tongue cannot reach. The cat sits up and licks a paw until it becomes damp, then passes the paw over its face, over and into the ear, across the forehead and eye, and down the cheek to the chin. It repeats the procedure with the opposite paw to clean the other side of the face. It licks and grooms each shoulder and foreleg in turn, then attends to its flanks and underside, the anus, genital region, and hindlegs, and finishes by washing the tail from the base to the tip. It teases out tangles and knots with its teeth, and bites out patches of dirt from between its paws.

In addition to keeping its coat clean and well groomed, the cat's washing technique has another important purpose. The effect of sunlight on the coat produces its nutritional requirement of Vitamin D, which it transfers from the coat into the body by the licking and washing action.

The cat licks a paw, then uses it to wash one side of its face.

Friendly cats often indulge in mutual grooming of each other's fur, which both seem to enjoy.

Communication

Cats recognize each other initially by smell. Friendly cats greet one another by touching noses or rubbing their foreheads together. They may rub their bodies together and sniff at each other's genital regions.

The alert cat has a direct gaze and points its ears and whiskers forward. If it is also slightly nervous, it will twitch its nostrils, attempting to identify by scent. When a person has been identified as a friend, the cat's expression relaxes, and its tail rises in greeting.

A cat under threat first freezes, staring at the aggressor with wide eyes. Its tail flicks slowly from side to side. If further threatened, the cat pulls in its chin, lays back its ears, and gradually runs sideways onto the enemy. Simultaneously, the hairs on the body and tail begin to erect, presenting the largest possible body area. The cat draws back its lips to reveal its teeth and growls an unmistakable warning. Its muscles are poised for either fight or flight, the weight of the body taken on three legs while the fourth is held ready to strike.

An agitated, nervous cat is dangerous to touch, for it may react as violently as if receiving an electric shock. Such a cat will be crouched down with tucked-in chin, wide eyes, and ears held sideways. It must be talked out of this state and calmed down, or left in peace and quiet to recover its composure.

The mechanism of purring is not fully understood, but it must be one of the most endearing characteristics of the domestic cat. Some cats purr softly and only rarely, but many cats regularly purr with content-

Cats recognize each other basically by smell, and when two friendly cats meet up, they generally touch noses or rub their foreheads together.

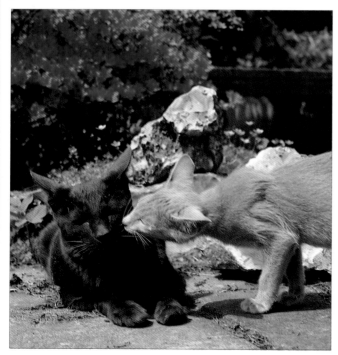

FELINE BODY LANGUAGE

Cats are masters in the art of body-language, conveying their moods and intentions by a series of well-defined postures, clearly understood by humans, as well as fellow felines.

Cats use a variety of sounds in communicating with humans. This cat is voicing feelings of nervousness.

This Blue Smoke Persian is obviously upset and emitting an extremely loud yowl.

An unhappy lilac Burmese squats into a defensive posture with wide eyes and flattened ears.

30

ment and to show affection. Even tiny kittens are able to purr as they nurse, though they will not purr in response to human handling until about six weeks old. Cats may purr in response to their owner's voice or touch, and some purr when suffering the pains of labor or terminal illness.

Most cats can make a range of sounds in three basic categories. The quietest is similar to a human murmur and includes soft purring. Murmurs are made with the mouth closed. The middle category of feline sounds may be thought of as vowel sounds, each being a variation of the "meow," and each being used to express a different need, such as asking to be let out.

The most interesting range of cat talk is that made by a mother cat teaching her kittens to eat solid food, to follow her from the nest, and to behave properly. The kittens themselves are able to purr, spit, and growl, and also have a loud distress call with which they cry to their mother when they are lost or frightened.

The typical tail-up greeting of a cat indicating its pleasure and soliciting a stroke from its owner.

An American Wirehair rolls over to solicit attention.

FACIAL EXPRESSIONS

A contented cat with upright ears and relaxed whiskers.

Nervous or apprehensive, ears start to go back and whiskers tense slightly forward.

A frightened or very angry cat. Ears flat, eyes narrowed, and whiskers forward, it is ready for defense or attack.

Alert and ready to pounce on its prey, the cat assumes an expression midway between normality and fear.

Relaxed and contented while being petted with half-closed eyes and relaxed whiskers.

SEXUAL BEHAVIOR

Both male and female domestic cats reach sexual maturity when very young, little more than kittens in fact, and will readily reproduce unless confined or neutered. Females are able to produce two or three litters each year.

FEMALE KITTENS MAY reach sexual maturity as early as five months old and may then come into season every three weeks during the breeding season, even though they will not be physically fully grown until they are over a year old. Male kittens may reach sexual maturity from six to eight months old, although in some pedigree breeds this may be delayed for as long as eighteen months. Domestic cats destined for life in the family home make much better pets when they are de-sexed, which removes their (often antisocial) sexual behavior patterns.

Male

A mature male cat is able to mate at any time, though he will be more sexually active in the spring and summer months. He is initially attracted to the female by the special evocative odor that she emits during estrus, and also responds to her inviting cries. The scent and cry of the female cat in estrus is said to carry over long distances, and any mature male cats in the vicinity will respond. When the cats meet, the rolling

and posturing of the female further excites the male, who will mount and mate with her as quickly as possible. In a natural environment, several males may be attracted to one female, and will bicker and fight for dominance and the privilege of mating. Sometimes a subordinate male will mate with the female while his superiors are engaged in battle. During her estrus period, the female cat will mate many times, either with the same male, or with several different males.

Entire male cats which roam freely treat their homes as bases for food and shelter only. They are totally motivated by their strong sexual drive and spend their days patrolling their territories, marking their boundaries with spurts of pungent urine to deter interlopers. They constantly search for sexually receptive females to fight over and mate with, but often need to take time off for rest and recuperation. When male cats fight, their long, sharp, canine teeth inflict deep puncture wounds in their opponents, and the raking of their hooked claws causes deep scratches, all of which take a long time to heal. A cat fight between

---

SEXUAL DIFFERENCES

FEMALE KITTEN

The vulva is a vertical slit almost joined to the circular anal opening.

FEMALE ADULT

The vulva is a vertical slit about half an inch from the circular anal opening.

MALE KITTEN

The tiny round opening in which the penis is concealed is about half an inch below the circular anal opening, with an indication of the scrotal sacs as slightly raised areas.

MALE ADULT

The testicles are clearly visible in the male, set between two openings at least an inch apart.

CAT FIGHTS

1 Cats meeting and investigating each other by smell and observation of body posturing.
2 One cat may take the initiative and advance to investigate more thoroughly. The less confident cat cringes in a defensive posture.
3 As the dominant cat advances further, the defendant cat backs away, perhaps lifting a paw to fend off a likely attack.
4 The defendant decides not to back down, both cats growl and wave their fluffed-out tails.
5 The dominant cat presses forward, turning sideways to present a bigger threat and the

defendant flattens his ears and hisses loudly.
6 The aggressive cat finally attacks in earnest and leaps onto the defending cat which turns onto its back extending its claws. Both cats are locked together in a growling mass, gripping each other with jaws and forelegs, and each raking at the other's body with the claws of the powerful hind legs. Eventually, the less powerful cat breaks away and escapes.

two males is bitter and serious. The cats confront each other, making huffing sounds, with cheeks puffed out, sometimes salivating and emitting low, fierce growls. They hunch up their shoulders and hips to look as large and powerful as possible. They circle, stiff-legged; then each cat lunges at the other's throat, biting hard. The cats lock together in a rolling ball and rake each other with the back claws, causing lots of flying fur. When they break apart, one may run away and receive a final, deep bite at the root of the tail or the testes. On subsequent meetings with the vanquished cat, the dominant male may underline his superiority by biting the submissive male on the neck and mounting him briefly, before releasing him and walking away with stiff legs and tail. A male previously beaten into submission usually does his best to avoid any such confrontations, or will crouch down, offering the scruff of his neck to the dominant cat. Males rarely fight with females, but females will fight, particularly in defense of their kittens.

As they approach puberty, kittens will often show the first signs of sexual gestures in their usual greeting and play behavior.

Female

Estrus, or breeding condition, in the female cat is easy to recognize and consists of four stages. In pro-estrus, the reproductive organs undergo changes in preparation for mating and pregnancy. The cat is extra affectionate, solicits stroking, and restlessly roams around the house seeking a way out. After five days of the first stage, true estrus begins, lasting for about seven days, during which time the cat will be ready and willing to mate. When stroked, she assumes the mating position (see page 34). She may become agitated and roll on the floor as if in pain. Most cats wail, and in some pedigree breeds, such as the Siamese, the wailing can be indescribably loud and prolonged. If mating does not take place, the third stage, meto-estrus, begins and the reproductive system relaxes until the fourth stage of anestrus is reached. During anestrus, the female cat's behavior is contented and calm until the next cycle begins.

When the breeding queen reaches the receptive part of estrus, she exhibits the typical mating position known as lordosis.

MATING

When a female cat is ready to mate, she adopts a characteristic hollowed back position, crouching and presenting her hindquarters, with her tail bent to one side. The male approaches her from the side and rear, running forward and grasping her by the loose skin at the scruff of the neck. He mounts her by straddling her body with his front legs, then arches his back in order to correctly position his penis for mating. The female also maneuvers her pelvis to help penetration. After a few pelvic thrusts, the male achieves penetration and quickly ejaculates. The female immediately pulls forward, growling fiercely, and attempts to turn and attack the male, who leaps away to safety. The female rolls, sometimes still growling, then both cats sit apart from each other and lick their own genital areas clean. After a few minutes, they will probably mate again.

Mating can occur up to ten times in an hour, or until the male is exhausted. If there are several males present, the female will mate with one or more of them in succession.

1 *The male approaches from the side and rear.*
2 *He mounts by straddling the queen's body and grasping the loose skin at her scruff.*
3 *The queen assists mating by raising her pelvis and turning her tail to one side.*
4 *After mating, the male leaps away, and the female turns, spits, and fiercely growls.*

MATERNITY

The female cat or queen makes a model mother, secreting her litter away from harm within a nest area. She feeds the kittens at regular intervals, keeps them spotlessly clean, and curls around them, purring, to rest and sleep. She will devote herself to their every need for as long as she needs to.

FELINE MOTHERS CARE for their kittens in a completely dedicated way until the kittens are able to take care of their own needs. Male cats are not involved in the rearing of kittens, though they have been observed playing with kittens in feral cat colonies.

After mating, the fertilized ova become implanted in the uterine wall of the female cat, and glands secrete hormones giving rise to certain patterns of behavior. The cat becomes even more sensitive to danger, she grooms herself even more thoroughly than before, and her appetite gradually increases. If she is a free-roaming cat, she will hunt with more dedication, and she will also nibble selected grasses and herbage. As her pregnancy advances, the cat chooses secluded sleeping areas. Her self-grooming sessions increase, and she pays particular attention to her genital area and gradually enlarging breasts. As the period of gestation of about sixty-three days reaches its end, the cat searches for a suitable site in which to give birth. The first stage of labor can extend for many hours. The cat is restless and will not eat, though she will drink from time to time. Eventually, when the second stage of labor commences, with typical contractions, the cat will generally go to the place she has chosen to give birth. The contractions gradually become stronger and

The mother cat constantly grooms her kittens, washing them by licking them all over with her rough tongue.

Kittens are born blind and deaf, but have a strong sense of smell which enables them to find a nipple, and to start feeding even before they are perfectly dry.

more frequent, and prior to the expulsion of the first kitten, a sac of fluid may be passed, preparing the passage for the birth.

Kittens may be born head first or tail first, both presentations being equally normal. The head or rump appears, and the cat licks at the membranes as contractions push the tiny kitten out. Sometimes, particularly with the first-born, the kitten seems to be held back by its shoulders or hips, but it is normally expelled without human interference as the cat shifts her position and bears down. She licks away all the membranes encasing the newly born kitten and chews the umbilical cord to within about half an inch of the kitten's body. The stump of cord dries and drops off, leaving a neat navel within about a week. The placenta may be passed still attached to the kitten, or may be expelled later, after the kitten is clean, dry, and nursing. The mother cat will normally eat the placenta, which is rich in nutrients, and which, in the wild, would sustain her until she was fit enough to hunt for food.

A mother cat may decide to move her litter to a new nest and carries the kittens one at a time, holding them firmly by the scruff of the neck.

After the birth of the first kitten, the rest of the litter follow at regular or irregular intervals, and the mother cat deals with each in the same way. She licks and washes each kitten, clearing the membrane from its body, cleaning the mucus from its nose and mouth, and stimulating it to breathe. She also licks vigorously at the kitten's anal region, stimulating the tiny animal to pass the meconium, a dark plug which stops up its bowel until released.

When the last kitten of the litter has been born, the mother cat washes her own genital region, legs, and tail. She gathers her kittens together and lying on one side, encourages them to suckle. She may not leave the nest for up to twenty-four hours for food and a drink. Young kittens urinate and defecate only when stimulated to do so by being licked in the genital and anal regions by the mother cat. She has a set routine for kitten care. After nursing the kittens, she washes and grooms them in turn, and swallows all the excreted material they produce, to make sure that the nest remains clean. This would be a safety factor in the wild, preventing scent-leaving clues as to the kittens' whereabouts and thus attracting predators.

Even after centuries of domestication, cats often revert to the innate behavior patterns of their wild ancestors. Three weeks or so after the birth of her litter, the cat may suddenly decide to move the kittens to another, often quite unsuitable, location. She grasps

DEVELOPMENT OF KITTENS

Kittens are born blind and deaf. They have a strong sense of smell, however, which enables them to locate their mother's nipples, and a strong sucking reflex, which means that they take in enough milk to satisfy their needs. About one week to ten days after birth, the eyes open and the hearing starts to develop, and until the litter is three weeks old, the queen looks after the kittens constantly, feeding and grooming them, and stimulating them to urinate and defecate by licking at their genital regions. The queen ingests the kittens' wastes at this time and spends about 70 percent of her time curled up with, and attending to, her family.

At two weeks, the kittens can scrabble around their nest box and at three weeks start to stand up on their legs and pay attention to what is going on around them. Between three and six weeks, they make great advances, learning to play, to make sounds, and show an interest in solid food. From about four weeks, they will use a corner of their box for toilet purposes and by six weeks can be taught to use a litter box. Having learned to eat a variety of foods and to spend less time with their mother, most kittens are fully independent and self-sufficient by about eight to ten weeks of age.

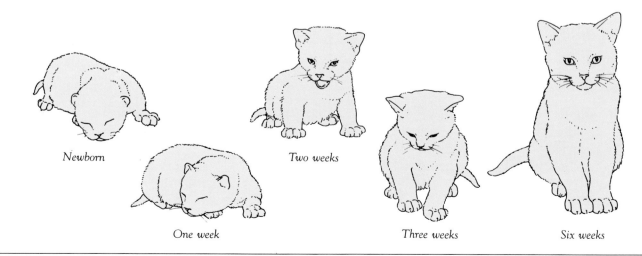

Newborn

One week

Two weeks

Three weeks

Six weeks

each kitten around the neck, holding in in her jaws, but not piercing the skin with her teeth, then lifts the kitten by raising her head and carries it between her straddled forelegs to its new resting place. The cat will carry each kitten in turn until she is satisfied that the litter is in a new, safe haven. When kittens are grasped around the neck, their natural response is to assume the fetal position and go completely limp. This means that they are rarely harmed by being carried by their mother.

Until the kittens are about three weeks old, the mother cat looks after all their needs. She leaves the litter only for short periods to eat, drink, and relieve herself, and returns as quickly as possible to her babies. By ten days, the kittens have opened their eyes and gradually begin to respond to various stimulae. During their third and fourth weeks, they try to leave the nest area, and as they become stronger and more mobile, and gradually accept solid food, the mother spends less time with them.

During their early weeks of life, their mother teaches the kittens a great deal about being feline. She encourages play behavior, including mock hunting and killing moves, and she initiates the first stages in toilet training, calling them to follow her away from the nest when they want to urinate and defecate. By the time the kittens are weaned and ready to go to new homes, their mother will have made sure that each is an independent and self-assured little cat with good feline manners.

Once her kittens are fully mobile, the mother cat encourages them to explore and to broaden their play and hunting behaviors.

NEUTERING

Unless a cat is destined for breeding purposes, it should be neutered in order to make a loving and carefree pet. Neutered cats can be shown in most cat associations and are easier to maintain in peak show condition than their entire male and female counterparts.

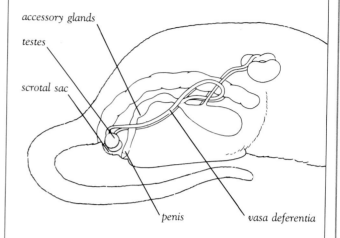

accessory glands

testes

scrotal sac

penis   *vasa deferentia*

Castration Castration or orchidectomy is the removal of the male sex organs. Such surgery is best carried out just before the male kitten reaches sexual maturity, when he has formed his masculine character, but has not shown signs of being interested in the opposite sex.

ovary

horn of the uterus

body of the uterus

kidney

Spaying Spaying or ovariohysterectomy involves the surgical removal of most of the female cat's sex organs – the ovaries, fallopian tubes, and uterus. Spaying may be carried out at a very early age in the female cat and is better performed before she has her first period of estrus, and definitely before she has kittens.

BREEDING PEDIGREE CATS

Breeding pedigree cats is a hobby that should not be undertaken lightly. Only cats of the very best quality and with strong constitutions should be kept for breeding, and they must be expertly and considerately cared for.

ALTHOUGH ORDINARY DOMESTIC cats seem to become pregnant and produce kittens without much bother, often against their owners' wishes, the production of pedigree kittens under controlled conditions can prove difficult, and cat breeding should not be undertaken lightly. Despite its many generations of domestication, a cat can resent the unnatural restrictions placed upon her during mating and pregnancy. She may prove unwilling to mate with the stud cat chosen for her; she may have a stressful gestation period or a difficult delivery. She could reject her kittens, have little or poor-quality milk, or be so unsettled as to spend her time anxiously moving the kittens to new nest sites.

A successful cat breeder will be someone for whom financial gain is not important. Breeding pedigree cats is a hobby full of rewards, but none of these is financial. There is a great sense of pride and achievement in planning a special litter, seeing it born and rearing it. A true cat lover will gain a great deal from caring for the female cat, known as the brood queen, helping her through the weeks of pregnancy, attending the birth, and looking after the needs of the growing family. On the debit side is the problem of parting with the kittens when they are fully independent and ready to go to new homes at about three months old.

It may seem logical to buy a pair of cats in order to start breeding, but this is impractical. Keeping a stud male is not a job for the novice. He will not be content with a monogamous relationship with one queen and needs special accommodation of his own, so that his habit of spray-marking his territory with strong-smelling urine does not become a serious household problem.

Starting out

To start breeding it is best to buy one or two females of the breed you have chosen, seeking advice from an experienced breeder or show judge, and purchasing the very best females that you can afford. Two females will keep each other company, and if they are unrelated, you will have a good foundation to lines of your own in future years. A kitten for breeding should be purchased at about three months old. She should be of sound conformation, with a good temperament and an impeccable pedigree, and should be properly registered with an acceptable cat association. She should be well grown for her age and should have received a suitable course of vaccinations for which you will be provided with certificates. Until she grows to adulthood, the kitten should lead a normal life, with good food, correct grooming, and lots of play opportunities combined with tender loving care. Kittens vary as to

Oriental cats such as the Siamese often have more than the average number of kittens in a litter and need extra care in order to rear them successfully. This superb seal point has eight strong and healthy youngsters.

GESTATION CHART

The average gestation period of the domestic cat is 65 days, so if the precise date of mating is known, the chart shows on which date the kittens are expected to be born. A variation of up to four days either way is not unusual, and it is important to check the pregnant cat at regular intervals in the week leading up to the expected birth.

To check the expected date of birth, refer to the date of mating in the green column. The birth date may be read from the yellow column. For example, a cat mated on May 1 will be due to have her kittens on July 5.

JAN	MAR	FEB	APR	MAR	MAY	APR	JUN	MAY	JUL	JUN	AUG	JUL	SEP	AUG	OCT	SEP	NOV	OCT	DEC	NOV	JAN	DEC	FEB
1	7	1	7	1	5	1	5	1	5	1	5	1	4	1	5	1	5	1	5	1	5	1	4
2	8	2	8	2	6	2	6	2	6	2	5	2	6	2	6	2	6	2	6	2	6	2	5
3	9	3	9	3	7	3	7	3	7	3	6	3	7	3	7	3	7	3	7	3	7	3	6
4	10	4	10	4	8	4	8	4	8	4	7	4	8	4	8	4	8	4	8	4	8	4	7
5	11	5	11	5	9	5	9	5	9	5	8	5	9	5	9	5	9	5	9	5	9	5	8
6	12	6	12	6	10	6	10	6	10	6	9	6	10	6	10	6	10	6	10	6	10	6	9
7	13	7	13	7	11	7	11	7	11	7	10	7	11	7	11	7	11	7	11	7	11	7	10
8	14	8	14	8	12	8	12	8	12	8	11	8	12	8	12	8	12	8	12	8	12	8	11
9	15	9	15	9	13	9	13	9	13	9	12	9	13	9	13	9	13	9	13	9	13	9	12
10	16	10	16	10	14	10	14	10	14	10	13	10	14	10	14	10	14	10	14	10	14	10	13
11	17	11	17	11	15	11	15	11	15	11	14	11	15	11	15	11	15	11	15	11	15	11	14
12	18	12	18	12	16	12	16	12	16	12	15	12	16	12	16	12	16	12	16	12	16	12	15
13	19	13	19	13	17	13	17	13	17	13	16	13	17	13	17	13	17	13	17	13	17	13	16
14	20	14	20	14	18	14	18	14	18	14	17	14	18	14	18	14	18	14	18	14	18	14	17
15	21	15	21	15	19	15	19	15	19	15	18	15	19	15	19	15	19	15	19	15	19	15	18
16	22	16	22	16	20	16	20	16	20	16	19	16	20	16	20	16	20	16	20	16	20	16	19
17	23	17	23	17	21	17	21	17	21	17	20	17	21	17	21	17	21	17	21	17	21	17	20
18	24	18	24	18	22	18	22	18	22	18	21	18	22	18	22	18	22	18	22	18	22	18	21
19	25	19	25	19	23	19	23	19	23	19	22	19	23	19	23	19	23	19	23	19	23	19	22
20	26	20	26	20	24	20	24	20	24	20	23	20	24	20	24	20	24	20	24	20	24	20	23
21	27	21	27	21	25	21	25	21	25	21	24	21	25	21	25	21	25	21	25	21	25	21	24
22	28	22	28	22	26	22	26	22	26	22	25	22	26	22	26	22	26	22	26	22	26	22	25
23	29	23	29	23	27	23	27	23	27	23	26	23	27	23	27	23	27	23	27	23	27	23	26
24	30	24	30	24	28	24	28	24	28	24	27	24	28	24	28	24	28	24	28	24	28	24	27
25	31	25	1	25	29	25	29	25	29	25	28	25	29	25	29	25	29	25	29	25	29	25	28
26	1	26	2	26	30	26	30	26	30	26	29	26	30	26	30	26	30	26	30	26	30	26	1
27	2	27	3	27	31	27	1	27	31	27	30	27	31	27	1	27	31	27	31	27	1	27	2
28	3	28	4	28	1	28	2	28	1	28	1	28	1	28	1	28	2	28	1	28	1	28	3
29	4			29	2	29	3	29	2	29	2	29	2	29	2	29	3	29	2	29	2	29	4
30	5			30	3	30	4	30	3	30	3	30	3	30	3	30	4	30	3	30	3	30	5
31	6			31	4			31	4			31	4	31	4			31	4			31	6
	APR		MAY		JUN		JUL		AUG		SEP		OCT		NOV		DEC		JAN		FEB		MAR

39

when they have their first season or period of estrus, so she must be carefully observed and not allowed to roam free. Whe her first season occurs, she should be carefully watched. At the next period of estrus, if she is at least ten months of age, it is feasible for her to be mated if your veterinary surgeon agrees that she is well enough and physically fit.

Pedigree male cats kept for breeding are called stud cats. They have usually proved their superior qualities in the show ring, attaining high show status because they conform so closely to the standard of points for their respective breeds. Because a working stud male will habitually spray his habitat with spurts of pungent urine as territorial marking behavior, he has to be confined in his own living quarters.

Matings must be strictly controlled, witnessed, and recorded by the stud's owner, who will issue a breeding certificate to the queen's owner, who pays an agreed stud fee. The two cats are given some hours to become accustomed to one another, and once the stud's owner is assured that the cats are relating and not aggressive, and that the queen is really ready, she is released from the pen and the cats are allowed to mate. This procedure is repeated to insure that a completely successful mating has taken place, usually over two or three days, then the queen is returned to her owner.

SELECTIVE BREEDING

From time to time anomalies occur in litters of kittens, in both pedigrees and domestics, and quite often, breeders fascinated by all things new or unusual may decide to try to perpetuate the unusual features and perhaps produce a new breed. It is possible, after selectively breeding one or several generations, to determine the genetic make-up of a new feline feature, and then to set out a formal and constructive breeding program to develop a new breed. Some features which are clearly detrimental to a cat's well-being would be frowned upon by true cat lovers and would thus prove unacceptable to most associations for registration and breeding purposes.

AMERICAN CURL
The curled ears of this breed do not appear to present any problems, and the breed is accepted by some associations in the United States.

SPHYNX
Those who love the apparently hairless Sphynx work tirelessly for its recognition for show and registration. Others consider that a breed which might not be viable in the wild should not be encouraged.

SCOTTISH FOLD
Refused recognition by some associations on the premise that the tightly folded ears are impossible to keep clean and healthy, and because some skeletal anomalies were apparent in some early Fold kittens.

SYMBOLIZING GENES

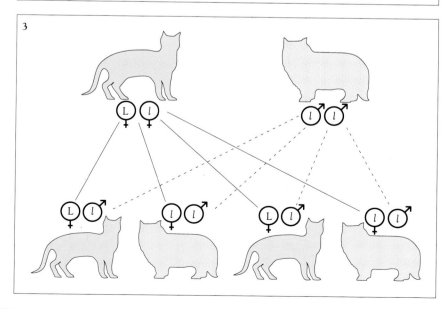

As in the human, genes in the domestic cat exist in pairs – one received from each parent – for each feature. The genes for each feature are either dominant or recessive to its opposite feature. For example, the normal "wild-type" coat of the *Felis catus* is shorthaired and is symbolized, for convenience sake, as *L*. The opposing genetic feature to short hair (*L*) is long hair, which is recessive to short hair and is symbolized *l*. Dominant genes are symbolized with an upper-case letter, and their corresponding recessive gene with the lower-case version of the same letter.

Sperm and ova contain one of each pair of the parents' genes, so it may be seen that some features are passed on in a fairly random fashion. Once the dominance or recessivity of the genes is understood, however, it is fairly simple to deduce methods of manipulating the genes by careful selection of breeding partners in order to produce offspring with the desired traits.

A simple example is the production of long-hair in cats, as is demonstrated in these charts.

1 *A homozygous shorthaired female is mated to a homozygous longhaired male (LL × ll).*

2 *A heterozygous shorthaired female is mated to a heterozygous shorthaired male (Ll × Ll).*

3 *A heterozygous shorthaired female is mated to a homozyous longhaired male (Ll × ll).*

KEY

ⓛ♂ gene from male

Ⓛ♀ gene from female

L short-hair
l long-hair

SHOWING

Throughout the world, various cat bodies and associations organize shows and exhibitions. At these functions, like-minded people are able to meet, to enter their prized pets, and to compete for awards and championships.

A PERSON WHO breeds or shows cats is called a cat fancier and usually takes up the hobby through an all-consuming love of all things feline. Cat fanciers share a common bond and interest in wanting to breed or own the perfect cat. Most cats show complete indifference to being put on public display, but owners derive great personal satisfaction in gaining top awards with their pets. There is little financial reward for the successful exhibitor; entry fees are high and prize money is often non-existent. Rosettes, ribbons, and trophies are eagerly sought after, and proudly displayed at home. Exhibitors enjoy cat shows as regular social functions. All members of the family are able to attend and enjoy the proceedings, and some cats actually appear to enjoy being pampered and admired by judges and the receptive audience of the show hall.

The first cat show ever recorded was held in 1598 at St. Giles Fair in Winchester, England, but the first properly benched show, with cats being placed in individual cages, took place at London's Crystal Palace in 1871. The first benched American cat show was held in Madison Square Garden, New York, in 1895. The vogue for exhibiting cats and competing for prizes spread slowly around the world, and nowadays hun-

Though there is no monetary gain in showing cats, the winning of first-place awards is the aim of most exhibitors. Here a lovely Chinchilla neuter and a kitten pose with their awards.

HOW TO USE THIS BOOK

All cat associations judge each individual cat breed using a system of points. The total is always one hundred, but the breakdown of points allocated to particular features varies from breed to breed, and from association to association. In the Breed Directory on pages 56 to 251, you will find the standards broken down and annotated for each breed.

The Introduction gives the background to the breed and how it developed

The Penalties box lists the features for which a cat will be penalized or disqualified in the show ring

The Key Characteristics box gives specific descriptions

The annotated points are those set in the USA.

dreds of shows take place in many different countries. Each country with an active band of cat fanciers has one or more governing bodies which accept cats for registration and promote the running of licensed cat shows.

Each registering body has its own rules and guidelines for breeding, registration, and showing cats, and often publishes information on all aspects of cat care, breeding, and exhibiting. In North America, cat lovers have a wide choice of cat organizations from which to choose.

The best way to enter the world of showing is to start by reading one of the many specialist cat magazines available. Shows are listed, and a day or two watching the proceedings can be invaluable. Most exhibitors are more than delighted to talk about their cats, and about show procedures. All shows have information desks with helpful assistants, and once you become a member of an association you have access to a vast wealth of data. Each association has its own rules and methods of show organization, but in one aspect they are all identical – the cat's welfare is the first priority at all times.

Show procedures vary, but the end result is the same. Cats are assessed by qualified judges who relate each cat's qualities to an official standard of points for its breed or variety, and then rank each cat in a class

At GCCF shows, cats are individually judged at their show pens after the exhibitors have been asked to vacate the main body of the show hall.

in order of merit. Various groups have their own nomenclature for top award-winning cats – Champion, Supreme Champion, and so on. Even non-pedigree domestic cats may be shown and have a special section at most shows. As they cannot be assessed against any breed standard, they are judged on temperament, condition, and overall esthetic appeal.

FELINE ASSOCIATIONS AND GOVERNING BODIES

Countries where pedigree cats are bred and exhibited have one or more associations or governing bodies which keep a register of cats and their lineage, and set down rules and regulations for cat shows. Britain has the Governing Council of the Cat Fancy (GCCF) and The Cat Association of Britain, which is the British member of FIFe. American cat fanciers have nine associations, the largest being the Cat Fancier's Association (CFA), which also has affiliated clubs in Canada and Japan.

In Europe, Australasia, and South Africa, there are national bodies and other associations, and generally one in each country is a member of the Federation Internationale Feline (Fife), which is the largest and most powerful of the feline associations in the world. Fife has thousands of members, covering the entire world of cats, and trains and licenses judges of high caliber throughout the world.

CANADA

- **CCA** The **Canadian Cat Association** is the only all-Canadian registry, with activities centered mainly in eastern Canada. It publishes a bilingual quarterly newsletter in French and English.

UNITED STATES

- **ACA** America's oldest cat registry, having been active since 1899, the **American Cat Association** is a fairly small association which holds shows in the southeast and southwest of the United States.

- **ACC** Based in the southwest, the **American Cat Council** is a small association which has modified "English-style" shows in which exhibitors must vacate the show hall during judging.

- **CCFF** Although it is one of the smaller associations in the United States, the **Crown Cat Fanciers' Federation** has many shows each year in the northeast and southeastern regions, and also in western Canada.

- **CFA** The **Cat Fanciers' Association** is the largest US association, incorporated and run by a board of directors. It produces an impressive annual yearbook full of articles, breeders' advertisements, and beautiful color photographs. There is a CFA show somewhere in the United States almost every weekend of the year.

- **CFF** With activities centered in the northeastern region of the United States, the **Cat Fanciers' Federation** is a registering body of medium size.

- **UCF** A medium-sized association, the **United Cat Federation** is centered in the southwest of the United States.

UNITED KINGDOM

- **CA** Formed on February 20, 1983, as an alternative body to the GCCF, the **Cat Association of Britain** keeps a register of all pedigree, half-pedigree, and non-pedigree cats belonging to its members, and holds cat shows all over Britain. Formerly run as an independent association, CA became a member of FIFe (below) in 1991.

- **GCCF** Formed on March 8, 1910, the **Governing Council of the Cat Fancy** is run by an executive committee, and its sixty or so affiliated clubs send delegates to represent their members at council meetings. Until 1983, GCCF was the sole body responsible for the registration of cats and licensing of cat shows in Britain.

WORLDWIDE

- **ACFA** An international association and run very democratically, the **American Cat Fanciers' Association** has affiliated clubs in Canada and Japan, and produces a monthly news bulletin for members.

- **FIFe** Most European countries have at least two bodies for the registration of cats, and licensing of shows. One body is almost certain to be affiliated to the **Federation Internationale Feline**, an enormous and well-organized incorporated and chartered society which also has affiliates in countries beyond Europe. Fully established in 1949, FIFe is today the largest cat body in the world, uniting more than 150,000 breeders and exhibitors in the world of show cats.

- **TICA The International Cat Association** produces a bi-monthly newsletter and a yearbook. It has a modern approach to showing and has shows throughout the United States and affiliates in Canada and Japan.

CAT CARE

The domestic cat is quite easy to care for within the confines of the home. It must be provided with some basic equipment, such as feeding and drinking bowls, a comfortable bed, a litter tray, and scratching post.

KEEPING YOUR CAT healthy is mainly a matter of commonsense and proper husbandry. In the first place, the cat needs to have been properly reared as a kitten and should be regularly vaccinated against the most dangerous feline diseases such as panleukopenia, or infectious enteritis, rhinotracheitis and calicivirus, often called cat 'flu, and feline leukemia virus. All cats should be fed a well-balanced diet and receive regular courses of anthelmintics to make sure that they are free from internal parasites. External parasites such as fleas should be controlled by the application of pest powder or sprays when necessary, or by dosing with a product designed to curtail the fleas' breeding cycle. The cat's toilet tray must be maintained in spotless condition at all times, as must its food and water bowls. Given such care, and lots of love and attention, the cat should always remain in good health.

disposable cardboard carrier

Petcraft

PET CARRIER
for
DOGS, CATS, BIRDS,
RABBITS etc.

CODE No. A2932

soft padded sleep igloo

WHAT YOUR CAT NEEDS
A vast range of equipment is available for the comfort of the pet cat, and in a broad price band.

elasticized safety collar and identity tag

hygienic ceramic water bowl

LIFESPAN OF A CAT

The length of a cat's life varies enormously. Those living wild as strays may only survive for two years or so, while a cherished pet may live well into its teens, a senior citizen in human terms.

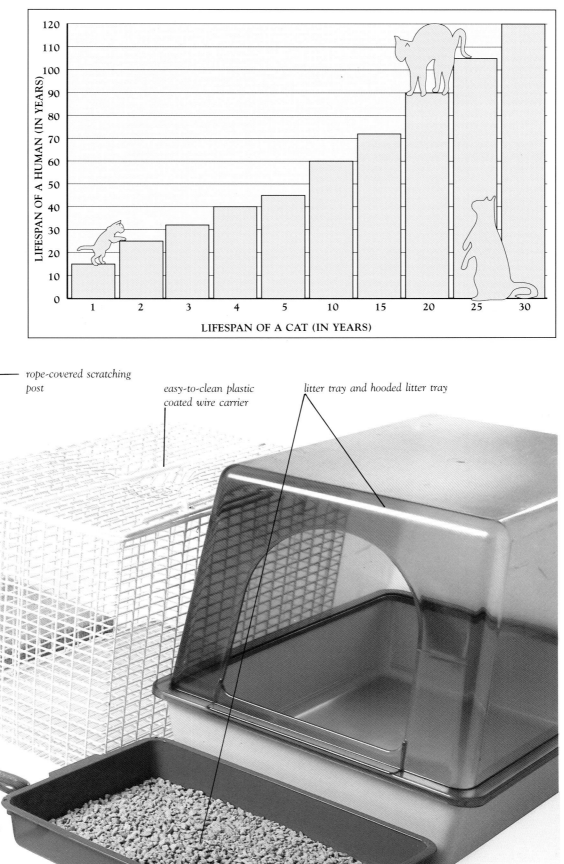

LIFESPAN OF A HUMAN (IN YEARS)

LIFESPAN OF A CAT (IN YEARS)

rope-covered scratching post

easy-to-clean plastic coated wire carrier

litter tray and hooded litter tray

non-toxic unbreakable toys

pure bristle grooming brush

GROOMING

Most cats benefit from grooming, and longhaired breeds such as the Persian must be groomed daily to keep the full coat in good condition and to prevent the soft undercoat from matting. Start grooming routines when the cat is very young. Weaning kittens should be gently brushed and handled all over so that they never resent being groomed in later life. It is essential to make the grooming routine a pleasant one, making sure that the cat never becomes resentful, particularly when its tender parts, such as the inside of the thighs, are being combed through. Different coat types need different grooming tools, and these should be reserved for the cat's own use. A wide variety of equipment is available, and items of better quality are less likely to damage the cat's coat or skin.

 1 2 3 4 5

GROOMING A LONGHAIRED CAT

1 Apply grooming powder to the coat.
2 Rub powder into the coat starting from the tail and working toward the head.
3 Brush the coat thoroughly, removing the powder and lifting the coat away from the skin.

4 Use a wide-toothed comb from tail to head to make sure there are no tangles; pay particular attention to the underparts.
5 Clean the eyes, nostrils, and inside the ear flaps with a series of moist swabs or small brush.

 1 2 3 4

GROOMING A SHORTHAIRED CAT

1 Remove dust, loose hairs, and any debris or parasites, using a metal fine-toothed comb from head to tail.
2 A rubber brush may be used for cats with thick short coats.

3 A soft bristle brush is best for cats with very fine short coats.
4 Buff the coat with a special grooming mitt, a piece of silk or velvet, or a chamois leather.

wire and bristle brush

slicker brush

wide- and fine-toothed comb

toothbrush

HEALTH

Though basically strong, healthy, and built for survival, the cat is susceptible to a host of diseases. Luckily, the most deadly of these may be guarded against by means of effective vaccines, generally given from kittenhood.

GIVING A CAT the correct care is basically a question of common sense. A cat must be given a clean, warm environment in which to live; the correct amount of suitable, nourishing food; constant access to fresh, clean drinking water; and facilities for play and exercise.

A cat should have a bed of its own in a quiet, secluded place, and it should be left in peace to sleep for undisturbed periods during the day. Meals should be fed regularly, on clean dishes, and any food not eaten within a reasonable time, should be removed and disposed of. Cats will not eat stale food. Fresh water should be provided every day and left down for the cat to drink whenever it wishes.

Even if the cat has access to the outdoors, it should be provided with a toilet tray and fresh litter at all

WATCHING OUT FOR PROBLEMS

EARS
The inside of the pinna or ear flap should look and smell clean and fresh. Dark grit or a discharge are signs of the presence of earmites, or infection.

NOSE
Discharge from the nose may indicate the onset of upper respiratory disease or an allergic reaction.

MOUTH
The mouth should be clean and fresh with sharp white teeth. Bad breadth indicates oral problems or kidney disease. An ulcerated mouth or tongue may be an early sign of upper respiratory infection.

EYES
Eyes should be bright with an alert expression. Any discharge should be treated without delay as it could indicate the onset of disease. The nictitating membrane may appear as a third eyelid at the inner corner of each eye and is a sure sign of illness in the cat.

SKIN
The skin should be loose and elastic. If it stays pinched when lifted between the finger and thumb, the cat is dehydrated and needs veterinary attention. Any grit on the spine at the base of the tail indicate the presence of fleas, and sore areas under the body may be an allergic reaction or due to parasitic mites.

ANUS
Any soiling, staining, or soreness may indicate that the cat is suffering from diarrhea.

SIGNS OF ILL HEALTH

Pain Often the first sign of disease. Locating the site of pain may need diagnosis. Pain from skin, muscle, or bone damage is easier to detect than that from the deeper structures.

Fever A rise in body temperature generally indicates infection, but may be caused by heatstroke. A cat's normal temperature at rest is 101.5° F, but 102.5° F is not uncommon.

Change in Behavior Often the first sign of a serious illness, a change in the personality or behavior of a cat should be monitored.

Loss of Balance or Body Control Lameness is detected fairly easily, denoting an injury to a muscle, tendon, or bone; other signs of painful movement may be more difficult to detect – the cat may just stop jumping up to or down from a chair.

Breathing Labored breathing, wheezing, coughing, or sneezing must not be ignored. Note changes in the cat's voice. Any of these symptoms could denote the onset of respiratory disease.

Defecation and Urination Any changes such as the presence of blood in the feces or urine must be taken seriously. A cat straining on its litter tray without producing any results must see a veterinarian without delay.

Eating and Drinking A change in appetite may be transitory, but should not be disregarded. Constant drinking, vomiting, or dribbling are all symptoms of feline diseases. Take note of the cat's behavior pattern and if it persists, seek veterinary advice. It may point to a dental problem or indicate the onset of illness.

Skin and Fur Most cats normally shed their coats twice a year, but any severe hair loss, perhaps leaving bald patches, should be reported to your veterinarian. If the cat scratches at its neck, it may have a parasitic infestation of fleas, ticks, or mites, which need to be treated. Ear mites infest the inside of the ear and must not be neglected. Ringworm, a fungal infection, often produces circular lesions and is transmissable to humans. Cats are also susceptible to various allergies from such things as household disinfectants and flea bites. A skin condition should never be neglected.

CALL THE VET IMMEDIATELY IF THE CAT IS:

- Shocked or hemorrhaging
- Thought to have ingested a poisonous substance
- Partially or completely unconscious
- Falling about, with uncoordinated movements, or appears partly or completely paralyzed
- Obviously injured
- Vomiting frequently or has constant diarrhea

times. It is more hygienic for the cat's wastes to be disposed of than for it to soil the yard. Various types of litter boxes are available, some with hooded lids, and the wide choice of cat litter includes some made from fresh smelling wood chips, as well as the original products made from Fuller's earth. The litter tray should be washed and dried when the litter is changed, and sterilized with diluted household bleach or a safe disinfectant recommended by the vet.

Cats need to strop their claws from time to time, to keep them in good condition and to remove any loose scale. Various types of scratching posts are available, from simple cardboard strips to ingenious constructions of shelves and posts covered with rope or carpet. A cat prefers to strop its claws on an upright post rather than one laid flat on the floor.

Although most cats which are correctly cared for and properly fed, housed, and vaccinated remain fit and well, it is important to be able to recognize the first signs of infection or trauma. Any change in a cat's normal behavior patterns should be treated with suspicion, for while this may be caused by something as simple as a change in the weather, it could also point to the first stages of a specific illness. All signs and symptoms should be carefully noted, and if necessary, veterinary advice should be sought. It is important to avoid any delay in seeking advice in the event of one of the more serious feline diseases, when early treatment is most effective.

The veterinarian should be a cat's best friend, diagnosing and treating any problems and providing preventative care in the form of feline vaccinations and constructive advice.

FELINE DISORDERS

	Gynecological disorder FP	Pregnancy	Queen in distress: "calling"	Trauma: fracture, dislocation, etc.	Ear infection	Conjunctivitis	Dental problems	Incorrect diet	Fleas and other external parasites	Intestinal worms	Heat stroke	Kidney disease	Hairball	Gastroenteritis	Urolithiasis FUS	Feline infectious peritonitis FIP	Feline leukemia virus FeLV	Feline infectious anemia FIA	Respiratory virus infection – cat 'flu, FOV, FVR	Feline infectious enteritis FIE
Vomiting	?	?		?				*		?		×	*	*	×	?	?	?		×
Diarrhea		?						*		?			?	*		?	*	?		×
Apparent constipation				?				×					?	?	*					?
Excessive thirst	×											*	?	?		?		?		?
Loss of appetite	×	×	×	×		?	*	×		?		×	×	×	×	×	×	×	?	*
Abnormal urination	?			?								*			*					
Dehydration	?											×				?	×		×	*
Coughing/sneezing							?					?	?	?		?			*	
Breathing problems		?		×				?	*							×	×	?	?	
Fever	?				?						*			?		×		?	×	?
Lowered temperature	×	?		?								?		?	?	×	?	?	?	*
Pale lips/gums	?			×				?				×				?	?	*		×
Abdominal swelling	×	*		?				?		×			?		×	*	?			
Shaking head				?	*		?		?											
Scratching head/neck				?	×		×	?	*											
Apparent pain	?		*	*	×		×					?	?	×	?					×
Lameness				*				?				?								
Salivation				?			*	×			*			×	?					?
Localized discharge	*		×	*	*	*	?												*	
Noticeable weight loss	?							?				?				*	*	?	?	?

SYMPTOMS
* MAJOR
× COMMON
? POSSIBLE

Feeding Your Cat

An adult cat requires about 50 calories per pound of its body weight each day. Active cats may need more calories, and sedentary cats may need less. Entire cats which are breeding require more calories than neutered cats, and a queen that is lactating and feeding four or more kittens may need as much as 150 calories for each pound of her body weight.

Adult cats generally fare better when given two regular daily meals, and as they grow old, they are best fed three or four small meals daily. Old cats with digestive problems often need special diets as advised by a veterinarian.

A cat's general appearance is the best guide to whether or not its diet is suitable for its size and lifestyle. The signs of a poor diet include dull eyes; a warm, dry nose; bad breath; a dry scurfy coat; flaking claws; and diarrhea or offensive-smelling stools.

There are a number of excellent ways of feeding cats. Canned food is comparatively expensive, but it is formulated to be highly acceptable to cats, and checking the label will show whether the quality and nutritional components are adequate.

Semi-moist diets are very convenient to store and serve, and are highly acceptable to most cats. How-

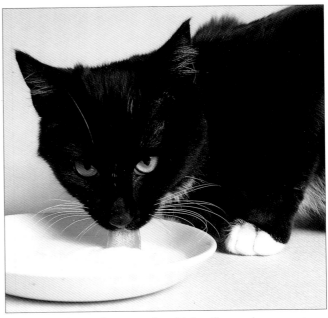

Though adult cats do not need to drink milk, most cats, except those unable to digest it like many Orientals, really enjoy this special treat.

CAT DETAILS		FOOD REQUIREMENTS	
AGE of CAT	WEIGHT OF CAT OUNCES	FEEDS	OUNCES PER FEED
KITTEN			
Newborn	3¾ oz	10	1
5 weeks	16 oz	6	3
10 weeks	32 oz	5	5
20 weeks	4½ lb	4	6
30 weeks	6½ lb	3	7
ADULT			
Male/Female	6½–10 lb	1–2	6–8½ oz
Pregnant	7–8 lb	2–3	8½
Lactating	5½ lb	4	14
Neuter	8–10 lb	1–2	6–7¾

NUTRITIONAL REQUIREMENTS

Proteins are essential substances for growth and repair; they are found in muscle meat, fish, cheese, eggs, and milk. At least 35–40 percent of the entire cat's diet should consist of protein; neutered cats need 25 percent. Cats which cannot digest milk or milk products may be able to accept yogurt as an alternative.

Carbohydrates are not essential in the cat's diet; if they are given, they should consist of cooked grains and vegetable fiber.

Fats provide concentrated forms of energy, and the cat is capable of digesting a diet containing 25 to 30 percent fat. Fats contain the fatty acids necessary for a healthy skin and coat, and fat-soluble vitamins A, D, E, and K. Fats may be added to the cat's diet in the form of butter, margarine, bacon fat, or pure vegetable oils.

Vitamins and minerals are found in a wide variety of foods. Cats need a lot of Vitamin A, but too much can be dangerous. If using canned cat food, check the label for the Vitamin A level. If feeding fresh meat, add one ounce of lightly cooked liver on one or two days each week.

Vitamin B is important to cats, and you should check the labels of canned food to make sure that the B group content is adequate.

Vitamin C is generally considered to be unnecessary in the feline diet, though it may help recovery after illness. Most cats accept Vitamin C in the form of an orange-flavored syrup sold for human babies.

Vitamin D is essential, but cats need a very small amount compared to the requirements of dogs and humans, and most of this need is obtained from sunlight. It is rarely necessary to supplement the diet with additional vitamins and minerals if an adequate diet is fed.

ever, they contain humectants and preservatives which can cause digestive disturbances in some cats. Owners often get around this problem by feeding one meal of canned food and one of semi-moist food each day.

Dry diets are very popular, particularly for pet cats. They are inexpensive, and very easy to store and serve. It is important to make sure that cats fed solely on dry diets are seen to drink plenty of water every day. Some brands may be slightly deficient in fat, so extra fat may be given if necessary.

ENERGY REQUIREMENTS

An adult cat needs 200 to 300 calories per day, depending on its size and amount of exercise. Kittens have a higher demand in relation to their body weight due to their rapid growth rate. Neutered cats need less energy in relation to their body weight as they are not reproducing and generally lead rather sedentary lives.

FOOD TYPE

KEEPING YOUR CAT HEALTHY

A regular regime of care for your cat will help it to stay in good condition and be less likely to become ill.

DAILY
- Observe the cat's general appearance and behavior; any dramatic change may indicate the need for immediate veterinary attention.
- Feed a well-balanced diet of good-quality food.
- Provide fresh water in a clean container.
- Dispose of soiled litter; clean toilet tray; check cat's stools (and urine if possible) for any sign of abnormality.
- Groom the cat according to its requirements in respect of coat type and hair length.
- In free-ranging cats, check the coat for the staining which could indicate diarrhea and for foreign bodies such as grass seeds or parasites such as ticks; check the feet for sore or cracked pads and for foreign bodies such as splinters or thorns; check all over the head, body, underparts, and legs for signs of fighting – bites and scratches can lead to abcesses if not treated with an antiseptic wash.

WEEKLY
- Examine ears and coat for parasites. If present, check with the veterinarian for appropriate treatment.
- Check mouth and throat; clean teeth if necessary.

MONTHLY
- Check the cat all over from head to tail with your fingertips, feeling for any lumps, bumps, lesions, or foreign bodies. Any worrying anomalies should be discussed with the vet.

SIX-MONTHLY
- Check the cat's records to see if blood tests or vaccinations are due and mark the dates in your diary: free-ranging cats should have a sample of feces analyzed for the presence of parasitic worms, and treatment administered where appropriate.

YEARLY
- Have a complete veterinary check carried out. This can be arranged in conjunction with an annual booster vaccination program.

58 Persian
78 Colorpoint

LONGHAIRED BREEDS

LONGHAIR

ALTHOUGH THEY HAVE been officially classified by the GCCF in Britain as Longhairs, these cats are popularly referred to as Persians, and are officially classified as such in the United States.

The typical Persian is a substantial, strong cat, with a full and flowing coat of long, dense fur concealing a sturdy body and thick legs. The head is large and round with tiny ears and large, round eyes. The fur around the neck is extra long, forming the typical ruff or frill, and the long hair on the tail makes it resemble a fox's tail or brush.

Persian cats first arrived in Europe in the sixteenth century and became more popular than the imported Angoras. Charles H. Ross reported, in a book published in 1868: "The Persian is a variety with hair very long and silky; perhaps more so than that of the Angora; it is however differently coloured, being of a fine uniform grey on the upper part with the texture of the fur as soft as silk and the lustre glossy; the color fades off on the lower parts of the sides and fades, or nearly does so, on the belly." This preceded the first cat shows.

Over the years, selective breeding standardized the type of the Persian breed so that all the varieties would closely conform to one basic standard. However, various cat associations designated different points awards for

BREAKDOWN OF 100 SHOW POINTS

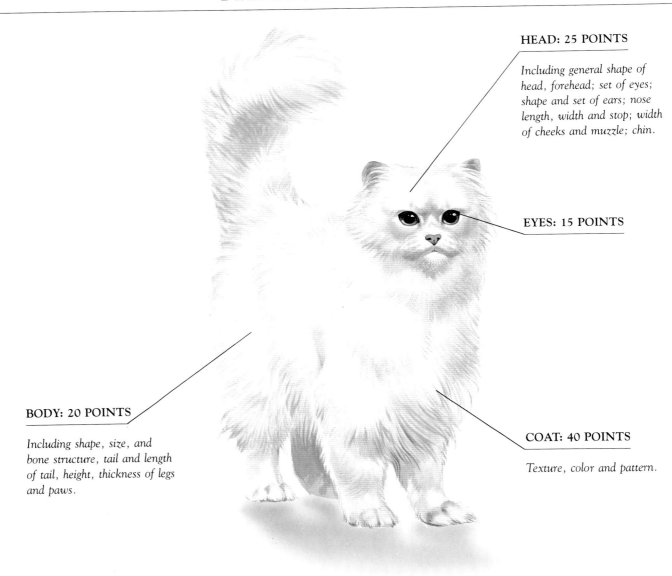

HEAD: 25 POINTS

Including general shape of head, forehead; set of eyes; shape and set of ears; nose length, width and stop; width of cheeks and muzzle; chin.

EYES: 15 POINTS

BODY: 20 POINTS

Including shape, size, and bone structure, tail and length of tail, height, thickness of legs and paws.

COAT: 40 POINTS

Texture, color and pattern.

different features as incentives for breeders to work toward refinement of those features.

Character and Care

Persian cats are generally placid and gentle by nature, and as kittens are playful and mischievous. They make very affectionate and loving pets, and are generally quiet and restful to have in the home. The females make excellent mothers, and the kittens rarely give problems during lactation and weaning.

The long, dense coat must be brushed and combed daily to prevent tangles and matting, and kittens must be accustomed to being groomed all over, including their underparts, from a very early age. In adults, particular attention must be paid to the frill or ruff, under the belly, and the flowing hair of the tail.

PENALTIES

The Persian is penalized for having a kinked or abnormal tail; a locket or button; any apparent weakness in the hindquarters; any apparent deformity of the spine; asymmetrical appearance of the head, and incorrect eye color.

KEY CHARACTERISTICS

- **CATEGORY** Longhair.

- **OVERALL BUILD** Medium to large, with massive shoulders and back, muscular.

- **COAT** Long and dense, standing off from the body, fine and silky texture, with a full ruff (frill) over shoulders and chest.

- **HEAD** Round and massive with a broad skull, round forehead, full cheeks, and powerful jaws.

- **NOSE** Short and broad with a definite stop.

- **CHIN** Strong and well-developed.

- **EYES** Large, round and full, set wide apart.

- **EARS** Small, round-tipped, set wide apart and rather low on the head.

- **BODY** Of cobby type, low on the legs, with a broad chest, massive shoulders, and well-muscled back.

- **LEGS** Short, thick, and strong.

- **PAWS** Large, round, and firm. Toe tufts preferred.

- **TAIL** Short, but in proportion to the length of the body, carried without a curve.

- **COLORS** White with blue, orange or copper, odd eyes; black, red, cream, blue, chocolate, lilac; smoke: black, blue, red, torbie, blue-cream; cameo: shell, shaded, shell tortoiseshell, shaded tortoiseshell; bicolor: black, blue, red, cream, and Van patterns; tabby (Classic and Mackeral patterns): silver, brown, red (*UK and US*), blue, cream, cameo, silver patched, brown patched, blue patched (*US only*).

WHITE

ODD-EYED WHITE

In this variety of Persian, one eye should be orange or copper, and the other deep blue, and both eyes should be of equal color intensity.

THIS VARIETY HAS been popular for more than a hundred years, and is the result of matings between the earliest imported Angora and Persian cats. The original white longhairs had blue eyes. Because of a genetic anomaly connected to blue eye color in cats, many of them were deaf. Eventually, efforts were made to improve the overall type and conformation of the whites, and cross-matings were made with Blue Persian and Black Persian show winners. Not only did the resulting offspring have more solid bone and better body and head type, some cats had orange or copper eye color, and in some cases, were odd-eyed, having one blue eye and one of orange or copper. An added bonus was that these cats had good hearing,

BLUE-EYED WHITE

These cats are sometimes found to be deaf, due to a genetic factor.

although some of the odd-eyed whites were found to be deaf in the ear adjacent to the blue eye. Today's White Persians are judged as three separate varieties, according to eye color, in Britain.

Special care is needed in grooming these white varieties, as they can easily become soiled with yellow staining around the eyes, nostrils, lips, and under the tail. If neglected, the stains may prove impossible to remove, spoiling the beauty of the coat. Fanciers generally use a white grooming powder to clean and enhance their pets' white coats, and this helps to prevent staining.

Coloring

The coat should be pure, glistening white, without markings or shadings of any kind. Nose leather and paw pads are pink. In the blue-eyed White, eye color is deep blue. In the copper-eyed (USA) or orange-eyed (UK) White, eye color is brilliant copper (USA) or orange or copper (UK). The odd-eyed White has one eye of deep blue, the other of copper or orange.

ORANGE-EYED WHITE

Cats with this copper or orange eye color are not affected by problems with their hearing and often appear more responsive than their blue-eyed cousins.

BLACK

ONE OF THE oldest of the pedigree breeds, the Black Persian is one of the most difficult to produce in top show condition. It is a massive, handsome cat, and the glossy, raven-black coat is complemented by the large glowing eyes. The black hair is prone to developing rusty tinges, thought to be caused by strong sunlight or damp conditions, and periods of molting cause brownish bars to appear in the flowing coat. Young black kittens are often quite disappointing, with lots of shading in the undercoat and rustiness in the top coat, but these defects usually disappear with maturity.

Coloring

The coat should be dense coal black from roots to tips of hair, free from any tinge or markings or shadings of any kind, and with no white hair. The nose leather is black, and the paw pads black or brown. Eye color is brilliant copper (USA) or copper or deep orange (UK), with no green rim.

BLACK PERSIAN
The eyes of the Black Persian should be brilliant copper or deep orange, setting off the jet-black coat to perfection.

RED

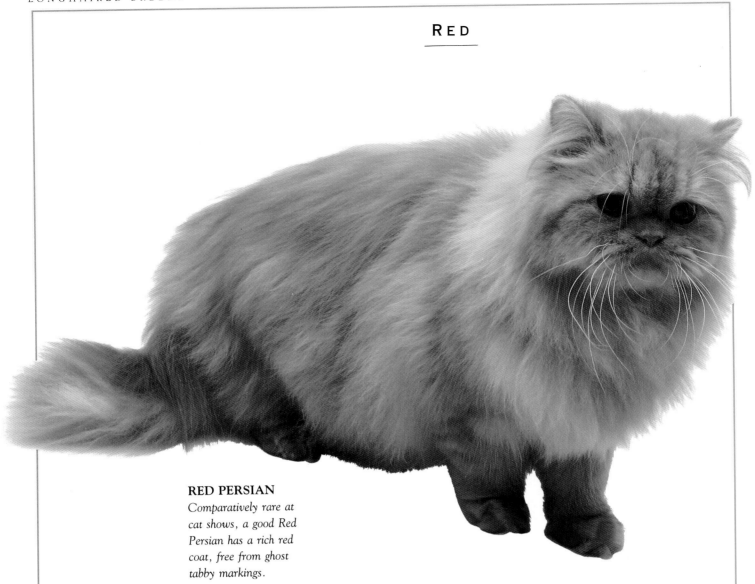

RED PERSIAN

Comparatively rare at cat shows, a good Red Persian has a rich red coat, free from ghost tabby markings.

ALTHOUGH THIS HAS been a favorite show breed for over a hundred years, in the days of the first cat shows there was some confusion in contemporary writings as to the true description of the variety's color. Until 1894, shows at London's Crystal Palace offered classes for Brown or Red Tabby Persians, but in 1895 a class for Orange and Cream was added. The Orange, Cream, Fawn and Tortoiseshell Society revised the standard for the Orange Persian, requiring "the colour to be as bright as possible, and either self or markings to be as distinct as can be got." Judges obviously selected their winners irrespective of markings. Over the years breeders selected for either self-colored or tabby in the reds, and by 1912 they had separate classes, still being described as Orange Self or Orange Tabby. The deeper color was selected, and although World War II decimated the variety's numbers, the past fifty years have seen wonderful improvements in Red Persians in the world's show rings.

Coloring

The coat should be deep, rich, clear, brilliant red without markings or shadings or ticking. Lips and chin are the same color as the coat. Nose leather and paw pads are brick red and eye color is brilliant copper (USA) or deep copper (UK).

CREAM

IN THE EARLY DAYS, cream cats were often called "fawns" and were often discarded by keen exhibitors in favor of cats with stronger coat colors. Some of the first Angoras were probably cream, for Charles H. Ross, writing in 1868, describes the Angora as "a very beautiful variety, with silvery hair of fine silken texture . . . some are yellowish, and others olive, approaching the colour of a lion . . ."

In 1903, Frances Simpson wrote that creams were becoming fashionable, but the first cats of this variety had been considered "freaks or flukes" and were given away. Cream cats were eventually imported into the United States from Britain and soon established themselves as successful show winners. Today's exhibition Cream Persian is a refined and sophisticated breed, exemplifying all the best features of the typical Longhair.

Coloring

The requirements for coat color differ between the United States, the United Kingdom, and Europe in general. The CFA standard requires one level shade of buff cream, sound to the roots, without markings, and with lighter shades preferred. Britain's GCCF calls for pure and sound pale to medium color, without shadings or markings. The FIFe standard requires pale, pure, pastel cream with no warm tone or any lighter shadings or markings, the color to be sound and even from roots to tips. Nose leather and paw pads are pink; eye color is brilliant copper (*USA*) [deep copper (*UK*)].

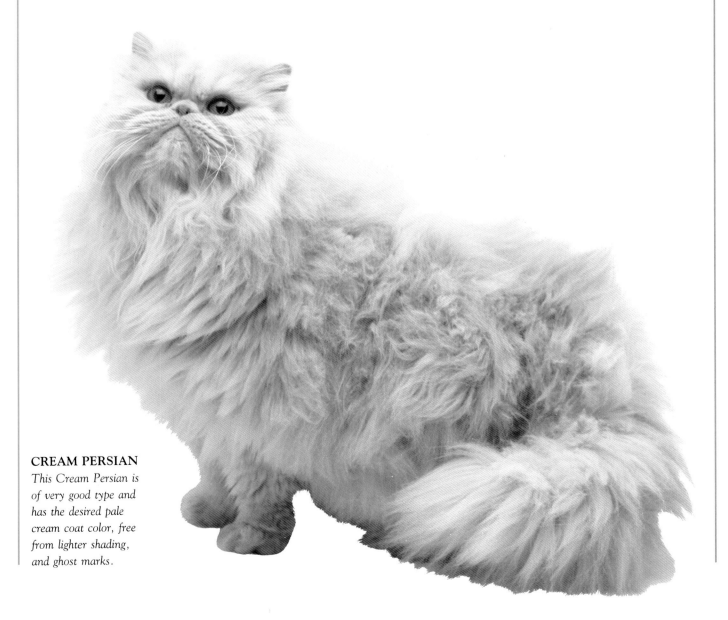

CREAM PERSIAN
This Cream Persian is of very good type and has the desired pale cream coat color, free from lighter shading, and ghost marks.

BLUE

THE BLUE COLOR in cats is caused by the action of the dilution factor on black, and some of the earliest Persian imports had this attractive coat color. In the first cat shows, lots of blue cats were exhibited, but they did not closely resemble the cats seen in the show rings today. By the turn of the century, early show faults such as white lockets and tabby markings had been largely eliminated, and in 1901 the Blue Persian Society was founded to promote the breeding and exhibiting of cats of this variety. Members of society, including Queen Victoria, owned Blue Persian cats, and this added to their general status and popularity, which remains to this day.

Coloring

The blue coat should be of one level tone from nose to tail tip, and sound from roots to tips of hair. Any shade of blue is allowed, but in the USA the lighter shades are preferred. The coat must be free from all markings, shadings, or white hairs. The nose leather and paw pads are blue; the eye color is brilliant copper (*USA*); deep orange or copper without any trace of green (*UK*).

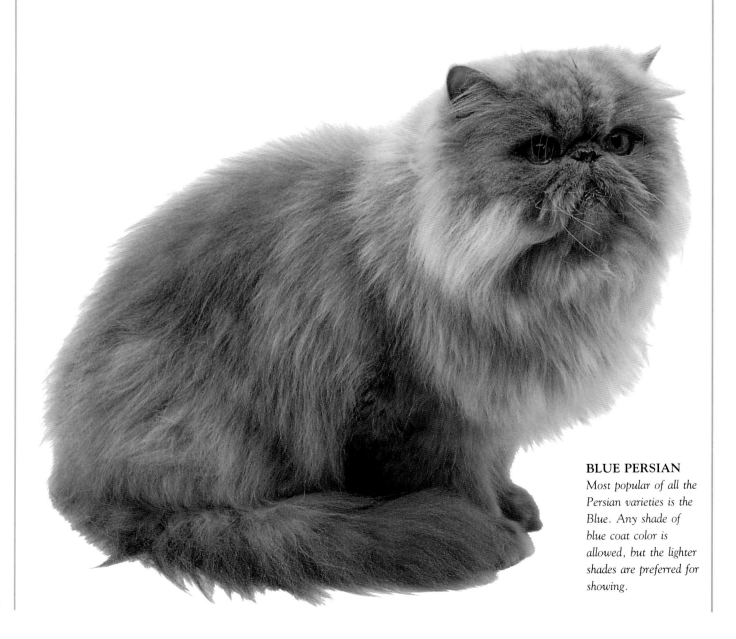

BLUE PERSIAN
Most popular of all the Persian varieties is the Blue. Any shade of blue coat color is allowed, but the lighter shades are preferred for showing.

BLUE-CREAM

**BLUE-CREAM
PERSIAN**
*In American shows,
this variety is required
to have cream patches
on its blue coat, while
the GCCF expects an
intermingled coat.*

CONSIDERED TO BE a fairly new variety, the
Blue-cream Persian was not recognized in
Britain until 1930, although reports of kittens
with blue and cream markings appeared at the
turn of the century. Blue-cream coloring is the
dilute equivalent of tortoiseshell. Just as a
tortoiseshell has patches of black and red, so
the blue-cream cat has corresponding dilute
patches of blue (from black) and cream (from
red). Although early cat fanciers understood
little of feline genetics, some, by careful
observation, were able to deduce some of the
results to be expected by cross-matings between
cats of various colors. The biggest problem to
beset the early cat breeders was that they did
not recognize the fact that the "marked blue
cats," or blue-creams, were all female, and that
the color was sex-linked. Breeders waited
hopefully for similar male kittens to be born so
that like-to-like matings could take place, to
produce a "true" breed.

Coloring
The requirements for coat color and pattern
differ between the United States, the United
Kingdom, and Europe in general. In North
America, the coat is required to be blue with
clearly defined patches of solid cream, well
broken on both body and extremities. Britain's
GCCF requires the coat to consist of pastel
shades of blue and cream, softly intermingled.
In Europe, FIFe refers to Blue-cream as Blue
Tortie, and the coat requirement is for light
blue-gray and pale cream, patched and/or
mingled, both colors to be evenly distributed
over the body and extremities. Although
breeders and show judges like the Blue-cream
to have a facial blaze, USA and UK standards
do not stipulate this, though it is featured as
desirable by FIFe.

The eye color is brilliant copper (USA) or
deep copper or orange (UK).

SMOKE

FIRST GIVEN A breed class at a British cat show in 1893, a contemporary author wrote of the Smoke Persian, "The Smoke is a cat of great beauty, but unfortunately is very rare." Sadly, this remains as true today, though there was a time in the early 1900s when the variety enjoyed more popularity. One of the early successful breeders and exhibitors was Mrs. H.V. James, who wrote about her beloved breed in 1903 and later supplied information for a cat book published in 1948, showing clearly her dedication to Smoke Persians. Mrs. James bought a Blue Persian kitten which died, and the replacement she received from the breeder proved most disappointing, developing into a cat of "a deep cinder colour," nothing like a Blue Persian. Mrs. James thought he looked rather smoky in color and so entered him as a Smoke Persian in a show, where, to her surprise, he was placed first in all his classes.

The National Cat Club's stud book, published in Britain for the years 1900 to 1905, listed thirty Smoke Persians, but when the newly established GCCF published its first stud book in 1912, only eighteen such cats were

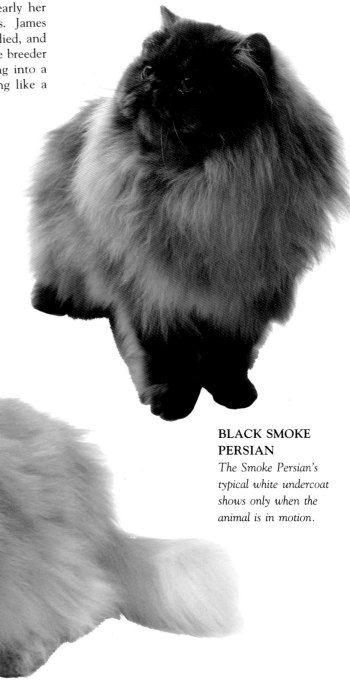

CREAM SMOKE PERSIAN

The cream variety is a dilute version of the Red Smoke. The cream coloring shades to white on the side and flanks.

BLACK SMOKE PERSIAN

The Smoke Persian's typical white undercoat shows only when the animal is in motion.

BLUE SMOKE PERSIAN

An excellent example of this variety with a full pale frill or ruff and ear tufts as required in the show standard.

listed. By the end of World War II, the Smoke Persian, like so many other minority breeds, had become practically non-existent.

Today's Smoke Persian is known as "the cat of contrasts" and though rare, is generally of excellent longhair type. The breed has always been popular in the United States, and in recent years has been bred in colors other than the original black.

BLACK SMOKE The undercoat is pure white, deeply tipped with black. In repose the cat appears black, but in motion the white undercoat is clearly apparent. The mask and points are black with a narrow band of white at the base of the hairs next to the skin, seen only when the hair is parted. The frill (ruff) and ear tufts are light silver. Nose leather and paw pads are black; eye color is brilliant copper (*USA*) or orange or copper (*UK*).

BLUE SMOKE The white undercoat is deeply tipped with blue so that in repose the cat appears blue, but in motion the white undercoat is clearly apparent. Mask and points are blue with a narrow band of white next to the skin which is seen only when the hair is parted. The frill (ruff) and ear tufts are all white; the nose leather and paw pads are blue; the eyes are a brilliant copper or orange or copper.

RED SMOKE The undercoat is white, deeply tipped with red. In repose the cat appears red, but in motion the white undercoat is clearly apparent. Mask and points are red with a narrow band of white next to the skin, seen only when the hair is parted. The frill (ruff) and ear tufts are white, the eye rims, nose leather and paw pads rose; eye color is brilliant copper.

LILAC SMOKE PERSIAN

Both Chocolate and Lilac Smoke Persians are accepted by several feline bodies and apart from color, should conform in every other way to the basic standard of points.

SMOKE TORTOISESHELL The white under-coat is deeply tipped with black, with clearly defined, unbrindled patches of red and light red hairs in the pattern of a Tortoiseshell. In repose the cat appears to be tortoiseshell, but in motion the white undercoat is clearly apparent. The face and ears are tortoiseshell patterned with a narrow band of white next to the skin, seen only when the hair is parted. A blaze of red or light red tipping on the face is desirable. The frill (ruff) and ear tufts are white and the eyes a brilliant copper.

BLUE-CREAM SMOKE The white undercoat is deeply tipped with blue, with clearly defined, unbrindled patches of cream in the pattern of a Blue-cream. In repose the cat appears to be blue-cream, but in motion the white undercoat is clearly apparent. Face and ears are blue-cream patterned with a narrow band of white next to the skin, seen only when the hair is parted. A blaze of cream tipping on the face is desirable. The frill (ruff) and ear tufts are white, and the eye color a brilliant copper.

CHOCOLATE SMOKE PERSIAN
Although only accepted as a provisional variety, this young cat has very good type and excellent eyes for both color and shape.

LILAC TORTIE SMOKE
The dilute version of the Blue-Cream Smoke, just beginning to develop the desired pale frill or ruff.

RED SMOKE PERSIAN
An excellent example of a variety that is difficult to breed without tabby markings. This fine cat has a superb coat and has been perfectly groomed.

CAMEO

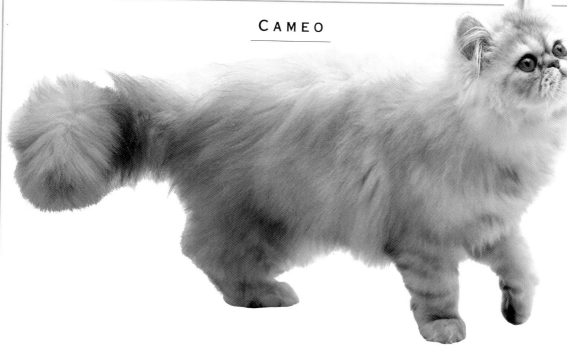

CAMEO PERSIAN

In kittens of the Cameo series, the full color effect takes some time to develop. This youngster has very good type.

FIRST BRED IN the United States in 1954, Cameo Persians were the result of matings between Smoke and Tortoiseshell cats of outstanding type. Cameo kittens are born almost white and develop their subtle color as they grow. There are three intensities of coloring within the Cameo group: Shell is very pale, Shaded somewhat darker, and Smoke is darker.

Cameo cats are naturally affectionate, and their unusual coloring soon gained popularity for the new varieties in countries outside the United States.

SHELL CAMEO (RED CHINCHILLA) The white undercoat must be sufficiently tipped with red on the head, back, flanks, and tail to give the characteristic sparkling appearance of the variety. The face and legs may be lightly shaded with tipping. The chin, ear tufts, stomach, and chest are white. Eye rims, nose leather, and paw pads are all rose, and the eye color a brilliant copper.

SHADED CAMEO (RED SHADED) A white undercoat has a mantle of red tipping shading the face, the sides, and the tail. The color ranges from dark on the ridge to white on the chest, stomach, under the tail, and on the chin. The legs are the same tone as the face. The general effect is much more red than the Shell Cameo. Eye rims are rose; eye color is a brilliant copper.

RED SHELL The white undercoat, delicately tipped with black, has well-defined patches of red and light red tipped hairs, in the tortoiseshell pattern, on the head, back, flanks, and tail. The face and legs may be slightly shaded with tipping. The chin, ear tufts, stomach, and chest are white. A blaze of red or light red tipping on the face is desirable. The eyes are brilliant copper.

RED SHADED The white undercoat has a mantle of black tipping and clearly defined patches of red and light red tipped hairs in the tortoiseshell pattern. This covers the face, down the sides and the tail, the color ranging from dark on the ridge to white on the chest, stomach, under the tail, and on the chin. The general effect is much darker than the Shell Tortoiseshell. Eye color is a brilliant copper.

BLUE-CREAM CAMEO

The softly intermingled blue and cream tipping of this variety may be of any intensity, overlaying the white undercoat.

BICOLOR

THE EARLIEST RECORDS of fancy cats give several examples of two-colored cats. Mainly Shorthairs, they include several colors, each with white. At the first cat shows, black and white cats were known as Magpies and were expected to have very precise and even markings. Such precise markings proved very difficult to achieve, and few breeders were prepared to persevere in order to produce the perfect Bicolor. Eventually, new standards were formulated by cat associations around the world.

The Bicolor may be of any solid color with white: black and white, blue and white, red and white, cream and white. In the United States, the cats are required to have white legs and paws, white on the chest, the underbody, and the muzzle, and an inverted "V" of white on the face is desirable. White is also allowed under the tail and as a marking resembling a collar around the neck.

The British standard is less precise in the requirements for the distribution of color and white. The patches of color should be clear and evenly distributed, with not more than two-thirds of the coat being colored, and not more than one half of the coat being white. The face must be patched with color and white. Faults in the bicolor include tabby markings, a long tail, or incorrect eye color.

RED AND WHITE BICOLOR
Red and Cream Bi-colored cats should be free from any shading in the colored areas of their coats.

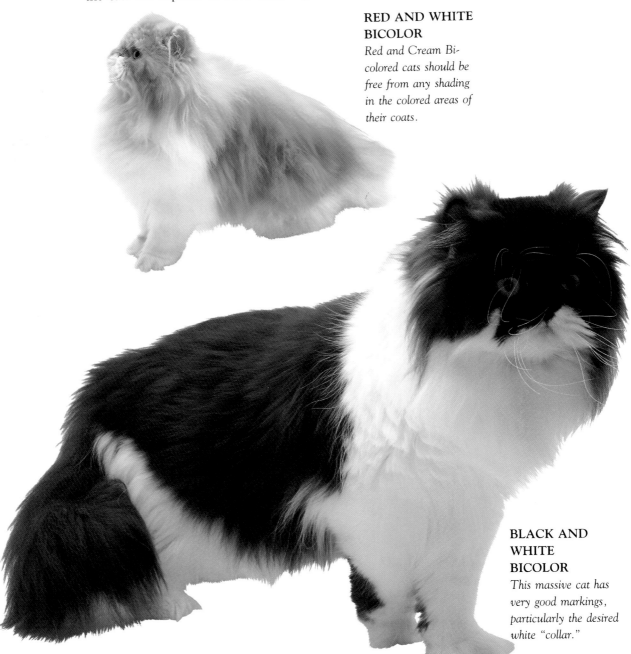

BLACK AND WHITE BICOLOR
This massive cat has very good markings, particularly the desired white "collar."

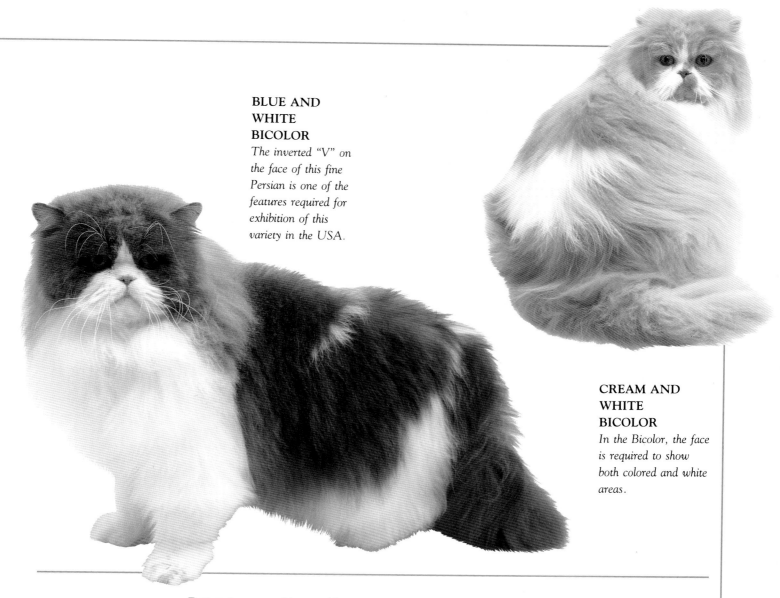

BLUE AND WHITE BICOLOR

The inverted "V" on the face of this fine Persian is one of the features required for exhibition of this variety in the USA.

CREAM AND WHITE BICOLOR

In the Bicolor, the face is required to show both colored and white areas.

PERSIAN VAN BICOLOR

THIS SUB-VARIETY may be shown in black and white, blue and white, red and white, or cream and white. The color distribution is quite different from that of the Persian Bicolor. The Van Bicolor is basically a white cat with the colour confined to the extremities – head, legs, and tail. Only one or two small colored patches on the body are allowed.

VAN BICOLOR

The distribution of color is unusual; the coat is basically white, with colored areas confined to the head, ears, and tail.

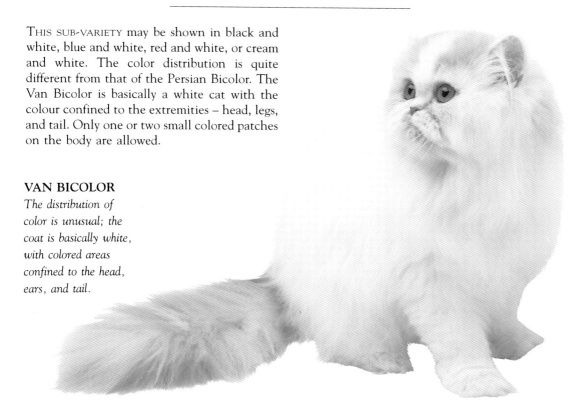

71

TABBY

PEDIGREE TABBY CATS have always caused controversy over their standards of points throughout the cat world. In the early days of the development of breeds, there were arguments about pattern and clarity of markings, and even more disagreement about the correct eye color. Tabby Persians are quite rare in the show rings of the world, possibly because it is difficult to reach the high standard demanded.

In Britain, the Tabby Persian is shown in three color varieties – Silver, Brown, and Red, whereas American show rings exhibit a wider variety of colors.

Coat Patterns

The Classic Tabby pattern, sometimes referred to as the "marbled" or "blotched," calls for precise dense markings, clearly defined and broad. The legs must be evenly barred, with bracelets extending as far as the body markings. The tail should be evenly ringed. Several unbroken necklaces ring the neck and upper chest, frown marks form a letter "M" on the forehead, and unbroken lines run back from the outer corner of each eye. Swirls on the cheeks and vertical lines over the back of the head extend to the shoulder markings, which are in the shape of a butterfly with both upper and lower wings distinctly outlined, and marked with dots inside the outline. Three parallel lines run down the spine from the butterfly to the tail, well separated by stripes of the coat's ground color. A large, solid blotch on each side is encircled by one or more unbroken rings. There should be a double vertical row of "buttons" on the chest and stomach.

In the Mackerel Tabby pattern, dense and clearly defined narrow penciling marks the coat. The legs are evenly barred, with narrow bracelets extending as far as the body markings. The tail is barred, and distinct chain-like necklaces encircle the neck. The head is barred, with a distinct "M" on the forehead. Unbroken lines run back from the eyes, and lines run back from the head to meet the shoulders. The spine lines form a narrow saddle, and pencilings run around the body.

SILVER TABBY A ground color of pure pale silver includes the lips and chin; the markings are dense black. Nose leather is brick red, paw pads black, and eye color green or hazel.

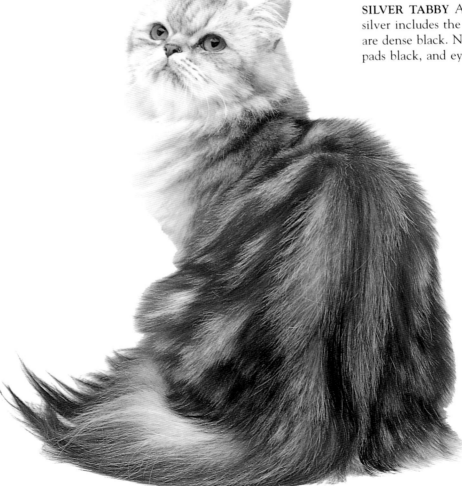

SILVER TABBY
The dense black markings of the longhaired Silver Tabby show up clearly on the pale silver base coat.

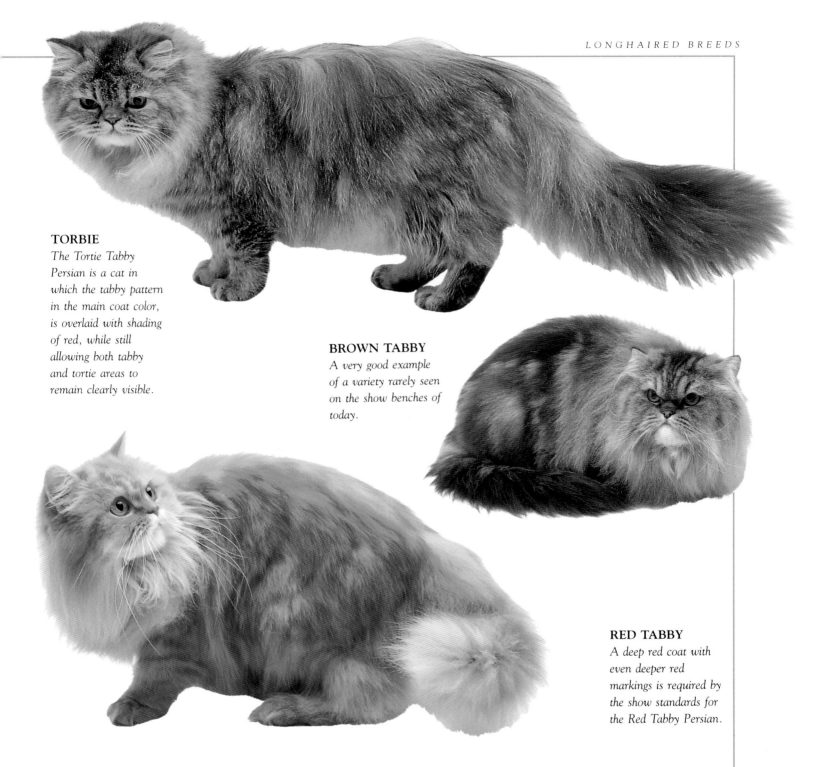

TORBIE
The Tortie Tabby Persian is a cat in which the tabby pattern in the main coat color, is overlaid with shading of red, while still allowing both tabby and tortie areas to remain clearly visible.

BROWN TABBY
A very good example of a variety rarely seen on the show benches of today.

RED TABBY
A deep red coat with even deeper red markings is required by the show standards for the Red Tabby Persian.

RED TABBY The ground color is red, including the lips and chin; the markings deep rich red. Nose leather is brick red, paw pads black or brown, and eyes brilliant copper.

BROWN TABBY The ground color is a brilliant coppery brown; the markings dense black. The lips and chin are the same color as the rings around the eyes. The backs of the legs should be black from the paw to the heel. Nose leather is brick red, paw pads black or brown, and the eyes copper or hazel (UK).

BLUE TABBY The ground color of pale bluish ivory includes the lips and chin; the markings are very deep blue, affording good contrast with the ground color. A warm fawn patina covers the whole of the cat. Nose leather is old rose, paw pads rose, and eye color copper.

CREAM TABBY The ground color is a very pale cream, and includes the lips and chin. The markings of buff or cream are sufficiently darker than the ground color to afford good contrast. Nose leather and paw pads are all pink; eye color is brilliant copper.

CAMEO TABBY The ground color is off-white, including the lips and chin. The markings are red. Nose leather and paw pads are rose and eye color is brilliant copper.

SILVER TORBIE TABBY A pale silver ground color includes the lips and chin. Classic or mackerel markings of black and patches of red and/or light red are clearly defined on the body and extremities. A blaze of red or light red on the face is desirable. Eye color is a brilliant copper or hazel.

BROWN TORBIE TABBY The ground color is a brilliant coppery brown with the lips and chin the same shade as the rings around the eyes; with classic or mackerel markings of dense black and patches of red and/or light red clearly defined on both body and extremities. Eye color is brilliant copper.

BLUE TORBIE TABBY A pale bluish ivory ground color includes the lips and chin. Classic or mackerel markings of very deep blue afford good contrast with the ground color. There are clearly defined patches of cream on the body and extremities, and a warm fawn overtone or patina over the whole of the cat. A blaze of cream on the face is desirable. Eye color is brilliant copper.

LILAC TABBY

In the dilute range of Tabby longhairs, the markings are less distinct.

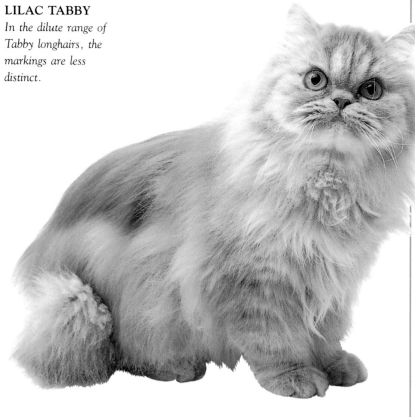

CHOCOLATE TORBIE

Warm markings on a bronze agouti base coat give this cat its glowing coat pattern.

BLUE TABBY

The Blue Tabby's strong blue markings are set on an unusual gray base coat with a slight fawn color cast, called "blue biscuit."

TORTOISESHELL AND WHITE

THE FIRST RECORDED tortoiseshell cats were short-coated, but around the early 1900s, long-coated tortoiseshells were seen at cat shows; they have always been popular as pets. Breeders are intrigued by the female-only variety, and enjoy the variety of colors a tortoiseshell queen can produce, depending on the recessive color genes she carries, and the color and genotype of the male to which she is mated. A similar situation exists with tortoiseshell-and-white cats, once known as Chintz cats in Britain, and referred to as Calico cats in the United States. In the Dilute Calico, the effect of the dilute gene replaces the black color with blue, and the red patches with cream, giving a blue, cream, and white cat. A dilute tortoiseshell (without white) is a blue-cream, which has been described on page 65. As there are no males in these varieties (very occasionally a male is born, but invariably proves to be sterile at maturity), solid-colored cats are generally used for stud purposes.

CALICO (USA) The body color is white with unbrindled patches of black and red; white is predominant on the underparts. The eye color is brilliant copper.

DILUTE CALICO *(USA)* The body color is white with unbrindled patches of blue and cream; white is predominant on the underparts. The eye color is brilliant copper.

TORTOISESHELL The body color is black with unbrindled and clearly defined patches of red and light red on both the body and extremities. A blaze of red or light red on the face is desirable. The eye color is brilliant copper.

TORTOISESHELL and WHITE *(UK)* The body color is black, red, and light red or their dilutions, (blue, cream and light cream), with the colors well distributed and interspersed with white. The eye color is deep orange or copper.

TORTOISESHELL
Popular since the pioneer days of cat breeding, the Tortoiseshell Persian always attracts public interest at shows by its striking coat of black patched with areas of red.

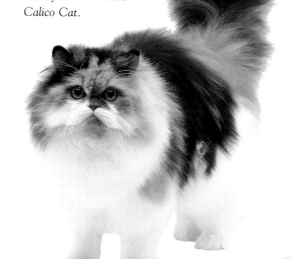

TORTOISESHELL AND WHITE
In America, this variety is known as a Calico Cat.

CHOCOLATE TORTIE
The black and red areas of the Tortie are replaced with warm chocolate and light red.

BLUE TORTIE AND WHITE
The patches of color are required to be distinct and free from scattered white hairs.

SILVER AND GOLDEN

PERHAPS THE MOST glamorous of the Persians, the Chinchilla has a characteristic sparkling, silvery appearance. It has a long history, being first recorded by John Jennings in 1893, who described it as "a peculiar but beautiful variety; the fur at the roots is silver and shades to the tips to a decided slate hue, giving it a most pleasing and attractive appearance." Exhibitors at London's first Crystal Palace cat shows described their cats variously as "Silver Grey," "Blue or Silver Striped," "Chinchilla Tabby," or "Silver Chinchilla."

The first Chinchilla cats were born by accident when silver tabbies were mated with cats of other colors. Early Chinchillas were much darker than those seen today, having heavier tipping, tabby markings on the face, and heavy barring on the legs. As the breed developed, the lighter cats came to be known as Chinchilla, and the darker ones, when successfully bred to a different standard, were designated the Shaded Silver. The question of

eye color proved difficult to resolve, the early specimens having a range of color from yellow, to amber and bright green. Chinchilla cats were imported into the United States from Britain from the early 1900s, and soon became well-established and popular on both sides of the Atlantic.

In recent years American breeders have found it possible to add the chinchilla and shaded silver appearance to other colors, and Chinchilla Golden and Shaded Golden cats have begun to appear at shows.

CHINCHILLA SILVER The cat has a pure white undercoat, sufficiently tipped with black on the head, back, flanks, and tail to give the characteristic sparkling silver appearance of this variety. The legs may be slightly shaded with tipping. The chin, ear tufts, chest, and stomach are pure white, and the rims of the eyes, lips, and nose are outlined with black. The nose leather is brick red; the paw pads are black; the eye color is green or blue-green.

SHADED SILVER/PEWTER The cat has a white undercoat with a mantle of black tipping shading down the face, sides and tail, from dark

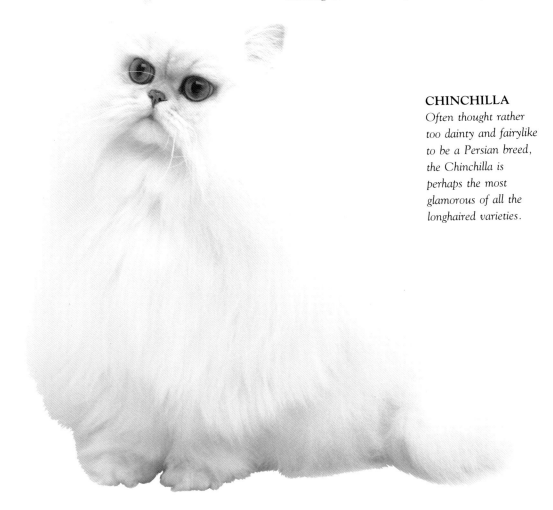

CHINCHILLA
Often thought rather too dainty and fairylike to be a Persian breed, the Chinchilla is perhaps the most glamorous of all the longhaired varieties.

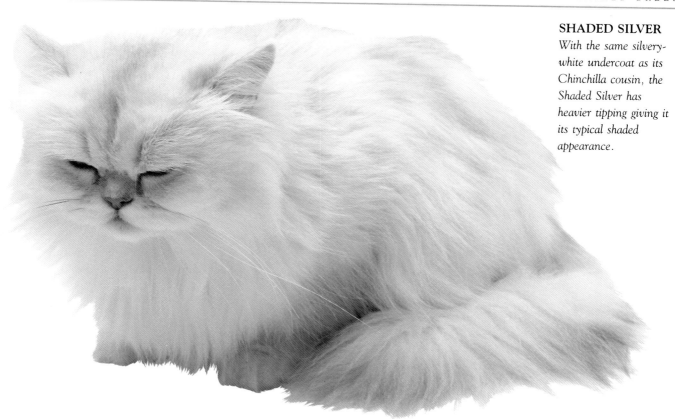

on the ridge to white on the chin, chest, stomach, and under the tail. The legs are the same tone as the face, and the general effect is darker than the Chinchilla. The rims of the eyes, lips and nose are outlined with black. The nose leather is brick red; the paw pads are black; the eye color is green or blue-green. Note that the Pewter Longhair (UK) eye color is orange or copper with black rims.

CHINCHILLA GOLDEN The cat has a rich, warm cream undercoat, sufficiently tipped with seal brown on the head, back, flanks, and tail to give a golden appearance. The legs may be slightly shaded with tipping, and the rims of the eyes, lips, and nose are outlined with seal brown. The nose leather is deep rose; the paw pads are seal brown; the eye color is green or blue-green.

SHADED GOLDEN The cat has a rich, warm cream undercoat and a mantle of seal brown tipping shading down the face, sides and tail, from dark on the ridge to cream on the chin, chest, stomach, and under the tail. The legs are the same tone as the face, and the general effect is darker than the Chinchilla. The rims of the eyes, lips, and nose are outlined with seal brown. The nose leather is deep rose; the paw pads are seal brown; the eye color is green or blue-green.

GOLDEN PERSIAN

Seal brown tipping on a base coat of golden apricot produces this unusual variety. As with the Chinchilla, this cat should have eyes of green or blue-green.

COLORPOINT

THIS BREED IS a cat of true Persian type with the markings first known in Siamese cats, where the true coat color is restricted to the cooler areas of the cat's body, known as the "points." These include the face, or mask, the ears, the legs and paws, and the tail. This coloring is produced by a recessive gene, often referred to as the Himalayan factor, hence the name used by American fanciers for Persian cats of this pattern.

The first crosses between Siamese and Persian cats were made in Sweden as long ago as 1922. Further experimental matings were made in the United States during the 1920s and 1930s, but it was not until the 1950s that breeders on both sides of the Atlantic, working with carefully planned breeding programs, produced cats with the desired type and coat pattern. In 1955, Britain's GCCF issued a breed number and approved a standard of points for the Himalayan-patterned Persians, but designated them as Colourpoint Longhairs. In the United States recognition of the Himalayan was approved by the CFA in 1957, and by the 1960s all other American associations

had accepted the variety. The Himalayan, or Colorpoint Longhair, in all its color subvarieties, soon became well established as one of the most popular of all the longhaired cats in the world's show rings.

Character and Care

The character of the Colorpoint combines the best traits of the cats used in its creation – the Siamese and the Persian. It is generally a little livelier and more entertaining than its solid-colored Persian cousins, but less vocal and boisterous than the typical Siamese. The precocious breeding tendencies of its Siamese ancestry have been passed on, with Colorpoint females coming into season and "calling" as early as eight months of age, though the males often do not reach maturity until they are 18 months old.

Regular grooming is essential to keep the long full coat in good condition, paying particular attention to the underparts, between the hind and fore legs, under the tail and around the neck, thoroughly brushing out the frill or ruff.

BREAKDOWN OF 100 SHOW POINTS

HEAD and EARS: 30 POINTS

EYES: 20 POINTS

BODY: 25 POINTS

COAT: 25 POINTS

KEY CHARACTERISTICS

- **CATEGORY** Longhair.

- **OVERALL BUILD** Medium or large, stocky.

- **COAT** Long and thick over the entire body, of fine texture and glossy; immense ruff (frill) around the neck and extending between the forelegs. Long tufts on the ears and between the toes.

- **HEAD** Round and massive, with very broad skull, round face, and set on a short, thick neck. Full cheeks.

- **NOSE** Short, broad nose with stop.

- **CHIN** Full, well-developed.

- **EYES** Large, full, round, and set far apart.

- **EARS** Small, round-tipped, tilted slightly forward and set far apart on the head.

- **BODY** Of stocky type, low on the legs, with a deep chest, and equally massive across the shoulders and rump.

- **LEGS** Short, thick, and heavy; straight forelegs.

- **PAWS** Large, round, and firm; toes not splayed.

- **TAIL** Short, but in proportion to body length; hair forms a "brush."

- **COLORS** Seal point, blue point, chocolate point, lilac point, red point, cream point, seal tortie point, chocolate tortie point, blue-cream point, seal tabby point, blue tabby point, chocolate tabby point, lilac tabby point, lilac-cream point; red tabby point, cream tabby point, seal tortie tabby point, blue-cream tabby point, chocolate tortie tabby point, lilac-cream tabby point.

PENALTIES

The Himalayan is penalized for lack of pigmentation in paw pads and/or nose leather; a locket or button; any abnormality of the tail; a squint; white toes; eye color other than blue; deformity of the skull and/or the mouth; any apparent weakness in the hindquarters.

SOLID POINTS

IN THE COLORPOINTS with solid points color, the standard requires that the coloring on all of the points should match in tone and be free from shadow markings or any patchiness.

SEAL POINT The body color is an even, pale fawn or cream, warm in tone, which shades gradually into lighter color on the chest and stomach. The points are deep seal brown. The nose leather and the paw pads are the same color as the points; the eye color is a deep, vivid blue.

BLUE POINT The body color is bluish-white, cold in tone, which shades gradually to white on the chest and stomach. The points are blue. The nose leather and paw pads are slate gray; the eye color is deep, vivid blue.

CHOCOLATE POINT The body color is ivory, with no shading. The points are milk chocolate, warm in tone. The nose leather and paw pads are cinnamon pink; the eye color is deep, vivid blue.

LILAC POINT The body color is glacial white, with no shading. The points are frosty gray with a pinkish tone. The nose leather and paw

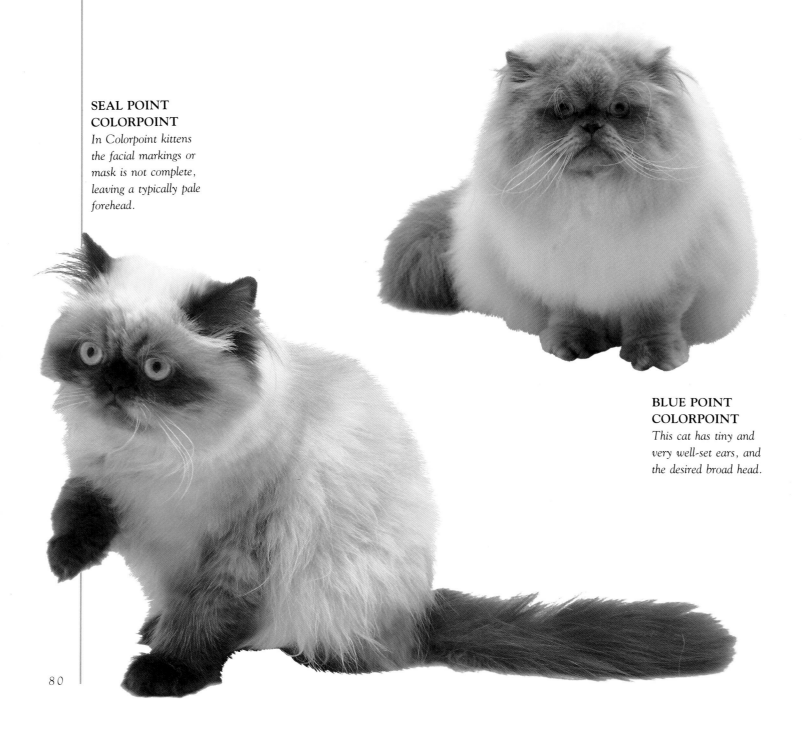

SEAL POINT COLORPOINT

In Colorpoint kittens the facial markings or mask is not complete, leaving a typically pale forehead.

BLUE POINT COLORPOINT

This cat has tiny and very well-set ears, and the desired broad head.

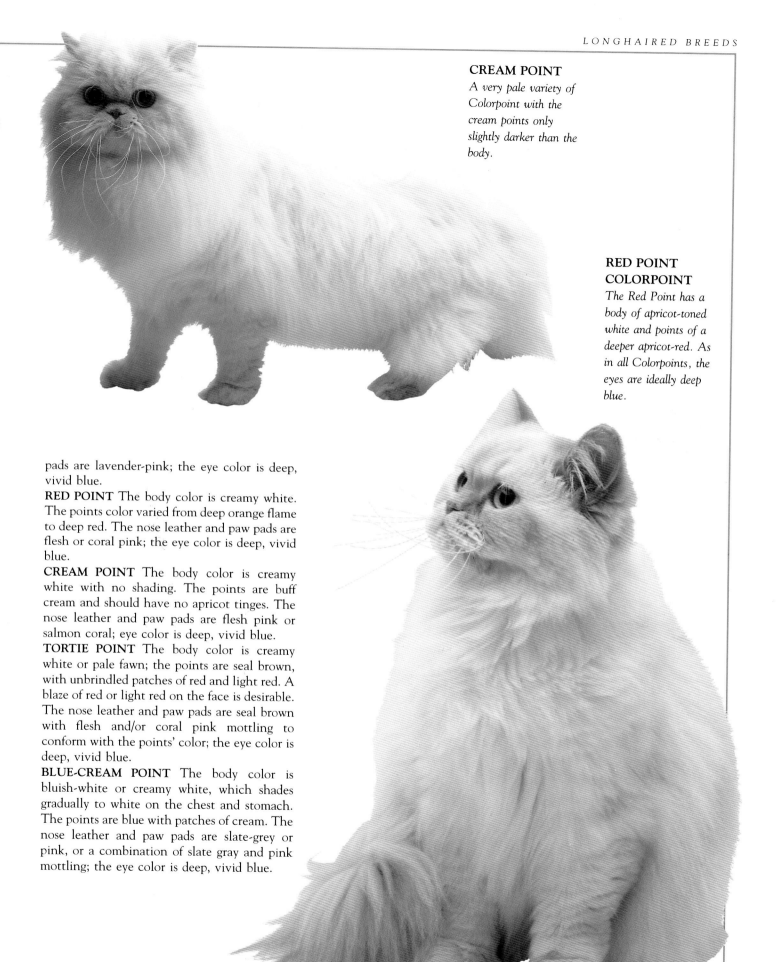

CREAM POINT
A very pale variety of Colorpoint with the cream points only slightly darker than the body.

RED POINT COLORPOINT
The Red Point has a body of apricot-toned white and points of a deeper apricot-red. As in all Colorpoints, the eyes are ideally deep blue.

pads are lavender-pink; the eye color is deep, vivid blue.

RED POINT The body color is creamy white. The points color varied from deep orange flame to deep red. The nose leather and paw pads are flesh or coral pink; the eye color is deep, vivid blue.

CREAM POINT The body color is creamy white with no shading. The points are buff cream and should have no apricot tinges. The nose leather and paw pads are flesh pink or salmon coral; eye color is deep, vivid blue.

TORTIE POINT The body color is creamy white or pale fawn; the points are seal brown, with unbrindled patches of red and light red. A blaze of red or light red on the face is desirable. The nose leather and paw pads are seal brown with flesh and/or coral pink mottling to conform with the points' color; the eye color is deep, vivid blue.

BLUE-CREAM POINT The body color is bluish-white or creamy white, which shades gradually to white on the chest and stomach. The points are blue with patches of cream. The nose leather and paw pads are slate-grey or pink, or a combination of slate gray and pink mottling; the eye color is deep, vivid blue.

TABBY POINTS

THE TABBY-POINTED varieties should have a clear "M" marking on the forehead, spotted whisher pads and typical "glasses" marks around the eyes. Tips of the ears and tail should match.

SEAL TABBY POINT The body color is pale cream to fawn, and warm in tone. The mask is clearly lined with dark stripes: vertical lines on the forehead form the classic "M" shape; horizontal lines bar the cheeks; dark spots appear on the whisker pads. The inner ear is light, and there is a "thumb-print" on the back of the outer ear. The legs are evenly barred with bracelets, and the tail is barred. All markings should be broad, dense, and clearly defined. No striping or mottling is allowed on the body, but consideration is given to shading in older cats.

The points are beige brown ticked with darker brown tabby markings. The nose leather is seal or brick red; the paw pads are seal brown; the eyes deep blue.

BLUE TABBY POINT The body color is bluish-white, and cold in tone. The mask is clearly lined with dark stripes: vertical lines on the forehead form the classic "M" shape; horizontal lines bar the cheeks; dark spots appear on the whisker pads. The inner ear is light, and there is a "thumb-print" on the back of the outer ear. The legs are evenly barred with bracelets, and the tail is barred. All markings should be broad, dense, and clearly defined. No striping or mottling is allowed on the body, but consideration is given to shading in older cats. The points are light silvery blue, ticked with darker

SEAL TABBY POINT

This variety is known as the Seal Lynxpoint in the United States, and this eat's head type conforms to the American standards.

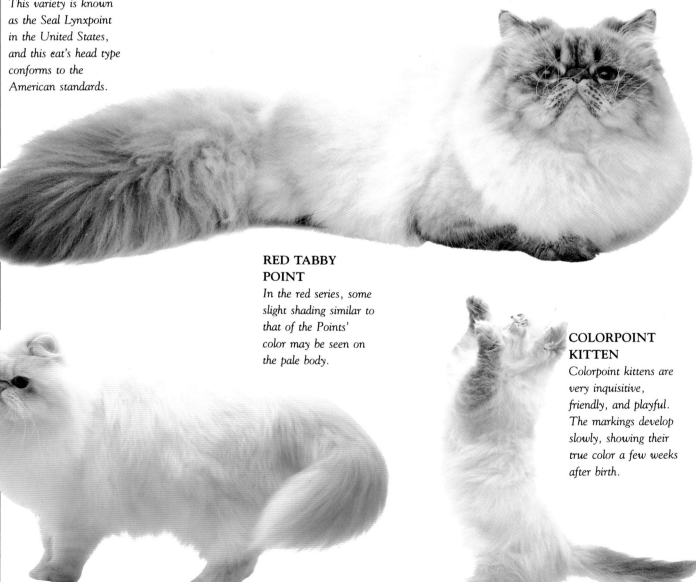

RED TABBY POINT

In the red series, some slight shading similar to that of the Points' color may be seen on the pale body.

COLORPOINT KITTEN

Colorpoint kittens are very inquisitive, friendly, and playful. The markings develop slowly, showing their true color a few weeks after birth.

blue tabby markings. The nose leather is blue or brick red; the paw pads are blue; the eye color is deep, vivid blue.

CHOCOLATE TABBY POINT The body color is ivory. The mask is clearly lined with dark stripes: vertical lines on the forehead form the classic "M" shape; horizontal lines bar the cheeks; dark spots appear on the whisker pads. The inner ear is light, and there is a "thumb-print" on the back of the outer ear. The legs are evenly barred with bracelets, and the tail is barred. All markings should be broad, dense, and clearly defined. No striping or mottling is allowed on the body, but consideration is given to shading in older cats. The points are warm fawn, ticked with milk-chocolate markings. The nose leather and paw pads are cinnamon pink; the eye color is deep, vivid blue.

LILAC TABBY POINT The body color is glacial white. The mask is clearly lined with dark

stripes: vertical lines on the forehead form the classic "M" shape; horizontal lines bar the cheeks; dark spots appear on the whisker pads. The inner ear is light, and there is a "thumb-print" on the back of the outer ear. The legs are evenly barred with bracelets, and the tail is barred. All markings should be broad, dense, and clearly defined. No striping or mottling is allowed on the body, but consideration is given to shading in older cats. The points are frosty gray ticked with darker frosty gray tabby markings. The nose leather and paw pads are lavender pink; the eye color is deep, vivid blue.

BLUE-CREAM POINT

Softly intermingled blue and cream pattern the points of this Colorpoint. It has a wonderfully full and well-groomed coat.

CHOCOLATE TORTIE COLORPOINT

This cute kitten shows the warm chocolate and light red markings on its points that identify the chocolate tortoiseshell coloration. As with all Colorpoint kittens, the markings take some time to develop fully.

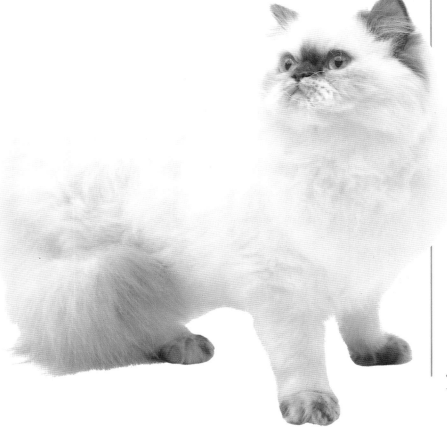

CHOCOLATE AND LILAC

DURING THE BREEDING and development of the Himalayan or Colorpoint Longhairs, breeders realized it might also be possible to produce self-colored chocolate and lilac longhaired cats. This proved quite simple to put into practice, and cats with the desired coat color were bred quite easily, but their body type and coat quality were extremely poor when judged against Persian standards. The pioneer breeders of these varieties also had to contend with the natural fading and bleaching effect on the coat color caused by the chocolate gene, and some of the early chocolate and lilac cats were very disappointing. Never to be outdone, the breeders determined to select for the characteristics they most desired in their dreamed-of color varieties, and eventually they succeeded in establishing chocolate and lilac longhaired cats of equal quality to their Himalayan cousins. Some North American associations decided to group the self-colored chocolate and lilac longhairs under the breed name of Kashmir; others grouped them with the Himalayans. Britain's GCCF preferred to call them the Chocolate Longhair and the Lilac Longhair.

CHOCOLATE LONGHAIR The color is a rich, warm, chocolate brown, sound from the roots to the tips of the hair, and free from markings, shading, or white hairs. The nose leather and paw pads are brown; the eye color is deep orange or copper (UK), or brilliant copper (USA).

LILAC LONGHAIR The color is a rich, warm, lavender with a pinkish tone, sound from the roots to the tips of the hair, and free from markings, shading, or white hairs. The nose leather and paw pads are pink; the eye color is pale orange in the UK, brilliant copper in the USA.

CHOCOLATE PERSIAN

Known as the Kashmir in some associations, the self-colored chocolate Persian is one of the most difficult cats to breed to the exacting standard of points.

LILAC-CREAM

This variety was created when the red or orange genetic factor was added to some breeding programs. Lilac and light cream hairs are patched or intermingled.

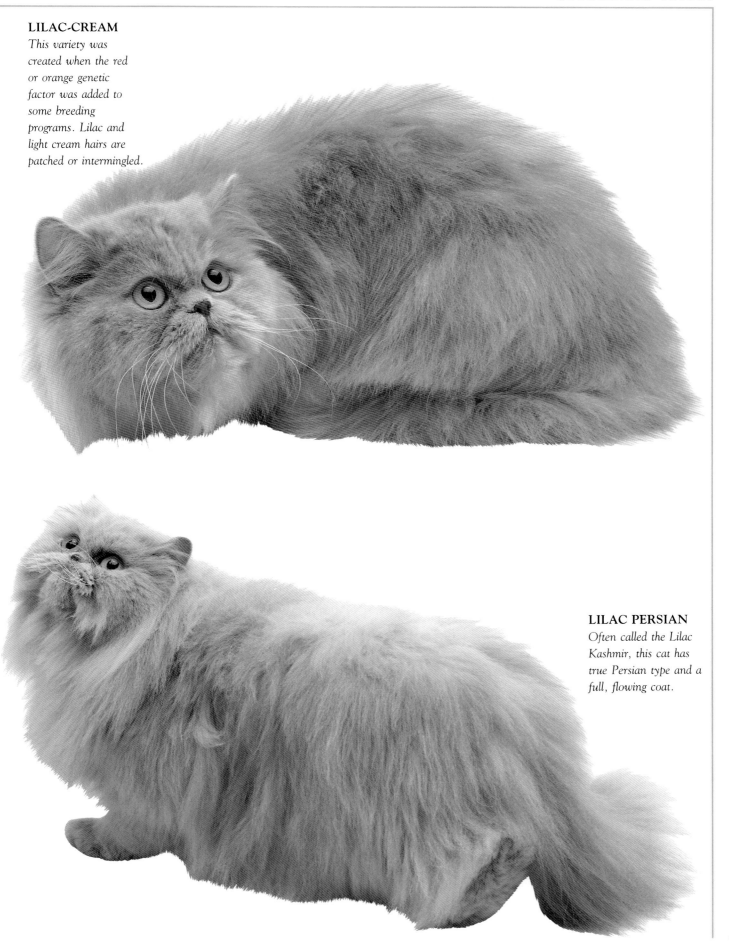

LILAC PERSIAN

Often called the Lilac Kashmir, this cat has true Persian type and a full, flowing coat.

88	Birman
94	Maine Coon
100	Ragdoll
105	Snowshoe
106	Norwegian Forest Cat
112	Angora
116	Turkish Van

SEMI LONGHAIRED BREEDS

BIRMAN

ALSO KNOWN AS THE Sacred Cat of Burma, the Birman is quite unrelated to the Burmese, despite the similarity in names. It is a unique breed, for although it bears a superficial resemblance to the Himalayan, or Colorpoint Longhair, it has stark white paws on all four feet. Its coat is silky, more like that of the Turkish Angora than the Himalayan, and its body type differs from that of the Persian, being longer and less cobby.

Legends about explaining the origins of this beautiful breed, and one in particular attempts to explain the Birman's coloring. Before the time of Buddha, the Khmer people built temples in honor of their gods. One such temple was raised to Tsun-Kyan-Kse, where a golden statue of the goddess so named was worshipped.

In the early 1900s the temple was raided, but it was saved by Major Gordon Russell and Monsieur Auguste Pavie. As a gesture of thanks, a pair of temple cats were sent to the two men, now living in France. The male cat died en route, but the female arrived safely and gave birth to kittens which founded the Birman breed in Europe.

Whatever the true origins of the breed, it survived in Europe and was imported into Britain and accepted for championship status by 1966. Separate breeding lines were established in the United States, with the first championship showing at the Madison Square Garden Cat Show, having been given official status by the CFA in 1967.

Character and Care

The Birman is quieter and more placid than a Siamese, but also less staid than a Persian. It is an inquisitive and affectionate cat, with a rather aloof appearance, giving the impression

BREAKDOWN OF 100 SHOW POINTS

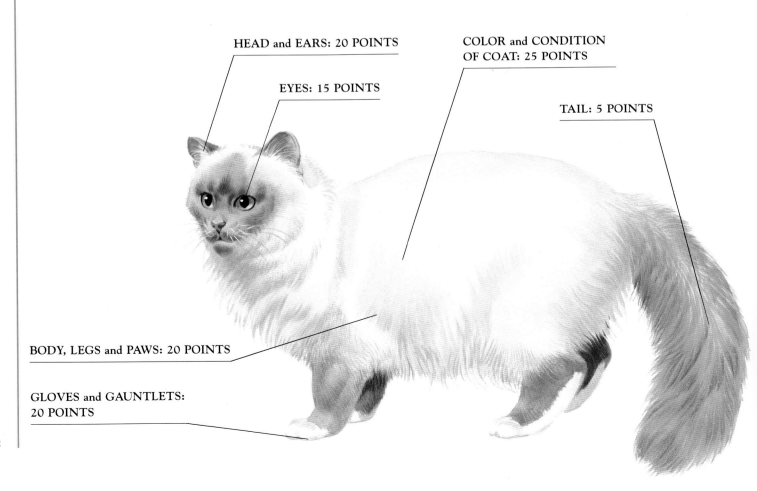

HEAD and EARS: 20 POINTS

EYES: 15 POINTS

COLOR and CONDITION OF COAT: 25 POINTS

TAIL: 5 POINTS

BODY, LEGS and PAWS: 20 POINTS

GLOVES and GAUNTLETS: 20 POINTS

that it is fully aware of its mystical origins. Unlike many other longhaired breeds, the Birman matures early, and the females often start to "call" as early as seven months of age. The queens make excellent caring mothers, and males kept at stud are often renowned for their extra-loving temperament.

The Birman coat is silkier and less dense than that of the Persian. It is comparitively easy to keep well groomed with regular brushing and combing. The white gloves and gauntlets must be kept free from staining by regular washing, careful drying, and the application of white grooming powder which is rubbed in, then completely brushed out, leaving the white areas spotlessly clean.

PENALTIES

The Birman is penalized for having white areas that do not run across the front paws in an even line; lack of white gloves on any paw; white shading on the stomach and chest; areas of pure white in the points (except the paws); a Siamese head type; and crossed eyes.

KEY CHARACTERISTICS

- **CATEGORY** Longhair.

- **OVERALL BUILD** Medium sized, long but stocky.

- **COAT** Long, silky texture; heavy ruff (frill) around the neck; long on the back and flanks, may curl slightly on the stomach; little undercoat; rarely becomes matted.

- **HEAD** Strong, broad, rounded skull with full cheeks.

- **NOSE** Medium length, roman in shape.

- **CHIN** Firm, with the lower lip forming a perpendicular line with the upper lip.

- **EYES** Almost round in shape.

- **EARS** Medium sized with rounded tips, set slightly tipped forward, not upright on the skull and with good width between.

- **BODY** Fairly long but not stocky, males more massive than females.

- **LEGS** Short to medium in length, and heavy.

- **PAWS** Large and rounded.

- **TAIL** Medium length, forming a plume.

- **COLORS** Seal point, blue point, chocolate point, lilac point, red point, cream point, seal tortie point, blue tortie point, chocolate tortie point, lilac tortie point solid points, tortie points, tabby points and tortie tabby all in the following colors: seal, blue, chocolate, lilac, red, cream.

SOLID POINTS

SEAL POINT BIRMAN

The characteristic white forepaws of this breed are called "gloves" and should end in a symmetrical line on or below the angle formed by the paw and leg.

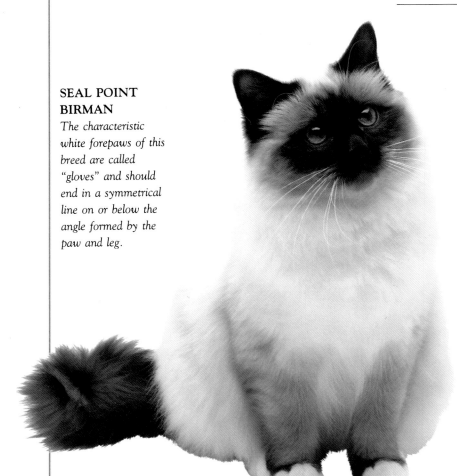

A LITTER OF BIRMANS normally consists of three, four, or five kittens which are born almost white all over. Within a few days, the points color starts to develop at the edges of the ears and on the tail. The eyes, when they open at seven to ten days, are a cloudy baby-blue which changes to the true blue color as the kittens grow.

SEAL POINT The body is even fawn to pale cream, warm in tone shading to lighter color on the stomach and chest. The points are deep seal brown apart from the gloves, which are pure white. The nose leather should match the points. The paw pads are pink, and eye color is blue, the deeper and more violet the better.

BLUE POINT The body is bluish-white, cold in tone, shading gradually to almost white on the stomach and chest. The points are deep blue except for the gloves, which are pure white. The nose leather is slate and the paw pads pink. Eye color should be blue, the deeper and more violet the better.

CHOCOLATE POINT The body is ivory with no shading. Points are milk-chocolate of warm tone except for the gloves, which are pure white. The nose leather is cinnamon pink and the paw pads pink. Eye color should be blue, the deeper and more violet the better.

BLUE POINT BIRMAN

The gloves on the hind paws are called "gauntlets." They cover the entire paw and taper up the back of the leg to a point just below the hock.

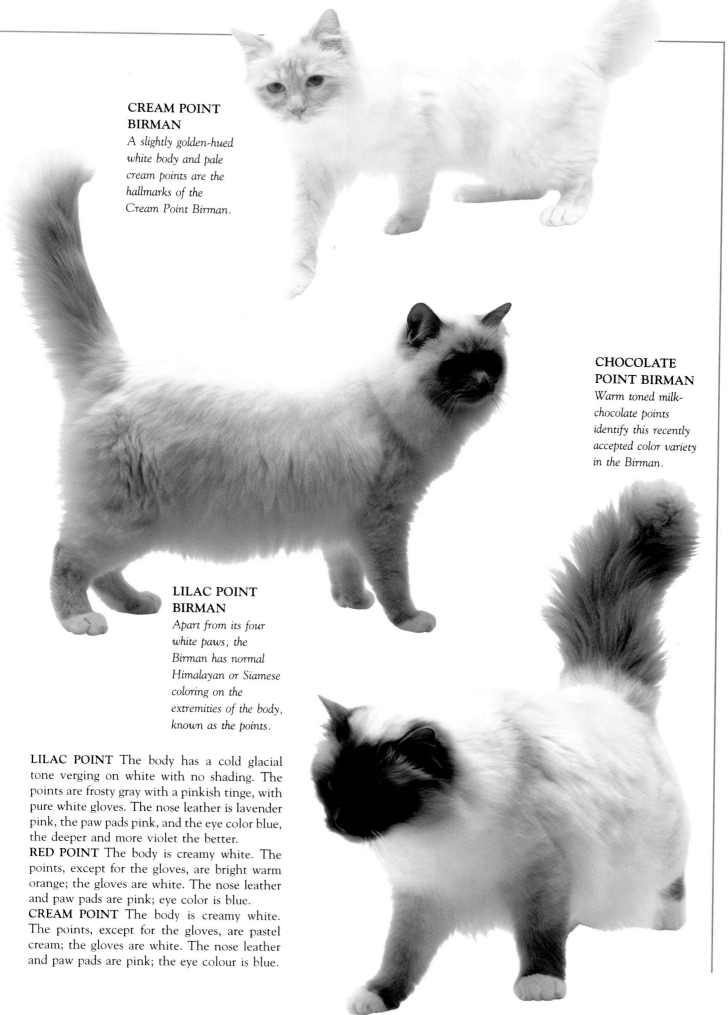

CREAM POINT BIRMAN
A slightly golden-hued white body and pale cream points are the hallmarks of the Cream Point Birman.

CHOCOLATE POINT BIRMAN
Warm toned milk-chocolate points identify this recently accepted color variety in the Birman.

LILAC POINT BIRMAN
Apart from its four white paws, the Birman has normal Himalayan or Siamese coloring on the extremities of the body, known as the points.

LILAC POINT The body has a cold glacial tone verging on white with no shading. The points are frosty gray with a pinkish tinge, with pure white gloves. The nose leather is lavender pink, the paw pads pink, and the eye color blue, the deeper and more violet the better.

RED POINT The body is creamy white. The points, except for the gloves, are bright warm orange; the gloves are white. The nose leather and paw pads are pink; eye color is blue.

CREAM POINT The body is creamy white. The points, except for the gloves, are pastel cream; the gloves are white. The nose leather and paw pads are pink; the eye colour is blue.

TABBY AND TORTOISESHELL POINTS

ALTHOUGH PURISTS CLAIM that only Seal Point and Blue Point Birman cats should be considered as the true Sacred Cats of Burma, the CFA in the United States also recognizes the Chocolate Point and Lilac Point varieties, and FIFe in Europe has produced standards of points for both the tabby and red series, including tortoiseshell, and tortoiseshell–tabbies in the four basic color combinations.

SEAL TABBY POINT The body is beige, with dark seal tabby points, except for gloves which are white. The nose leather is brick red, pink, or seal brown, and the paw pads are pink.

BLUE TABBY POINT The body is bluish-white, with blue-gray tabby points, except for the gloves which are white. The nose leather is old rose or blue-gray.

CHOCOLATE TABBY POINT The body is ivory. The points, except for the gloves, are milk-chocolate tabby; the gloves are white. The nose leather is pale red, pink, or milk-chocolate.

LILAC TABBY POINT The body is glacial white (magnolia) with lilac tabby (frosty gray with a slight pinkish tinge) points, except the gloves, which are white. The nose leather is pink or lavender-pink.

RED TABBY POINT The body is off-white with a slight red tinge. The points, except for the gloves, are warm orange tabby; the gloves are white. The nose leather is pink or brick-red.

CREAM TABBY POINT The body is off-white. The points, except for the gloves, are cream tabby; the gloves are white.

SEAL TORTIE POINT The body is beige, shading to fawn. The points, except for the gloves, are seal brown patched or mingled with red and/or light red. The gloves are white. The nose leather is pink and/or seal.

SEAL TORTIE TABBY POINT The body is beige. The points, except for the gloves, have tabby markings in seal brown patched or mingled with red and/or light red. The gloves are white and the nose leather seal, brick red or pink, or seal mottled with brick red or pink.

BLUE TABBY POINT BIRMAN

The Birman is alert and interested in everything that is going on. It makes an excellent pet, and its long coat is easier to care for than that of the cats of the Persian group.

SEAL TORTIE POINT BIRMAN
Seal brown overlaid and intermingled with red and light red produce the tortoiseshell coloring.

SEAL TABBY POINT BIRMAN
Tabby pointed Birman cats are now accepted with provisional status in Britain by GCCF.

BLUE TORTIE POINT The body is bluish white. The points, except for the gloves, are blue-gray patched or mottled with pastel cream. The gloves are white. The nose leather is blue-gray and/or pink.

BLUE TORBIE TABBY POINT The body is glacial white with a slight bluish tinge. The points, except for the gloves, have tabby markings in blue-gray patched or mingled with pastel cream. The gloves are white and the nose leather blue-gray, old rose or pink, or blue-gray mottled with old rose and/or pink.

CHOCOLATE TORTIE POINT The body is ivory. The points, except for the gloves, are milk-chocolate patched or mingled with red and/or light red; the gloves are white. The nose leather is milk-chocolate and/or pink.

CHOCOLATE TORTIE TABBY POINT The body is ivory. The points, except for the gloves, have tabby markings in milk-chocolate patched or mingled with red and/or light red; the gloves are white. The nose leather is milk-chocolate, light red or pink, or milk-chocolate mottled with light red and/or pink.

LILAC TORTIE POINT The body is glacial white (magnolia). The points, except for the gloves, are lilac (frosty gray with a slight pinkish tinge) patched or mingled with pale cream; the gloves are white. The nose leather is lavender pink and/or pink.

LILAC TORBIE TABBY POINT The body is glacial white (magnolia). The points, except for the gloves, have tabby markings in lilac (frosty gray with a slight pinkish tinge) patched or mingled with pale cream; the gloves are white. The nose leather is lavender pink or pale pink, or lavender pink mottled with pale pink.

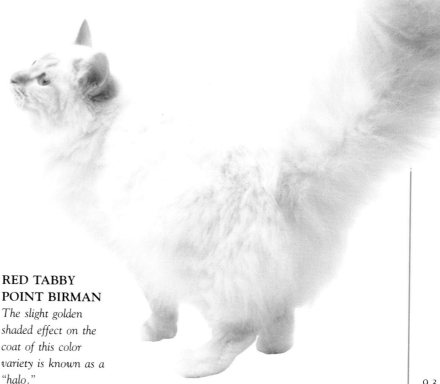

RED TABBY POINT BIRMAN
The slight golden shaded effect on the coat of this color variety is known as a "halo."

93

MAINE COON

ONE OF THE OLDEST NATURAL BREEDS of North America, the Maine Coon, or Maine Cat, has been known as a true variety for more than a hundred years. As its name implies, it originated in the state of Maine. At one time it was thought that the cat was the product of matings between semi-wild domestic cats and raccoons, hence the name "coon," though this is now known to be a biological impossibility. Another legend tells how Marie Antoinette, in planning her escape from the horrors of the French Revolution, sent her pet cats to be cared for in Maine until she could find herself, and them, a new home. Today's more enlightened felinophiles believe that long-coated cats such as the Angora were introduced to coastal towns as trade goods by visting seamen, and these cats bred with the local domestic cats, resulting eventually in the large and handsome American longhaired breed we know today.

A tabby Maine Coon is recorded as having won the Best in Show at the Madison Square Garden Cat Show in 1895, but with the introduction of more striking breeds from Europe at the turn of the century, the popularity of the Maine Coon declined. Though the breed flourished as a popular and hardy pet for some years, it was not until 1953 that the Central Maine Coon Cat Club was formed to promote the breed. By 1967 a show standard was accepted by some American cat associa-

BREAKDOWN OF 100 SHOW POINTS

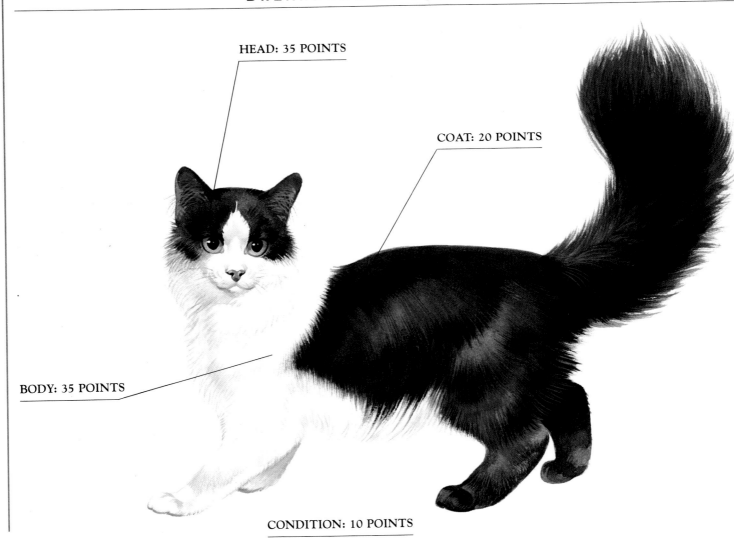

HEAD: 35 POINTS

COAT: 20 POINTS

BODY: 35 POINTS

CONDITION: 10 POINTS

tions. In 1976 the International Society for the Preservation of the Maine Coon was formed, and the Cat Fanciers' Association accepted the breed with full championship status.

Character and Care

Considered by their fans to be perfect domestic pets, typical Maine Coons have extrovert personalities and are very playful and amusing, often teaching themselves tricks. They may take three or four years to develop their full size and stature, being very slow to mature.

Although the coat is long and flowing, it rarely gets matted, and is easy to care for with occasional combing through.

KEY CHARACTERISTICS

- **CATEGORY** Longhair.

- **OVERALL BUILD** Medium to large.

- **COAT** Heavy and shaggy, with a silky texture. Short on the head, shoulders and legs, becoming gradually longer down the back and sides, shaggy on hind legs and belly fur; full ruff (frill).

- **HEAD** Medium sized with a squarish outline; gently concave in profile, with curved forehead and high, prominent cheekbones.

- **NOSE** Medium length.

- **CHIN** Firm, and in vertical alignment with the nose and upper lip.

- **EYES** Large, slightly oval but not almond shaped, set slightly slanted toward the outer base of the ear.

- **EARS** Large, wide at the base, moderately pointed and with lynx-like ear tufts, set high but well apart.

- **BODY** Long with substantial bone, large framed and well proportioned, muscular and broad chested. Males are larger than females.

- **LEGS** Medium length.

- **PAWS** Large, round, and tufted between the toes.

- **TAIL** At least as long as the body from shoulder-blade to the base of the tail; wide at the base tapering to the tip with full, flowing hair.

- **COLORS** The Maine Coon is recognized in all colors except the Himalayan and Burmese patterns, and chocolate, cinnamon, lilac or fawn. There is no relationship between coat color and eye color, though brilliant eye color is desirable. Any amount of white is allowed.

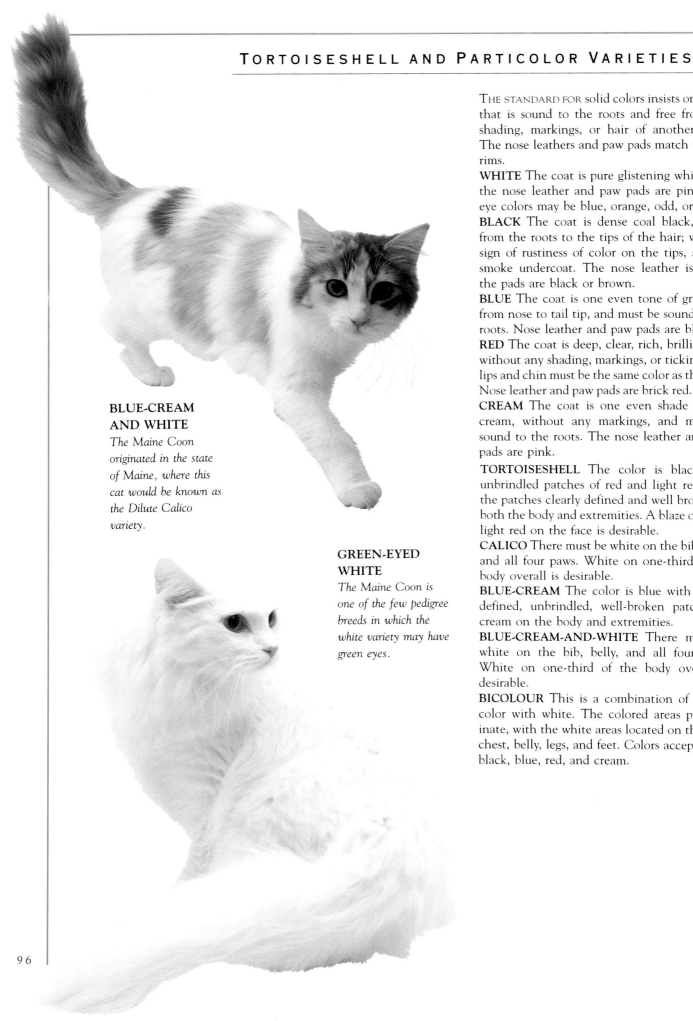

THE STANDARD FOR solid colors insists on a coat that is sound to the roots and free from any shading, markings, or hair of another color. The nose leathers and paw pads match the eye rims.

WHITE The coat is pure glistening white; and the nose leather and paw pads are pink. The eye colors may be blue, orange, odd, or green.

BLACK The coat is dense coal black, sound from the roots to the tips of the hair; with no sign of rustiness of color on the tips, and no smoke undercoat. The nose leather is black; the pads are black or brown.

BLUE The coat is one even tone of gray-blue from nose to tail tip, and must be sound to the roots. Nose leather and paw pads are blue.

RED The coat is deep, clear, rich, brilliant red without any shading, markings, or ticking. The lips and chin must be the same color as the coat. Nose leather and paw pads are brick red.

CREAM The coat is one even shade of buff cream, without any markings, and must be sound to the roots. The nose leather and paw pads are pink.

TORTOISESHELL The color is black with unbrindled patches of red and light red, with the patches clearly defined and well broken on both the body and extremities. A blaze of red or light red on the face is desirable.

CALICO There must be white on the bib, belly, and all four paws. White on one-third of the body overall is desirable.

BLUE-CREAM The color is blue with clearly defined, unbrindled, well-broken patches of cream on the body and extremities.

BLUE-CREAM-AND-WHITE There must be white on the bib, belly, and all four paws. White on one-third of the body overall is desirable.

BICOLOUR This is a combination of a solid color with white. The colored areas predominate, with the white areas located on the face, chest, belly, legs, and feet. Colors accepted are black, blue, red, and cream.

BLUE-CREAM AND WHITE

The Maine Coon originated in the state of Maine, where this cat would be known as the Dilute Calico variety.

GREEN-EYED WHITE

The Maine Coon is one of the few pedigree breeds in which the white variety may have green eyes.

SMOKE AND SHADED VARIETIES

ANY SOLID OR TORTIE color is accepted in this group. The base coat should be as white as possible, with the tips of the hairs shading to the basic color, darkest on the head, back, and paws. The Smoke is densely colored; while the shaded shows much more of the silver undercoat.

SHADED SILVER There is a white undercoat with a mantle of black tipping shading down the sides, face, and tail, with the color ranging from dark on the ridge to white on the chin, chest, stomach, and underside of the tail. The legs are the same tone as the face. The general effect is much darker than the Chinchilla. Eye rims, lips, and nose are outlined with black; nose leather is brick red; paw pads are black.

SHADED RED There is a white undercoat with red tipping shading down the sides, face and tail, with the color ranging from dark on the ridge to white on the chin, chest, stomach, and underside of the tail. Legs are the same tone as the face. Nose leather and paw pads are black.

BLACK SMOKE There is a white undercoat deeply tipped with black; in repose, the cat appears black; in motion, the white undercoat is clearly apparent. The points and mask are black, with a narrow band of white at the base of the hairs next to the skin. The ruff (frill) and ear tufts are light silver; the nose leather and paw pads are black.

BLUE SMOKE There is a white undercoat deeply tipped with blue; in repose, the cat appears blue; in motion, the white undercoat is clearly apparent. The points and mask are blue, with a narrow band of white hairs next to the skin. The ruff (frill) and ear tufts are white; nose leather and paw pads are blue.

RED SMOKE There is a white undercoat deeply tipped with red; in repose, the cat appears red; in motion, the white undercoat is clearly apparent. The points and mask are red, with a narrow band of white hairs next to the skin. The eye rims, nose leather, and paw pads are rose.

CREAM SMOKE This is a dilute version of the Red Smoke in which the red tipping is reduced to pale cream.

RED SHADED

In shaded varieties, the undercoat should be as white as possible, and the basic color should be deepest on the head, back, and the paws.

TABBY VARIETIES

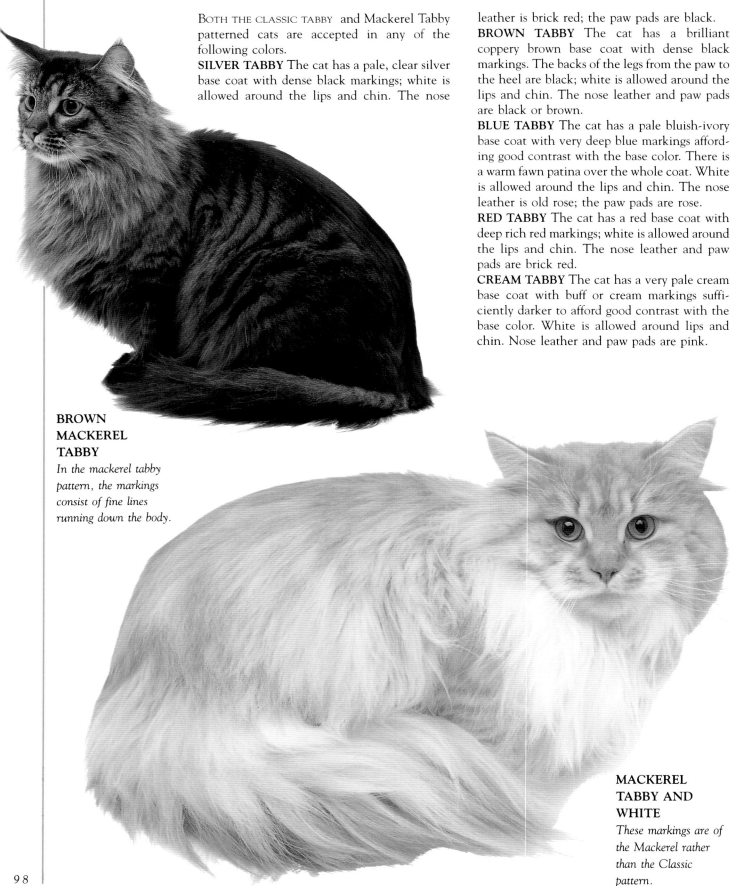

BOTH THE CLASSIC TABBY and Mackerel Tabby patterned cats are accepted in any of the following colors.

SILVER TABBY The cat has a pale, clear silver base coat with dense black markings; white is allowed around the lips and chin. The nose leather is brick red; the paw pads are black.

BROWN TABBY The cat has a brilliant coppery brown base coat with dense black markings. The backs of the legs from the paw to the heel are black; white is allowed around the lips and chin. The nose leather and paw pads are black or brown.

BLUE TABBY The cat has a pale bluish-ivory base coat with very deep blue markings affording good contrast with the base color. There is a warm fawn patina over the whole coat. White is allowed around the lips and chin. The nose leather is old rose; the paw pads are rose.

RED TABBY The cat has a red base coat with deep rich red markings; white is allowed around the lips and chin. The nose leather and paw pads are brick red.

CREAM TABBY The cat has a very pale cream base coat with buff or cream markings sufficiently darker to afford good contrast with the base color. White is allowed around lips and chin. Nose leather and paw pads are pink.

BROWN MACKEREL TABBY

In the mackerel tabby pattern, the markings consist of fine lines running down the body.

MACKEREL TABBY AND WHITE

These markings are of the Mackerel rather than the Classic pattern.

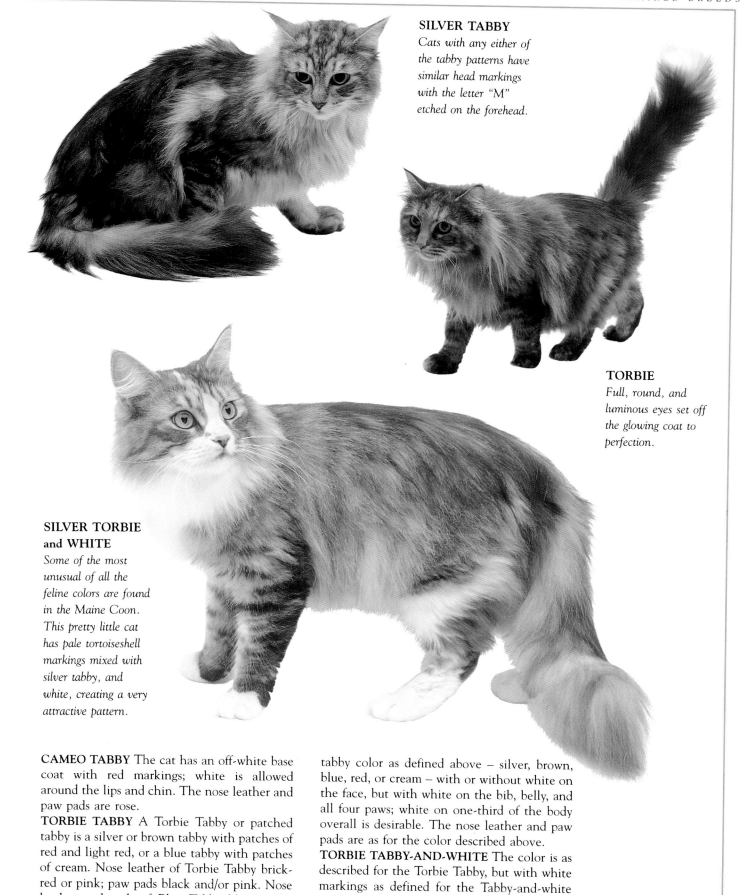

SILVER TABBY
Cats with any either of the tabby patterns have similar head markings with the letter "M" etched on the forehead.

TORBIE
Full, round, and luminous eyes set off the glowing coat to perfection.

SILVER TORBIE and WHITE
Some of the most unusual of all the feline colors are found in the Maine Coon. This pretty little cat has pale tortoiseshell markings mixed with silver tabby, and white, creating a very attractive pattern.

CAMEO TABBY The cat has an off-white base coat with red markings; white is allowed around the lips and chin. The nose leather and paw pads are rose.

TORBIE TABBY A Torbie Tabby or patched tabby is a silver or brown tabby with patches of red and light red, or a blue tabby with patches of cream. Nose leather of Torbie Tabby brick-red or pink; paw pads black and/or pink. Nose leather and pads of Blue Tabby blue and/or pink.

TABBY-AND-WHITE The cat may be any tabby color as defined above – silver, brown, blue, red, or cream – with or without white on the face, but with white on the bib, belly, and all four paws; white on one-third of the body overall is desirable. The nose leather and paw pads are as for the color described above.

TORBIE TABBY-AND-WHITE The color is as described for the Torbie Tabby, but with white markings as defined for the Tabby-and-white (above). Colors accepted are silver, brown, and blue. The nose leather depends on basic color; paw pads are pink.

RAGDOLL

THE FIRST RAGDOLL cats were bred by an American, Ann Baker, whose white long-haired cat Josephine was involved in a road accident which left her with permanent injuries. When Josephine eventually had kittens, they were found to have particularly placid temperaments and would completely relax when picked up and cuddled, reminiscent of a rag doll.

The name was chosen and recognized in 1965 by the National Cat Fanciers' Association, and later by other associations. Although this breed's alleged inability to feel pain or fear, or to fight with other animals is claimed to be due to Josephine's accident, this goes against all genetic reasoning. The specialized temperament is almost certainly due to the fact that only cats of a loving disposition were selected in the first matings. The three patterns found in the breed could certainly have been produced by Josephine if the stud cat used had carried genes for the Himalayan pattern and long coat, and if either Josephine or her mate had also carried the gene for white spotting.

Though some controversy remains over the breed, the Ragdoll has gained popularity around the world, and it has become an interesting addition to the show scene.

BREAKDOWN OF 100 SHOW POINTS

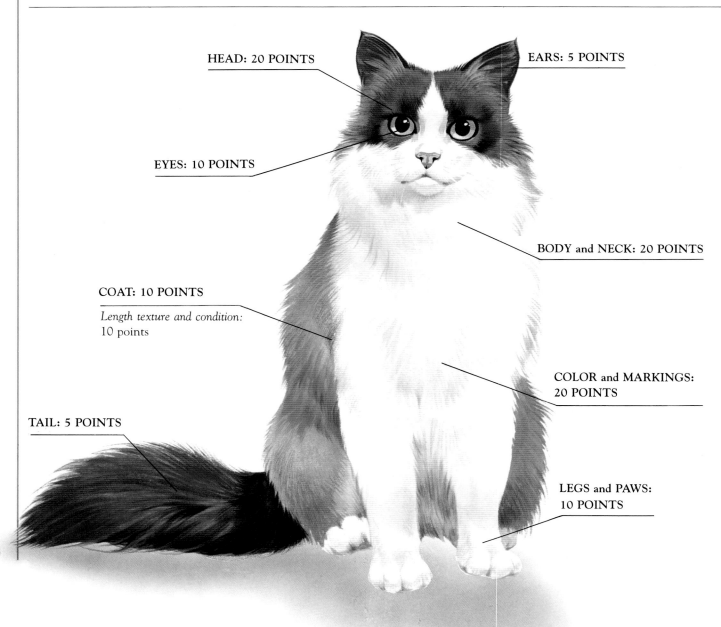

HEAD: 20 POINTS

EARS: 5 POINTS

EYES: 10 POINTS

BODY and NECK: 20 POINTS

COAT: 10 POINTS

Length texture and condition:
10 points

COLOR and MARKINGS:
20 POINTS

TAIL: 5 POINTS

LEGS and PAWS:
10 POINTS

Character and Care

The Ragdoll is an exceptionally affectionate, loving, and relaxed cat. Although it is generally calm and placid, with a quiet voice, it loves to play and to be petted. The thick coat does not form mats and is therefore quite easy to groom with regular gentle brushing of the body and combing through the longer hair on the tail and around the neck.

KEY CHARACTERISTICS

- **CATEGORY** Longhair.

- **OVERALL BUILD** Large, solid appearance.

- **COAT** Medium long, dense, soft, and silky in texture, lying close to the body and breaking as the cat moves. Longest around the neck and framing the face; short on the face; short to medium length on the front legs; medium to long over the body.

- **HEAD** Medium size, broad modified wedge shape with a flat plane between the ears; well-developed cheeks; medium long muzzle.

- **NOSE** Slightly curved in the upper third.

- **CHIN** Well developed.

- **EYES** Large and oval, with the outer corners being level with the base of the ears.

- **EARS** Medium size, broad-based, with rounded tips, set wide apart and tipped slightly forward.

- **BODY** Long, with medium bone structure. Muscular, broad chest, muscular hindquarters.

- **LEGS** Medium in length and of medium bone. Hind legs slightly higher than forelegs.

- **PAWS** Large, round, and compact; with tufts between the toes.

- **TAIL** Long, but in proportion to the body, medium broad at the base and slightly tapered toward the tip; bushy.

- **COLORS** Seal point, blue point, chocolate point and lilac point, all with clear blue eyes.

MITTED

SEAL MITTED RAGDOLL
Mitted Ragdolls may have a narrow white facial blaze in addition to white on the chin, chest, bib, and underbody, and the obligatory four white paws.

BLUE MITTED RAGDOLL
In the mitted pattern of the Ragdoll breed, the four paws are white to the same degree as that found in the Birman.

THE BODY IS LIGHT in color and only slightly shaded; the points (except the paws and chin) should be clearly defined, matched for color and in harmony with the body color. The chin must be white, and a white stripe on the nose is preferred; white mittens on the front legs and back paws should be entirely white to the knees and hocks. A white stripe extends from the bib to the underside between the front legs to the base of the tail.
LILAC POINT The body color is glacial white; the points are frosty grey of a pinkish tone, except for the white areas.

SEAL POINT The body color is pale fawn or cream; the points are deep seal brown, except for the white areas.
BLUE POINT The body color is cold-toned bluish-white; the points are blue, except for the white areas.
CHOCOLATE POINT The body color is ivory; the points are milk chocolate, except for the white areas.
LILAC POINT The body color is glacial white; the points are frosty gray of a pinkish tone, except for the white areas.

BICOLOR

THE BODY IS LIGHT in color; the points – ears, mask, and tail – should be well-defined. The mask has an inverted white "V"; the stomach is white; and the legs are preferably white. No white is allowed on ears or tail.

SEAL POINT The body color is pale fawn or cream; the points are deep seal brown, except for the white areas.

BLUE POINT The body color is cold-toned bluish-white; the points are blue, except for the white areas.

CHOCOLATE POINT The body color is ivory; the points are milk chocolate, except for the white areas.

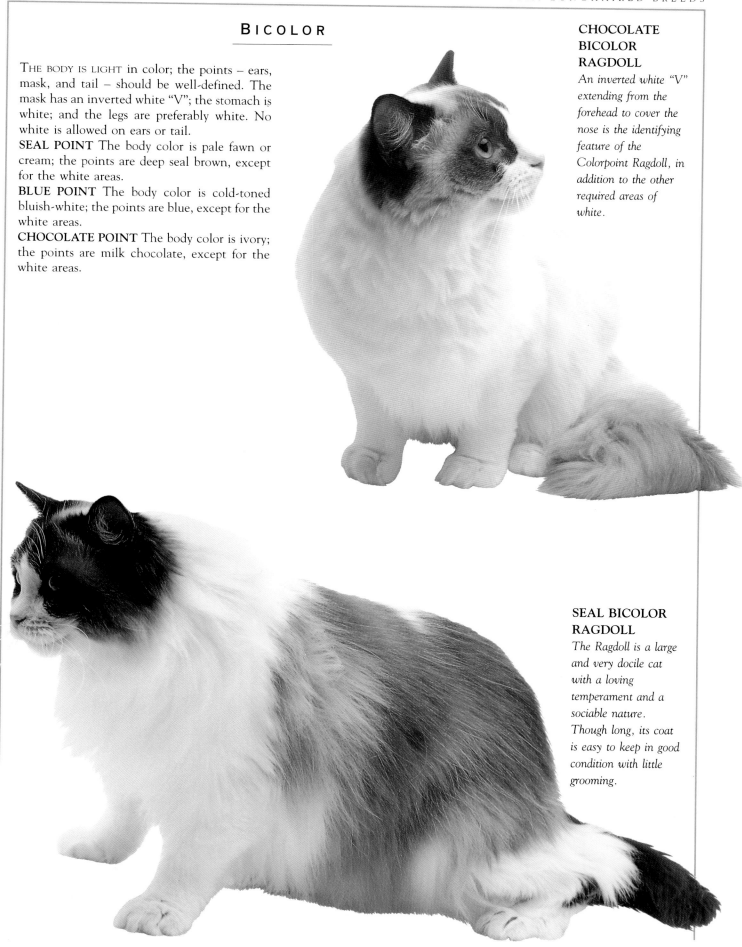

CHOCOLATE BICOLOR RAGDOLL
An inverted white "V" extending from the forehead to cover the nose is the identifying feature of the Colorpoint Ragdoll, in addition to the other required areas of white.

SEAL BICOLOR RAGDOLL
The Ragdoll is a large and very docile cat with a loving temperament and a sociable nature. Though long, its coat is easy to keep in good condition with little grooming.

COLORPOINT

THE BODY IS LIGHT in color and only slightly shaded; the points – ears, mask, legs, and tail – should be clearly defined, matched for color and in harmony with the body color. No white hairs allowed.

LILAC POINT The body color is glacial white; the points are frosty gray of a pinkish tone, except for the white areas.

SEAL POINT The body color is pale fawn or cream; the points are deep seal brown, except for the white areas.

BLUE POINT The body color is cold-toned bluish-white; the points are blue, except for the white areas.

CHOCOLATE POINT The body color is ivory; the points are milk chocolate, except for the white areas.

SEAL COLORPOINT
All the points are evenly matched, with no white markings anywhere.

BLUE COLORPOINT
The basic Himalayan colors of seal, blue, chocolate, and lilac are accepted in this breed.

LILAC COLORPOINT
Even in the lilac variety, good contrast between the body and points' color is required. The coat itself should be dense, of silky texture, and medium length.

SNOWSHOE

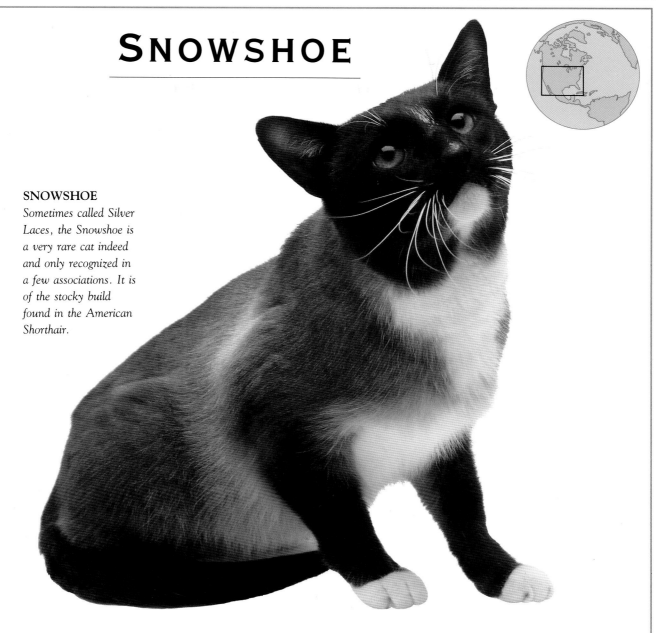

SNOWSHOE
Sometimes called Silver Laces, the Snowshoe is a very rare cat indeed and only recognized in a few associations. It is of the stocky build found in the American Shorthair.

THE SNOWSHOE OR Silver Laces is a rare cat, even in the United States where it was first bred. It combines the stocky build of the American Shorthair with the body length of the Siamese, and is Himalayan or Siamese in coloring, but with the white paws which are also found in the Birman.

Character and Care
The Snowshoe is a robust and lively cat. It is highly intelligent and loving and, like the Siamese, enjoys human company.

Its coat needs the minimum of grooming, and the white paws may be kept immaculate by dusting with grooming powder from time to time to prevent discoloration.

KEY CHARACTERISTICS
● **CATEGORY** Shorthair.
● **OVERALL BUILD** The Snowshoe is of medium size and well muscled.
● **COAT** Short, fine, close-lying coat.
● **COLORS** Any recognized points color.
● **OTHER FEATURES** The head is triangular with large pointed wide-based ears and large oval eyes of brilliant blue. The long body is well-muscled with a strong back, the legs are of medium bone with compact oval paws, and the tail is thick at the base, tapering to a pointed tip. There are no standards set either for the nose or for the chin.

NORWEGIAN FOREST CAT

KNOWN AS THE *Norsk Skaukatt* in its native Norway, the Norwegian Forest Cat is very similar to the Maine Coon in many ways. It is a uniquely Scandinavian breed whose origins are shrouded in mystery, and it is referred to in Norse myths and mid-nineteenth-century fairy stories. Having evolved naturally in the cold climate of Norway, it has a heavy, weather-resistant coat. The glossy, medium-length top coat hangs from the spine line, keeping out rain and snow, while the wooly undercoat keeps the body comfortably warm. Its strong legs, paws, and claws make the Forest Cat an extremely good climber in trees and on rocky slopes. It is highly intelligent, nimble, and an excellent hunter.

From these naturally evolved cats, a group of breeders set out in the 1930s to develop a pedigree breed, starting with some hardy farm cats. As a breed, the Forest Cat gained in popularity during the 1970s and was granted full Championship status in FIFe in 1977.

The ideal show cat differs from the Maine Coon in having hind legs longer than the forelegs, and the standard of points specifies a double coat, which is permitted but not desirable in the American breed.

BREAKDOWN OF 100 SHOW POINTS

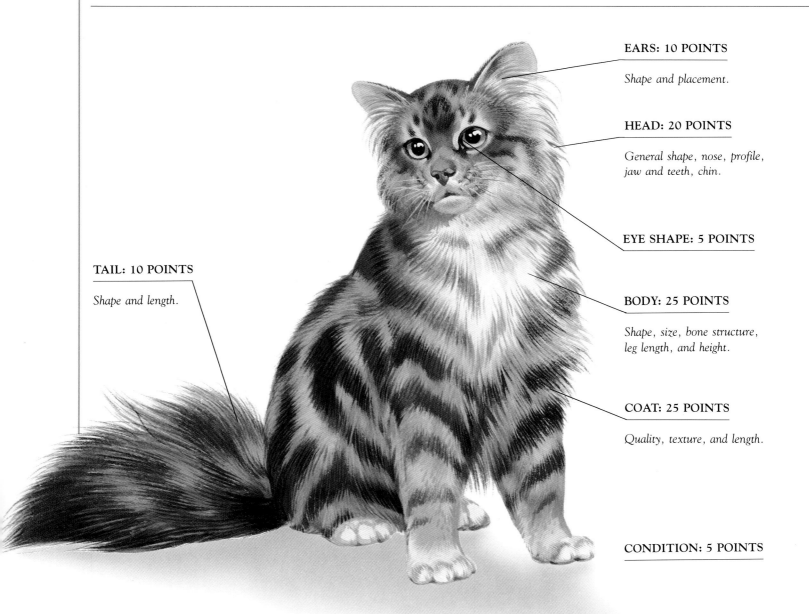

EARS: 10 POINTS

Shape and placement.

HEAD: 20 POINTS

General shape, nose, profile, jaw and teeth, chin.

EYE SHAPE: 5 POINTS

BODY: 25 POINTS

Shape, size, bone structure, leg length, and height.

COAT: 25 POINTS

Quality, texture, and length.

TAIL: 10 POINTS

Shape and length.

CONDITION: 5 POINTS

Character and Care

Strong and hardy, the Forest Cat can be very playful while retaining the strongly independent character of its semi-wild ancestors. It enjoys human company and can be very affectionate, but dislikes too much cosseting. The trouble-free coat periodically needs combing through to keep the undercoat in good condition and to clean the flowing tail and full ruff or frill.

KEY CHARACTERISTICS

- **CATEGORY** Longhair.

- **OVERALL BUILD** Large.

- **COAT** Semi-long; a wooly undercoat is covered with a smooth, water-repellent upper coat. The glossy hair covers the back and sides. The cat has a full ruff or frill.

- **HEAD** Triangular, with a long, straight profile and no stop.

- **NOSE** Long and straight.

- **CHIN** Firm.

- **EYES** Large, open, and set slightly obliquely.

- **EARS** Wide-based, with lynx-like tufts, set high, the outer edges of the ears following the lines of the head down to the chin.

- **BODY** Long, strongly built, with solid bone structure.

- **LEGS** Long, the hind legs longer than the forelegs.

- **PAWS** Tufted.

- **TAIL** Long and bushy.

- **COLORS** All colors except chocolate, cinnamon, lilac, and fawn are accepted, though neither the Himalayan pattern nor the Burmese factor is allowed. Type always takes preference over color. No relationship between coat and eye color, but clear eye color is desirable.

SOLID VARIETIES

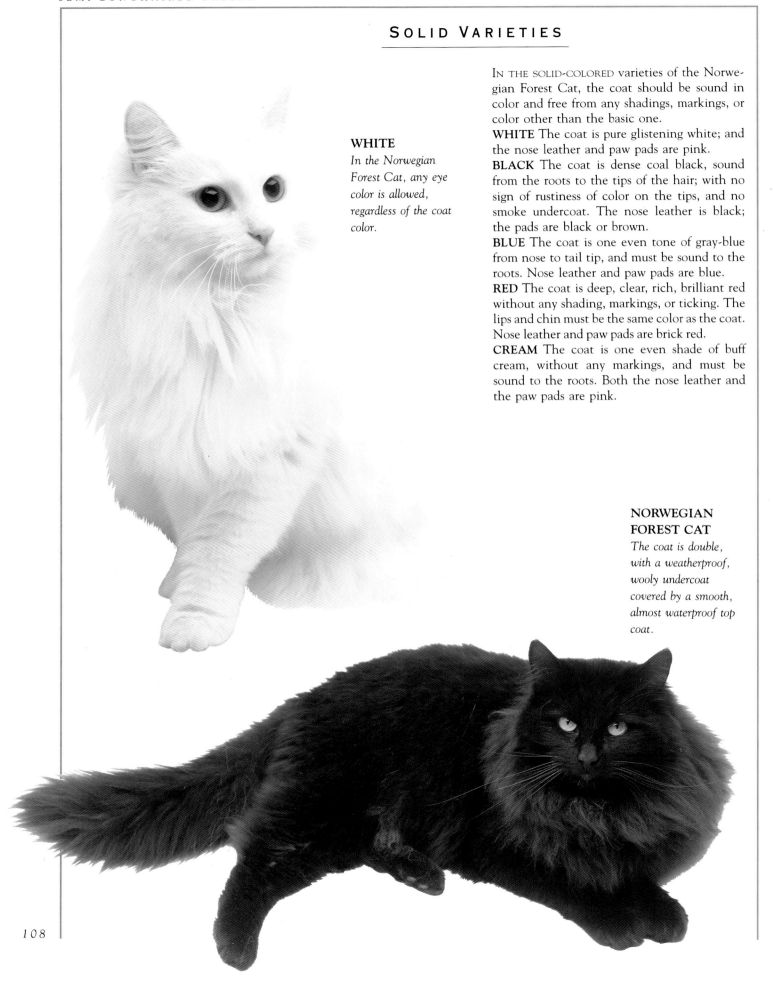

IN THE SOLID-COLORED varieties of the Norwegian Forest Cat, the coat should be sound in color and free from any shadings, markings, or color other than the basic one.

WHITE The coat is pure glistening white; and the nose leather and paw pads are pink.

BLACK The coat is dense coal black, sound from the roots to the tips of the hair; with no sign of rustiness of color on the tips, and no smoke undercoat. The nose leather is black; the pads are black or brown.

BLUE The coat is one even tone of gray-blue from nose to tail tip, and must be sound to the roots. Nose leather and paw pads are blue.

RED The coat is deep, clear, rich, brilliant red without any shading, markings, or ticking. The lips and chin must be the same color as the coat. Nose leather and paw pads are brick red.

CREAM The coat is one even shade of buff cream, without any markings, and must be sound to the roots. Both the nose leather and the paw pads are pink.

WHITE
In the Norwegian Forest Cat, any eye color is allowed, regardless of the coat color.

NORWEGIAN FOREST CAT
The coat is double, with a weatherproof, wooly undercoat covered by a smooth, almost waterproof top coat.

TABBY VARIETIES

ANY OF THE FOUR tabby patterns are accepted in the Norwegian Forest Cat, and a whole range of colors, except the chocolate and lilac series. Any amount of white on the body is also permitted.

SILVER TABBY The cat has a pale, clear silver base coat with dense black markings; white is allowed around the lips and chin. The nose leather is brick red; the paw pads are black.

BROWN TABBY Brilliant coppery-brown base coat with dense black markings. The backs of the legs from paw to heel are black; white allowed around lips and chin. Nose leather and paw pads are black or brown.

BLUE TABBY The cat has a pale bluish-ivory base coat with very deep blue markings affording good contrast with the base color. There is a warm fawn patina over the whole coat. White is allowed around the lips and chin. The nose leather is old rose; the paw pads are rose.

RED TABBY Red base coat with deep rich red markings; white allowed around lips and chin. Nose leather and paw pads are brick red.

CREAM TABBY The cat has a very pale cream base coat with buff or cream markings sufficiently darker to afford good contrast with the base color. White is allowed around lips and chin. Nose leather and paw pads are pink.

TABBY-AND-WHITE May be silver, brown, blue, red, or cream – with or without white on the face, but with white on the bib, belly, and all four paws; white on one-third of the body overall is desirable. The nose leather and paw pads are as above.

BLUE SILVER TABBY

Any amount of white is permitted on the paws, chest, or underbody, or as a facial blaze.

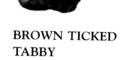

BROWN TICKED TABBY

All tabby patterns are accepted, including the Ticked as seen in this very full-coated cat.

BROWN TABBY

This handsome cat is marked with the Classic tabby pattern which shows clearly on the smooth semi-longhaired cat.

RED SILVER TABBY and WHITE

The addition of silver to other varieties adds to the range of pale, attractive shades.

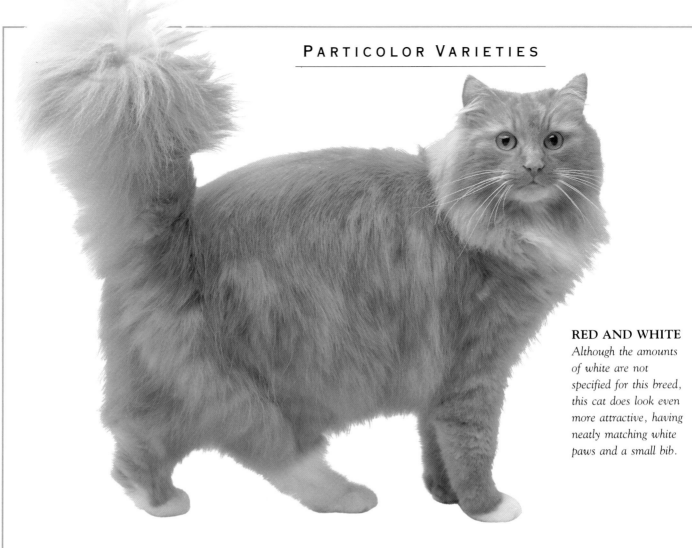

RED AND WHITE

Although the amounts of white are not specified for this breed, this cat does look even more attractive, having neatly matching white paws and a small bib.

DEVELOPED FROM THE indigenous domestic cat, the Norwegian Forest Cat is found in a wide variety of coat colors and patterns. There is no relationship between coat color and eye color as expected in most other pedigree breeds.

TORTOISESHELL Black with unbrindled patches of red and light red, the patches clearly defined and well broken on body and extremities. A blaze of red on the face is desirable.

CALICO Color as for the Tortoiseshell with or without white on the face, but there must be white on the bib, belly, and all four paws. White on one-third of the body overall is desirable.

BLUE-CREAM The color is blue with clearly defined, unbrindled, well-broken patches of cream on the body and extremities.

BLUE-CREAM-AND-WHITE The color is as defined for the Blue-cream, with or without white on the face, but there must be white on the bib, belly, and all four paws. White on one-third of the body overall is desirable.

BICOLOR Combination of a solid color with white. Color predominates, with white areas located on the face, chest, belly, legs, and feet. Colors are black, blue, red, and cream.

TORTOISESHELL

All colors of torties are accepted in the breed and may be with or without white markings.

SMOKE AND CAMEO VARIETIES

THE LONG COAT OF the Norwegian Forest Cat is particularly attractive in the colors which have a silver undercoat, such as the smoke, shaded, tipped and cameo series in all colors.

CHINCHILLA There is a pure white undercoat, and the coat on the back, flanks, head, and tail is sufficiently tipped with black to give the characteristic sparkling silver appearance. The legs may be slightly shaded with tipping. The chin, ear tufts, stomach, and chest are pure white; eye rims, lips and nose are outlined with black. Nose leather and paw pads are black.

SHADED SILVER There is a white undercoat with a mantle of black tipping shading down the sides, face and tail, the color ranging from dark on the ridge to white on the chin, chest, stomach, and underside of the tail. The legs are the same tone as the face. The general effect is much darker than the Chinchilla. The eye rims, lips, and nose are outlined with black; nose leather is brick red; paw pads are black.

RED SHELL CAMEO There is a white undercoat, and the coat on the back, flanks, head, and tail is sufficiently tipped with red to give the characteristic sparkling appearance. The face and legs may be very slightly shaded with tipping. The chin, ear tufts, stomach, and chest are white; the eye rims, nose leather and paw pads are rose.

RED SHADED CAMEO There is a white undercoat with a mantle of red tipping down the sides, face, and tail, with the color ranging from dark on the ridge to white on the chin, chest, stomach, and underside of the tail. The legs are the same tone as the face. The nose leather and paw pads are black.

BLACK SMOKE There is a white undercoat deeply tipped with black; in repose, the cat appears black; in motion, the white undercoat is clearly apparent. The points and mask are black, with a narrow band of white at the base of the hairs next to the skin. The ruff (frill) and ear tufts are light silver; the nose leather and paw pads are black.

BLUE SMOKE There is a white undercoat deeply tipped with blue; in repose, the cat appears blue; in motion, the white undercoat is clearly apparent. The points and mask are blue, with a narrow band of white hairs next to the skin. The ruff (frill) and ear tufts are white; the nose leather, and paw pads are blue.

RED SMOKE There is a white undercoat deeply tipped with red; in repose, the cat appears red; in motion, the white undercoat is clearly apparent. The points and mask are red, with a narrow band of white hairs next to the skin. The eye rims, nose leather, and paw pads are rose.

BLACK SMOKE
The Forest Cat's eyes should be large and held well opened, set slightly obliquely, and may be of any color.

ANGORA

ONE OF THE MOST ANCIENT of cat breeds, originating in Turkey, the Angora was the first of the longhaired cats to reach Europe. In the sixteenth century, a naturalist called Nicholas-Claude Fabri de Peiresc imported several cats into France from Angora (now Ankara) in Turkey. They were described in contemporary literature as "ash-colored dun and speckled cats, beautiful to behold." The cats were bred from, and some of the kittens went to England, where they were highly prized and known as French cats. When another type of long-coated cat arrived in Europe from Persia (now Iran), the Angora and the Persian were intermated quite indiscriminately.

The Persian type gradually superseded the Angora type in popularity, and by the twentieth century the Angora breed was virtually unknown outside its native land.

During the 1950s and 1960s, North America, Britain, and Sweden imported cats from Turkey to start breeding programs for the development of the Angora breed. In the United States, the Turkish Angora was officially recognized and granted championship status by some associations in the early 1970s, but until 1978, the CFA only accepted the white variety. Eventually, however, a wide range of colors was accepted.

Character and Care

Precocious as kittens, Angoras are playful and athletic. They are generally affectionate with their owners, but can be aloof with strangers.

Angoras molt excessively in summer, and the loose hair should be combed out daily. The lack of a fluffy undercoat means that the coat does not become matted.

BREAKDOWN OF 100 SHOW POINTS

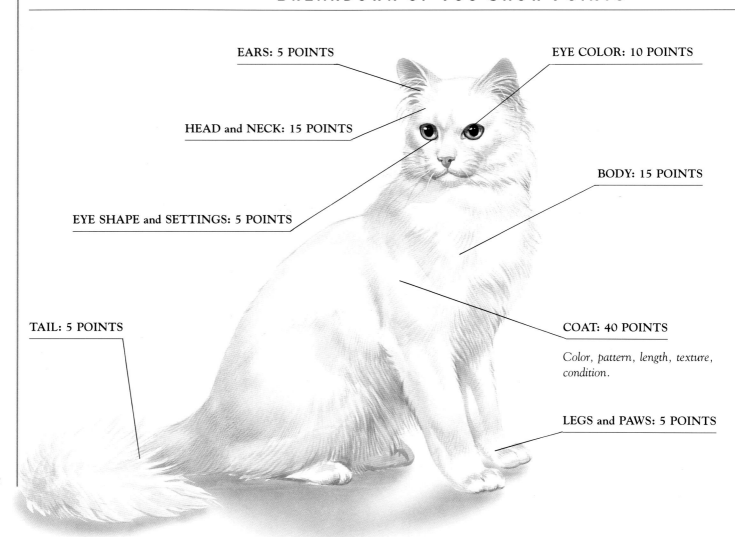

EARS: 5 POINTS

EYE COLOR: 10 POINTS

HEAD and NECK: 15 POINTS

BODY: 15 POINTS

EYE SHAPE and SETTINGS: 5 POINTS

TAIL: 5 POINTS

COAT: 40 POINTS

Color, pattern, length, texture, condition.

LEGS and PAWS: 5 POINTS

KEY CHARACTERISTICS

- **CATEGORY** Longhair.

- **OVERALL BUILD** Medium sized and well-proportioned, with males larger than females.

- **COAT** Medium length, silky and sleek, with no undercoat. Long at the ruff.

- **HEAD** Small to medium in size and wedge-shaped, wide at the top tapering toward the chin.

- **NOSE** Medium length, with a gentle slope and no stop or break.

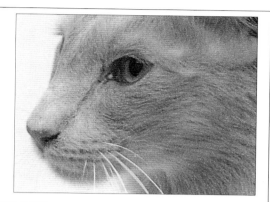

- **CHIN** Gently rounded, the tip forming a perpendicular line with the nose.

- **EYES** Large, almond shaped, slanting slightly upward.

- **EARS** Long and pointed, wide at the base, well-furred and tufted.

- **BODY** Fine boned, with a light-framed chest and slender torso. Lithe, with the hind part higher than the front.

- **LEGS** Long, with hind legs longer than forelegs.

- **PAWS** Small, round, and dainty with tufts between the toes.

- **TAIL** Long and tapering, wide at the rump and narrow at the tip; well-furred. It is carried horizontally over the body, sometimes touching the head.

- **COLORS** White with amber, blue green, or odd eyes; black, blue, chocolate red, cream, cinamon, caramel, fawn, blue-cream tabby in standard and silver, in any pattern and all colors; tortie, torbie tabby, smokes and shaded in all colors.

PENALTIES

The Angora (Turkish Angora) is penalized for having a kinked or abnormal tail.

DISQUALIFICATION FEATURES
- Persian body type

ANGORA VARIETIES

ODD-EYED WHITE

In the Angora, unlike most other Odd-Eyed cats, one eye should be blue and the other eye green.

IN THE BRITAIN, the Angora has been granted preliminary show status as the longcoated equivalent of the Oriental, the cat called Javanese by the Cat Association of Britain and FIFe of Europe.

WHITE The coat should be pure white with no other coloring, and the nose leather and paw pads pink. There are three sub-varieties – Amber-eyed, Blue-eyed, and Odd-eyed.

BLACK The coloring must be dense coal black, sound from the roots to the tips of the hair and free from any tinge of rust on the tips, or a smoke undercoat. Nose leather is black and paw pads black or brown; eye color is amber.

BLUE The denser shades of blue are preferred, the coat should be one even tone from nose to tail tip with the color sound to the roots. The nose leather and paw pads are all blue, and the eye color is amber.

RED A deep, rich, clear, brilliant red is required, without shading, markings, or ticking. Lips and chin should be the same color as the coat. Nose leather and paw pads are brick red; the eye color is amber.

CREAM One level shade of buff cream without markings must be attained, with the color sound to the roots. Lighter shades are preferred. Nose leather and paw pads should be pink, and the eye color is amber.

BLUE-CREAM Blue should be the predominant color with patches of solid cream. The patches should be clearly defined and well broken on both body and extremities. The eye color is amber.

TORTOISESHELL Black is the dominant color with unbrindled patches of red and light red. The patches should be clearly defined and well broken on both body and extremities. A blaze of red or light red on the face is desirable. The eye color is amber.

CALICO The coat should be mostly white, with unbrindled patches of black and red, and white predominant on the underparts. Eye color is amber. In the dilute calico, the dominant color is again white, with unbrindled patches this time of blue and cream; white is predominant on the underparts.

BICOLOR Varieties are black and white, blue and white, red and white, or cream and white.

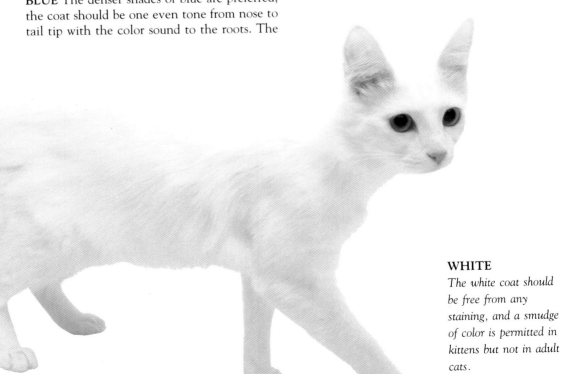

WHITE

The white coat should be free from any staining, and a smudge of color is permitted in kittens but not in adult cats.

LILAC ANGORA

This is an excellent example of the variety, showing very good type and a true lilac coat, which should be as the standard describes – frosty gray with a distinct pinkish tone giving the overall appearance.

The muzzle, chest, legs, feet, and underparts should all be white in each. White under the tail and a white collar are permissible. An inverted V-shaped blaze on the face is desirable. Eye color is amber.

BLACK SMOKE The undercoat is white, deeply tipped with black. In repose the cat appears black, but in motion the white undercoat is clearly apparent. The narrow band of white hairs next to the skin may be seen only when the hair is parted. The mask and points, nose leather, and paw pads are black, and the eye color is amber.

BLUE SMOKE The white undercoat is deeply tipped with blue. The cat in repose appears blue, but in motion the white undercoat is clearly apparent. Blue mask and points with a narrow band of white hairs next to the skin may be seen only when the hair is parted. The mask and points, nose leather, and paw pads are blue, and the eyes amber.

Tabby

The following colors apply to both the Classic and Mackeral tabby patterns.

SILVER TABBY This cat has a pale, clear silver base coat including lips and chin, with dense black markings. Nose leather is brick red and paw pads black. The eyes are green or hazel.

BROWN TABBY The brilliant coppery brown base coat should have dense black markings. Lips and chin should be the same shade as the rings around the eyes, and backs of the legs black from paw to heel. Nose leather is brick

red and paw pads black or brown. The eyes are amber.

BLUE TABBY The pale bluish-ivory base coat includes the lips and chin, with very deep blue markings affording a good contrast with the base color. A warm fawn patina should cover the whole coat. Nose leather is old rose, the paw pads rose, and the eyes amber.

RED TABBY The red base coat includes the lips and chin with deep, rich red markings. Nose leather and paw pads are all brick red; the eye color is amber.

BLACK

The jet black coat that is required in this variety is often difficult to produce, particularly in the young cat, for which judges make allowances in the show situation.

115

TURKISH

THE CAT KNOWN as the Turkish in Britain and the Turkish Van in Europe and the United States was first introduced to Britain and the cat fanciers of the world in 1955 by Laura Lushington. Traveling in the Lake Van district of Turkey, she and a friend were enchanted by these cats and eventually acquired the first breeding pair. Others of the breed were imported into Britain, and the necessary breeding programs were completed in order to apply for official recognition of the cats as a pure breed in their own right. This was achieved in 1969, and the cats attracted considerable attention.

Turkish Van cats were also introduced independently from Turkey directly to the United States, where they are now recognized by some associations.

Character and Care

The first cats imported from Turkey were inclined to be slightly nervous of human contact, but today's Turkish cats generally have affectionate dispositions. They are strong and hardy, and breeders were intrigued by the animals' natural liking for water – they will voluntarily swim if given the opportunity and have no objection to being bathed in preparation for show appearances.

The silky coat has no wooly undercoat, making grooming an easy task.

BREAKDOWN OF 100 SHOW POINTS

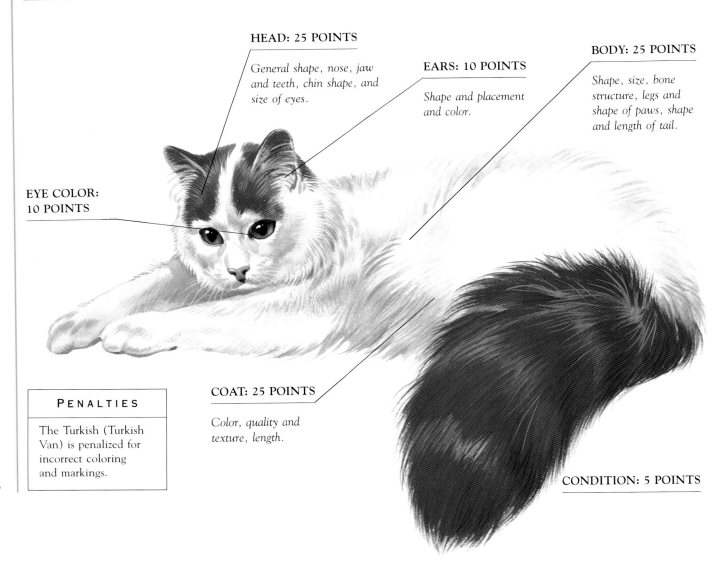

HEAD: 25 POINTS

General shape, nose, jaw and teeth, chin shape, and size of eyes.

EARS: 10 POINTS

Shape and placement and color.

BODY: 25 POINTS

Shape, size, bone structure, legs and shape of paws, shape and length of tail.

EYE COLOR: 10 POINTS

COAT: 25 POINTS

Color, quality and texture, length.

PENALTIES

The Turkish (Turkish Van) is penalized for incorrect coloring and markings.

CONDITION: 5 POINTS

**AUBURN
TURKISH**

*The markings of the
Turkish Van cat are
responsible for the
"Van" designation in
other varieties which
are mostly white, with
small and discrete
areas of color.*

CREAM TURKISH

*The cream Turkish cat
may have light amber
eyes, or blue eyes, and
the odd-eyed variety is
also accepted where
there is one blue eye
and the other of light
amber.*

KEY CHARACTERISTICS

- **CATEGORY** Longhair.

- **OVERALL BUILD** Of medium size and heavy build.

- **COAT** Fine and silky, semi-long on body, no wooly overcoat.
  Pattern Predominantly white, with auburn or cream markings on the face, and a white blaze; the tail is auburn or cream. Small, irregularly placed auburn or cream markings on the body are allowed in an otherwise good specimen.

- **COLORS** Auburn – chalk-white coat with no trace of yellow; auburn markings on face with a white blaze; white ears. Eye rims, nose leather, paw pads, and inside ears are shell pink; eye color is amber (*UK*), plus blue and odd-eyed (*Europe*). Cream – chalk-white coat with no trace of yellow; cream markings on face with a white blaze; white ears. Eye rims, nose leather, paw pads, and inside ears shell pink; eye color amber, blue, and odd-eyed.

- **OTHER FEATURES** Short, blunt head, triangular in shape. Straight nose, of medium length, with firm chin. Eyes are large and oval, set slightly obliquely. Ears are large and well-furred, wide-based with slightly rounded tips, set high and erect on the skull. The body is long, but sturdy and muscular, with medium-length legs and medium-length tail, well-furred but without undercoat. Paws are round and dainty, and well-tufted.

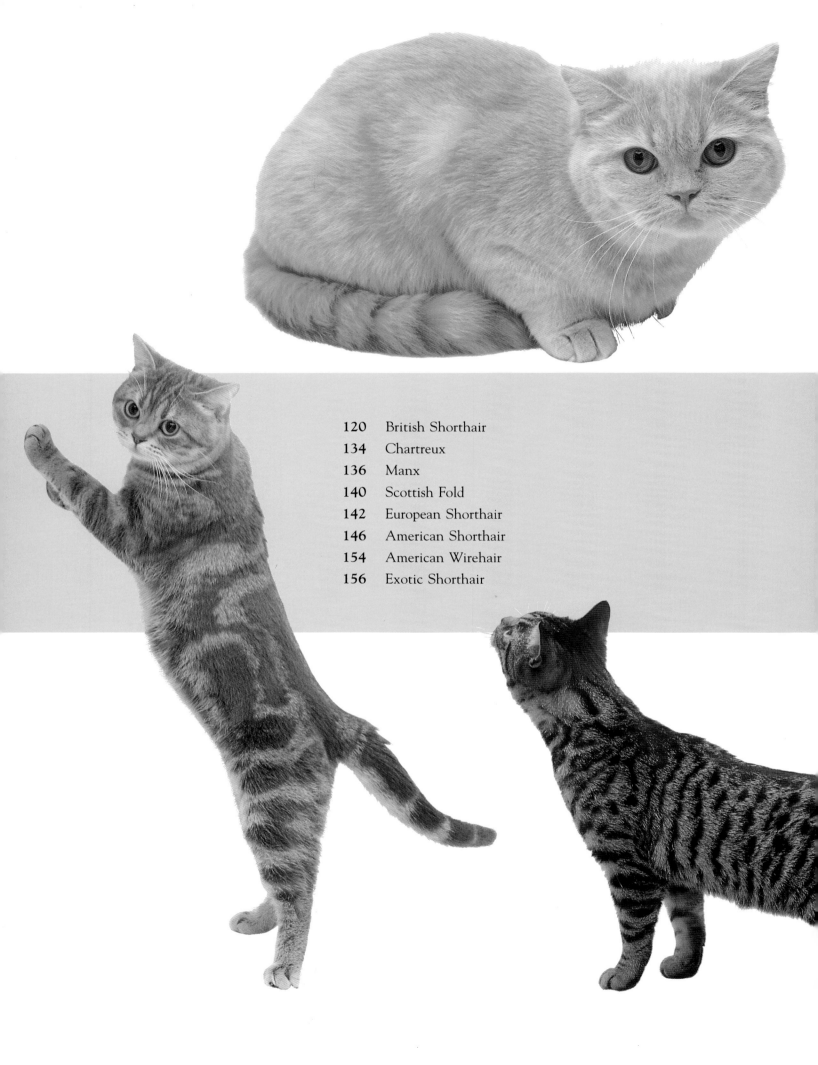

120 British Shorthair

134 Chartreux

136 Manx

140 Scottish Fold

142 European Shorthair

146 American Shorthair

154 American Wirehair

156 Exotic Shorthair

SHORTHAIRED BREEDS

BRITISH SHORTHAIR

THIS BREED PROBABLY evolved from domestic cats introduced to the British Isles by the Roman colonists some 2,000 years ago. However, today's pedigree Shorthairs must conform to strict standards of points and differ quite considerably from the common domestic or farm cat.

Shorthairs appeared in substantial numbers in the first cat shows held toward the end of the nineteenth century, then seemed to lose their popularity in favor of the Persian and Angora cats which were specially imported for the show scene.

It was not until the 1930s that a general resurgence of the breed began, and selective breeding produced cats of good type and the desired range of colors. In the early days, solid colors were preferred to the patterned varieties, the most highly prized of all being the blue-gray, sometimes given solitary breed status as

the British Blue.

British Shorthairs suffered a setback during World War II, when many owners had to give up breeding pedigree kittens and neutered their cats. In the post-war years, very few pedigree stud males remained, and the Shorthair's type suffered after outcrosses were made with short-haired cats of Foreign type. Matters were redressed during the early 1950s by careful matings with Blue Persians, and within a few generations the British Shorthair was brought up to the exacting standards existing today.

American stock came from the best of the British catteries. At first, the ACFA officially recognized only the blue and black varieties, and the CCA and CFF recognized only the British Blue. In 1976, the ACFA was the first to accept all colors, and it was followed by the remaining associations. In the United States, as in Britain, British Shorthairs are bred only to

BREAKDOWN OF 100 SHOW POINTS

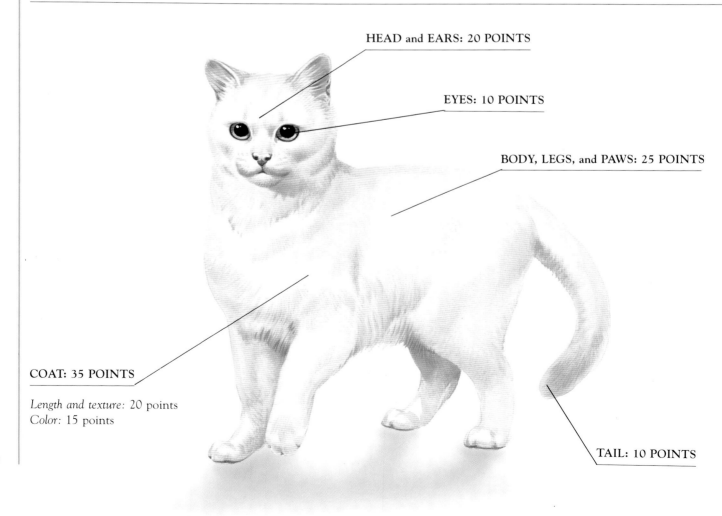

HEAD and EARS: 20 POINTS

EYES: 10 POINTS

BODY, LEGS, and PAWS: 25 POINTS

COAT: 35 POINTS

Length and texture: 20 points
Color: 15 points

TAIL: 10 POINTS

other British Shorthairs, and back-crossing to Persians is no longer allowed.

Character and Care

The typical British Shorthair has a sweet and gentle nature and makes an undemanding, quiet-voiced pet. It is generally calm and intelligent, and readily responds to affection.

Although it has a short coat, this is quite dense and needs regular grooming by brushing and combing right through to the roots every day. It is particularly important to accustom all kittens to this daily procedure from a very early age so that it is not resented later. The eyes and ears should be gently cleaned with a cotton swab whenever necessary, and the coat may be polished with a grooming mitt or a silk scarf.

KEY CHARACTERISTICS

- **CATEGORY** Shorthair.

- **OVERALL BUILD** Large and chunky (not coarse or overweight).

- **COAT** Short and dense, not double or wooly. Firm and resilient to the touch.

- **HEAD** Very broad and round with well-developed cheeks, set on a short, thick neck.

- **NOSE** Medium broad with gentle dip in profile.

- **CHIN** Firm and well-developed.

- **EYES** Large, round, and well opened.

- **EARS** Medium size, broad-based and round-tipped, set far apart.

- **BODY** Medium to large; powerful, with a level back and broad chest.

- **LEGS** Short to medium length, well boned.

- **PAWS** Round.

- **TAIL** Length in proportion to body, thick at the base and tapering to a rounded tip.

- **COLORS** White, black, blue, cream tortoiseshell, blue-cream, black smoke, bicolor, calico, tabby (Classic, Mackerel, and Spotted; all colors) chocolate, lilac, smoke (all colors), tipped (all colors), Himalayan or Colorpoint (all colors).

SOLID VARIETIES

THE MOST POPULAR of the British Shorthairs is the self-coloured British Blue, the color so well complemented by the orange or copper eyes. The Black and the British White have coats more difficult to produce to top show standard.

BLACK SHORTHAIR This is one of the oldest varieties known and is often mismarked with a white locket. In the show specimen, no white hairs are allowed anywhere. The true Black Shorthair must have a shining coat, jet black to the roots and with no rusty tinge. The nose leather is black, the paw pads black or brown, and the eye color gold, orange, or copper with no trace of green.

WHITE SHORTHAIR The White Shorthair of good show type is one of the most striking of British Shorthairs. The coat must be pure white with no sign of yellow tingeing; the nose leather and paw pads are pink. The Blue-eyed White has eyes of a deep sapphire blue and is penalized in the show ring for green rims or flecks in the eye. The Orange-eyed White has deep orange, gold or copper eye color.

BLACK

One of the oldest of the pedigree breeds, the Black British Shorthair is difficult to produce with the required black coat sound to the roots and with no white hairs.

BLUE-EYED WHITE

Occasionally found to be deaf, the Blue-Eyed White is a beautiful variety which, for showing, should have eyes of a deep blue.

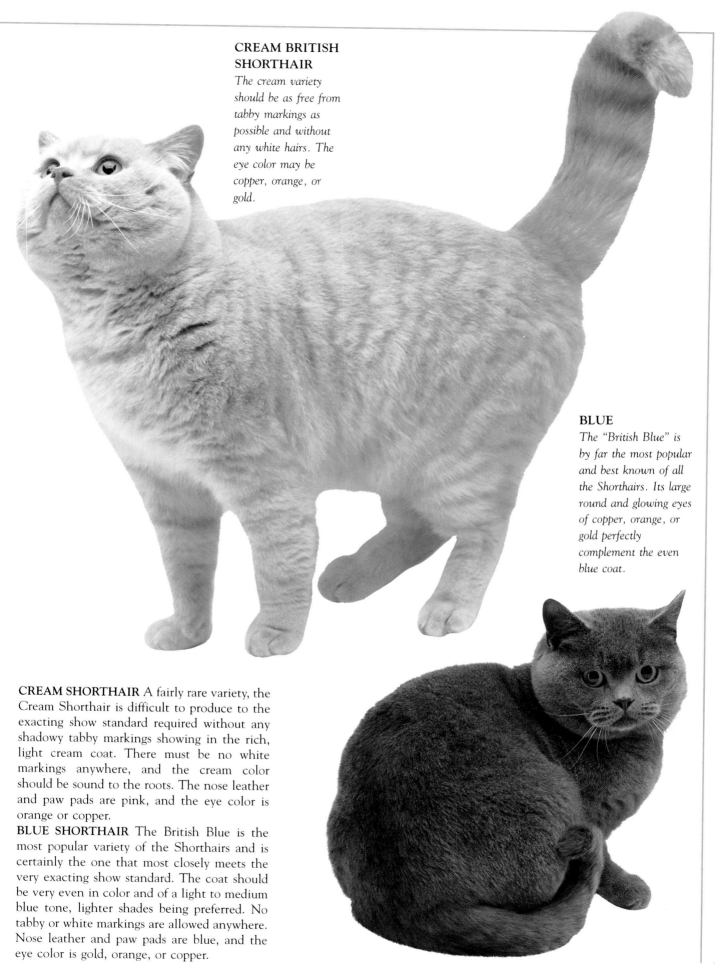

CREAM BRITISH SHORTHAIR

The cream variety should be as free from tabby markings as possible and without any white hairs. The eye color may be copper, orange, or gold.

BLUE

The "British Blue" is by far the most popular and best known of all the Shorthairs. Its large round and glowing eyes of copper, orange, or gold perfectly complement the even blue coat.

CREAM SHORTHAIR A fairly rare variety, the Cream Shorthair is difficult to produce to the exacting show standard required without any shadowy tabby markings showing in the rich, light cream coat. There must be no white markings anywhere, and the cream color should be sound to the roots. The nose leather and paw pads are pink, and the eye color is orange or copper.

BLUE SHORTHAIR The British Blue is the most popular variety of the Shorthairs and is certainly the one that most closely meets the very exacting show standard. The coat should be very even in color and of a light to medium blue tone, lighter shades being preferred. No tabby or white markings are allowed anywhere. Nose leather and paw pads are blue, and the eye color is gold, orange, or copper.

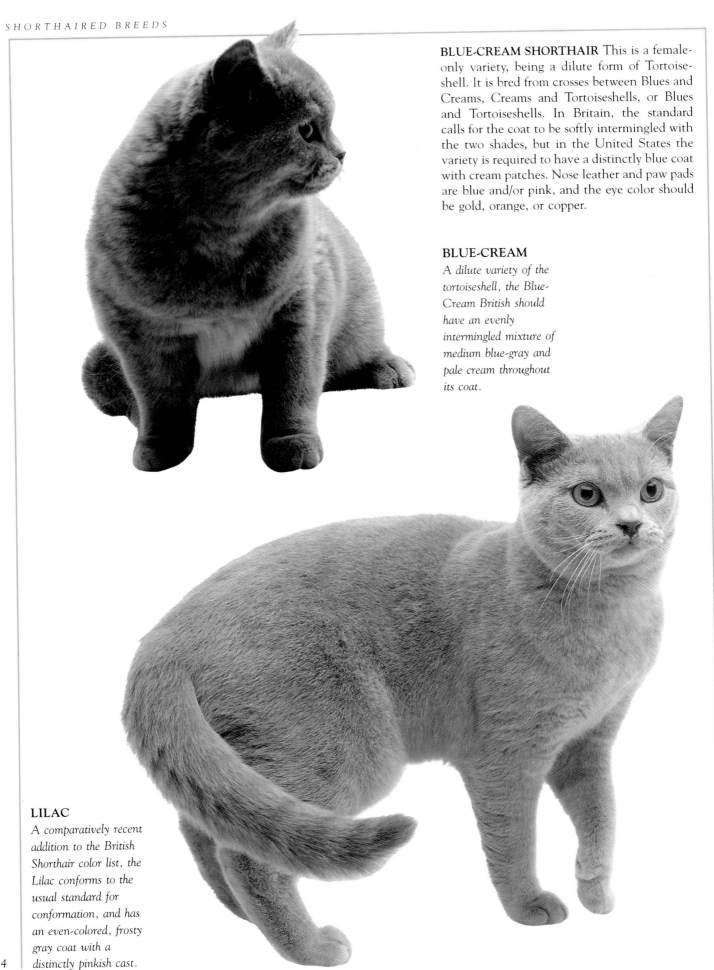

BLUE-CREAM SHORTHAIR This is a female-only variety, being a dilute form of Tortoise-shell. It is bred from crosses between Blues and Creams, Creams and Tortoiseshells, or Blues and Tortoiseshells. In Britain, the standard calls for the coat to be softly intermingled with the two shades, but in the United States the variety is required to have a distinctly blue coat with cream patches. Nose leather and paw pads are blue and/or pink, and the eye color should be gold, orange, or copper.

BLUE-CREAM

A dilute variety of the tortoiseshell, the Blue-Cream British should have an evenly intermingled mixture of medium blue-gray and pale cream throughout its coat.

LILAC

A comparatively recent addition to the British Shorthair color list, the Lilac conforms to the usual standard for conformation, and has an even-colored, frosty gray coat with a distinctly pinkish cast.

BICOLOR VARIETIES

CREAM AND WHITE BICOLOR
Symmetry of coloring is desired in the British Bicolor, with not more than half of the cat white.

BICOLOR SHORTHAIRS are cats of just two colors: a standard color with white. It is important for the markings to be as symmetrical as possible to present a balanced impression. The cats may be black-and-white, blue-and-white, red-and-white, or cream-and-white, and there must be no tabby markings in the self-colored areas. The markings which make up the self-colored portions should start immediately behind the shoulders around the barrel of the body and include the tail and hind legs, leaving the hind paws white. The ears and mask of the face should be in the self-color, while the shoulders, neck, forelegs and feet, chin, lips, and blaze should be white. The white area also extends as a blaze up the face and over the top of the head in the ideal specimen. The nose leather and paw pads are generally pink, and the eye color is gold, orange, or copper.

The Bicolor is penalized for brindling or tabby markings, and is disqualified if the white areas predominate.

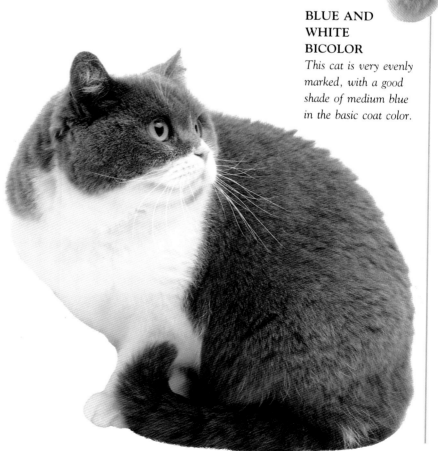

BLUE AND WHITE BICOLOR
This cat is very evenly marked, with a good shade of medium blue in the basic coat color.

TORTOISESHELL VARIETIES

BLACK AND RED markings, both dark and light, should be equally balanced over the cat's head, body, legs, and tail. Colors should be brilliant, free from blurring, brindling, and tabby patches, and with no white markings. A red blaze down the face is desired. The nose leather and paw pads should be pink and/or black. Eye color is gold, orange, or copper (hazel is also allowed by some associations).

This variety is penalized for brindling, tabby markings, unequal balance of color, and unbroken color on the paws, and is disqualified for any white markings.

TORTOISESHELL
Here the characteristic black and red colors are intermingled evenly.

CHOCOLATE TORTIE
Warm chocolate mixed with red and light red make up the bright coloring of the chocolate-tortoiseshell coat.

LILAC TORTIE
In the lilac tortoiseshell, there is an admixture of lilac and pale cream which produces a pleasing pastel effect over the body.

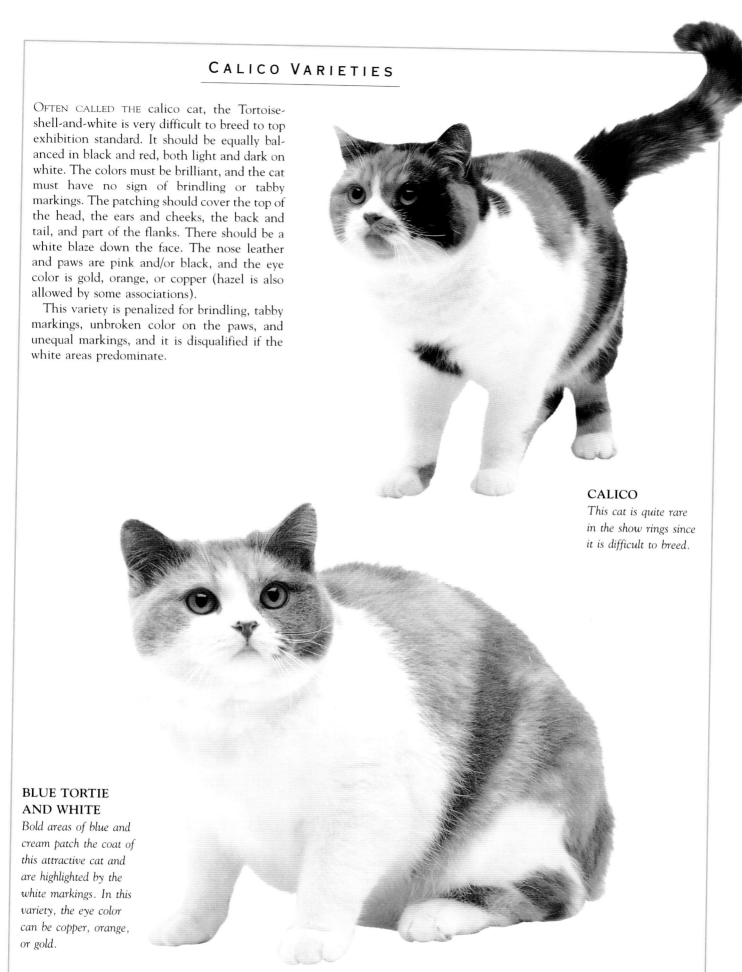

OFTEN CALLED THE calico cat, the Tortoise-shell-and-white is very difficult to breed to top exhibition standard. It should be equally balanced in black and red, both light and dark on white. The colors must be brilliant, and the cat must have no sign of brindling or tabby markings. The patching should cover the top of the head, the ears and cheeks, the back and tail, and part of the flanks. There should be a white blaze down the face. The nose leather and paws are pink and/or black, and the eye color is gold, orange, or copper (hazel is also allowed by some associations).

This variety is penalized for brindling, tabby markings, unbroken color on the paws, and unequal markings, and it is disqualified if the white areas predominate.

CALICO

This cat is quite rare in the show rings since it is difficult to breed.

BLUE TORTIE AND WHITE

Bold areas of blue and cream patch the coat of this attractive cat and are highlighted by the white markings. In this variety, the eye color can be copper, orange, or gold.

TABBY VARIETIES

**BROWN
SPOTTED**

*Clearly defined black
spots on a brown
ground color is the
requirement for this
variety.*

THERE ARE THREE acceptable tabby patterns in
the British Shorthair – the Classic, the Mackerel, and the Spotted. All three are found in a
wide variety of colors, only some of which are
recognized for show purposes, although associations around the world differ considerably in
their rules. Tabby varieties are penalized for
incorrect eye color; white anywhere; and
incorrect tabby markings.

Patterns
In the Classic tabby, markings should be dense
and clearly defined; the legs evenly barred with
bracelets and the tail evenly ringed, and the cat
should have several unbroken necklaces on the
neck and upper chest. On the head, frown
marks form a letter "M," and an unbroken line
runs back from the outer corner of each eye.
There are swirl markings on the cheeks, and
vertical lines run over the back of the head to
the shoulder markings, which resemble a butterfly, with both upper and lower wings distinctly outlined and marked with dots within
the outlines. The back is marked with a spine

**RED MACKEREL
TABBY**

*Lines run down from
the spine in the
Mackerel Tabby, but
the markings on the
head are the same as
for the other tabbies.*

**BROWN CLASSIC
TABBY**

*This chunky British cat
shows the Classic
Tabby pattern, which
is also known as the
Marbled or Blotched
Tabby.*

BLUE SPOTTED

*In the Blue Spotted,
the pattern consists of
blue-gray spots on a
lighter background,
with enough difference
in color to afford a
good contrast between
the markings and the
base coat.*

line and a parallel line on each side, all three
lines being separated by stripes of the coat's
ground colour. A large solid blotch on each side
of the body should be encircled by one or more
unbroken rings, and the side markings should
be the same on both sides of the body. A double
row of "vest" buttons should run down the
chest and under the stomach.

In the Mackerel tabby, markings should be
dense and clearly defined and all resemble
narrow pencil lines. The legs should be evenly
barred with narrow bracelets, and the tail
barred. There are several distinct narrow necklaces around the neck. The head is barred, with
a distinct "M" on the forehead, and unbroken
lines running back from the eyes. More lines
run back over the head to meet the shoulder
markings. Along the spine the lines run
together forming a dark saddle, and fine,
pencil-like markings run down each side of the
body from the spine. Clear spotting is essential

in the Spotted tabby: the spots can be round,
oval, oblong, or rosette-shaped. The head
markings should be the same as those required
for the Classic tabby. The legs should be clearly
spotted, and the tail spotted or with broken
rings. Spotted cats are penalized when the spots
are not distinct, and for having bars, except on
the head.

SILVER SPOTTED

*Perhaps the clearest of
all the spotted coats is
that of the Silver,
which has dense black
markings on a
background of very
pale silvery-white hair.*

129

RED TABBY

This richly colored Red Tabby has the typical Classic pattern on a slightly lighter red base. The desired unbroken "necklaces" can be seen quite clearly around the cat's neck.

SILVER TABBY

Like the Silver Spotted, the Silver Tabby's coat pattern shows up extremely well in black on pale silver. The necklaces and eye lines are easy to identify in this picture.

Colors

BROWN TABBY Ground color should be rich sable or brown with dense black markings. Lips and chin should be the same as the rings around the eyes. Backs of the legs should be black from heel to paw. Nose leather must be brick red and the paw pads black or brown. Eye color is gold, orange, or copper. (Some associations also allow green or hazel eye color.)

RED TABBY Ground color is red, including lips and chin. Markings are a deep, rich red, quite distinct from the ground color. Nose leather and paw pads are brick red. Eye color is gold, orange, or copper. (Some associations also accept hazel eye color.)

SILVER TABBY Ground color is a pale clear silver, including lips and chin, and markings are dense black. Nose leather is brick red; paw pads black. Eye color may be green or hazel.

BLUE TABBY Accepted by some associations. Ground color, including lips and chin, should be pale bluish-ivory, and markings a very deep blue, affording good contrast with the ground color. There should be an overall warm fawn patina. Nose leather is old rose; paw pads rose. Eye color is gold or copper.

CREAM TABBY Accepted by some associations. For this variety the ground color, including lips and chin, is very pale cream. Markings are of buff or cream sufficiently darker than the ground color to afford good contrast, while still remaining in the dilute color range. Nose leather and paw pads are pink. Eye color may be gold or copper.

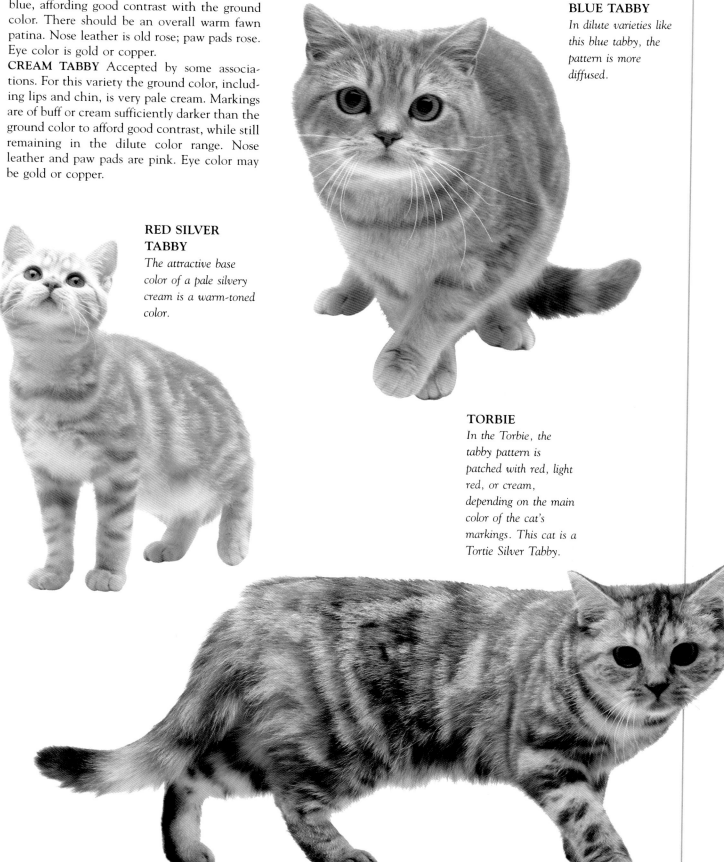

BLUE TABBY
In dilute varieties like this blue tabby, the pattern is more diffused.

RED SILVER TABBY
The attractive base color of a pale silvery cream is a warm-toned color.

TORBIE
In the Torbie, the tabby pattern is patched with red, light red, or cream, depending on the main color of the cat's markings. This cat is a Tortie Silver Tabby.

OTHER VARIETIES

SMOKE-PATTERNED CATS are of standard feline colors, but instead of the color being sound to the roots, the undercoat is white or silver. In repose the cat at first appears to be self-colored, but in motion the white or silver undercoat is apparent, giving a shot-silk appearance. In each sub-variety, the nose leather, paw pads, and eye color required is the same as for that of the relevant self-color. British Shorthair Smoke cats are bred in a variety of colors, but the various associations each have a limited range of those which are officially recognized.

BLACK SMOKE The white or silver undercoat is deeply tipped with black. In repose the cat appears black; in motion the pale undercoat is clearly apparent. The nose leather and paw pads are both black, and the eye color may be either gold or copper.

BLUE SMOKE The undercoat is white or silver, deeply tipped with blue. The cat in repose appears blue; but as with the black, in motion the pale undercoat is clearly apparent. Nose leather and paw pads are blue, and the eye color may be gold or copper.

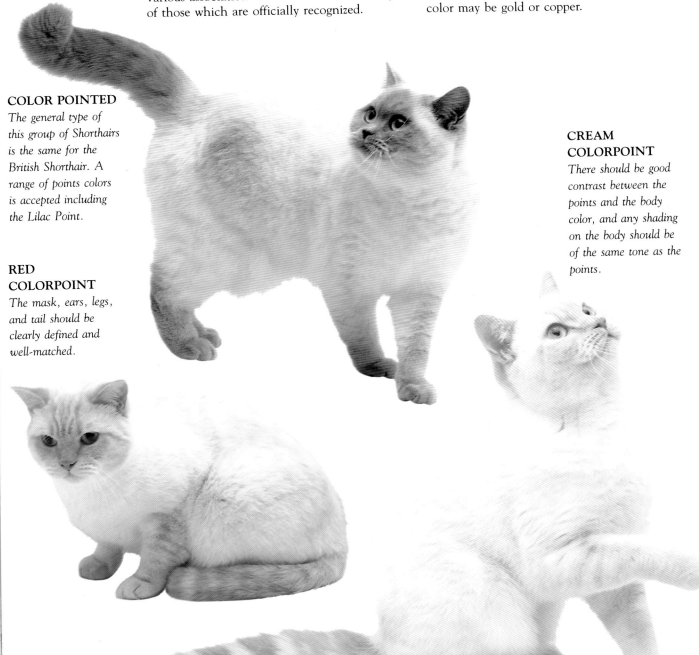

COLOR POINTED

The general type of this group of Shorthairs is the same for the British Shorthair. A range of points colors is accepted including the Lilac Point.

RED COLORPOINT

The mask, ears, legs, and tail should be clearly defined and well-matched.

CREAM COLORPOINT

There should be good contrast between the points and the body color, and any shading on the body should be of the same tone as the points.

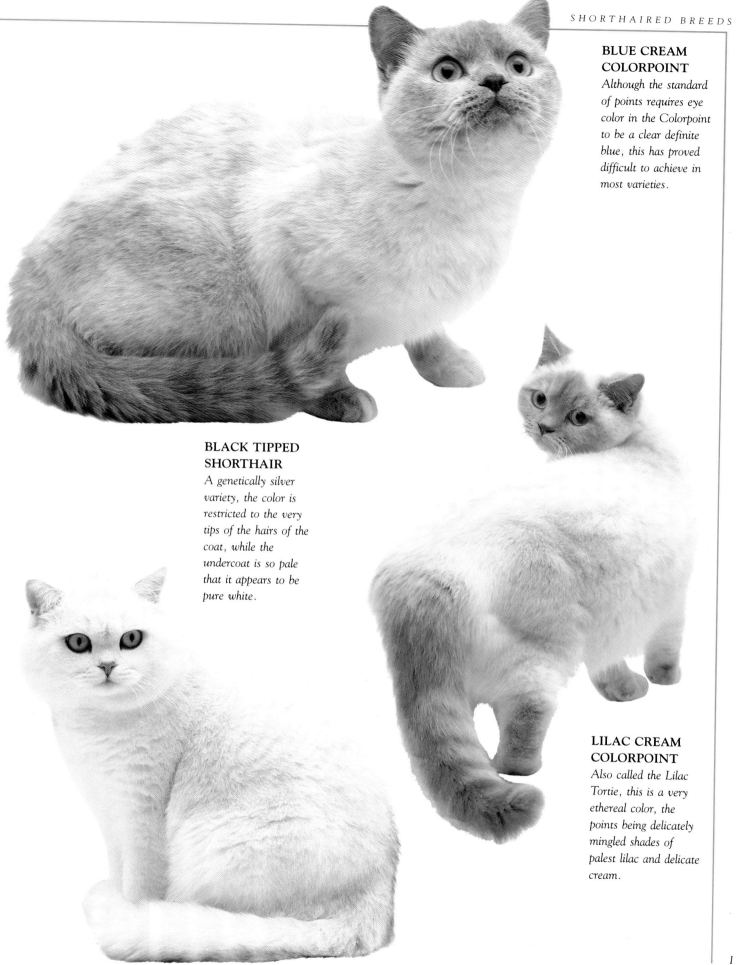

BLUE CREAM COLORPOINT

Although the standard of points requires eye color in the Colorpoint to be a clear definite blue, this has proved difficult to achieve in most varieties.

BLACK TIPPED SHORTHAIR

A genetically silver variety, the color is restricted to the very tips of the hairs of the coat, while the undercoat is so pale that it appears to be pure white.

LILAC CREAM COLORPOINT

Also called the Lilac Tortie, this is a very ethereal color, the points being delicately mingled shades of palest lilac and delicate cream.

CHARTREUX

NATIVE TO FRANCE, the Chartreux is said to have been bred exclusively by Carthusian monks as long ago as the sixteenth century. The monks lived in the monastery near the town of Grenoble, world-famous for its unique liqueur, known as Chartreuse. The naturalist Georges Louis Buffon's work *Histoire Naturelle*, published in 1756, records details of the self-blue feline, and in the 1930s a French veterinarian suggested that the breed should have its own scientific name, *Felis catus cartusianorum*. Today's Chartreux should not be confused with the British Blue or the European Shorthaired Blue. It is massively built, with a very distinctive jowled head, more pronounced in the male than in the female, and is a blue-only breed.

Character and Care
Self-assured and affectionate, the Chartreux has always been considered a cat for the connoisseur. It is quiet-voiced and will happily live confined to the house. The dense coat needs regular combing to keep the wooly undercoat in good condition, and brushing enhances the way in which the coat stands away from the body – a breed characteristic.

BREAKDOWN OF 100 SHOW POINTS

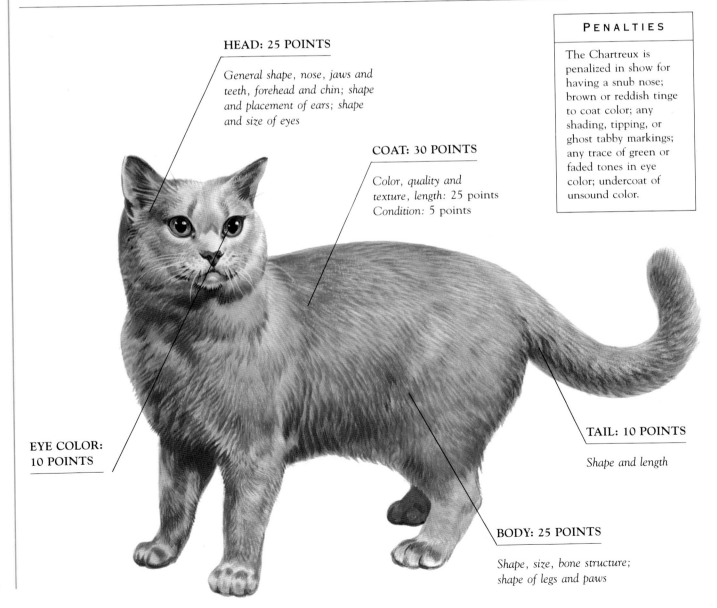

HEAD: 25 POINTS

General shape, nose, jaws and teeth, forehead and chin; shape and placement of ears; shape and size of eyes

COAT: 30 POINTS

Color, quality and texture, length: 25 points
Condition: 5 points

PENALTIES

The Chartreux is penalized in show for having a snub nose; brown or reddish tinge to coat color; any shading, tipping, or ghost tabby markings; any trace of green or faded tones in eye color; undercoat of unsound color.

EYE COLOR: 10 POINTS

TAIL: 10 POINTS

Shape and length

BODY: 25 POINTS

Shape, size, bone structure; shape of legs and paws

The strong head and broad skull of the blue cat known as the Chartreux.

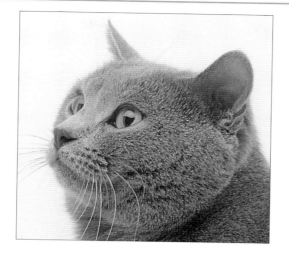

KEY CHARACTERISTICS

- **CATEGORY** Shorthair.

- **OVERALL BUILD** Medium to large, firm and muscular.

- **COAT** Dense and with slightly wooly undercoat; double coat makes the hair stand out from the body; glossy appearance.

- **COLOR** Any shade of blue from pale blue-gray to deep blue-gray, paler shades preferred. Uniform tone essential.

- **OTHER FEATURES** A wide head, with a narrow flat plane between the ears, and wide jowls. The nose is broad and straight, and the chin firm and well developed. Eyes are large and open, not too rounded and with the outer corner slightly uptilted; eye color is vivid deep yellow to vivid deep copper. The most intense color is preferred. Ears are medium sized, set high on the head and slightly flaring, giving an alert expression. The body is solid and muscular with a broad chest; the legs are strong, medium length in proportion to the body. Paws are large, and the tail is medium length in proportion to the body; it may taper and has a rounded tip.

CHARTREUX

One of the true blue cats of the world, the Chartreux is a massive breed with a very gentle nature and a quiet voice.

MANX

LEGENDS AND FAIRY-TALES explaining the origins of this unique tailless breed abound, but modern science agrees that its appearance is due to a mutant dominant gene. The original mutation must have occurred many years ago, for Manx cats have been known since 1900, with a specialist breed club being first established in Britain in 1901.

Although it is an old breed, Manx cats remain rare. The females produce small litters as a direct result of the gene for taillessness. This factor is a semi-lethal gene, and the homozygous Manx – one that inherits the tailless gene from both parents – dies within the womb at an early stage of fetal development. The Manx that is born alive is the heterozygote – one that inherits only one gene for tail-lessness, the other member of the gene pair being for a normal tail. Breeders usually cross tailless Manx with normal-tailed Manx offspring to retain the correct body type.

Character and Care

Manx cats are highly intelligent, playful and affectionate, and make ideal and unusual pets. A good specimen generally takes top awards in show when competing against other breeds, particularly if it is easy to handle and performs wells for the judges.

The Manx's double coat repays good feeding and regular grooming. It should be combed through to the roots over the entire body and given a final sheen by polishing with the hands, a grooming mitt, or a silk scarf.

BREAKDOWN OF 100 SHOW POINTS

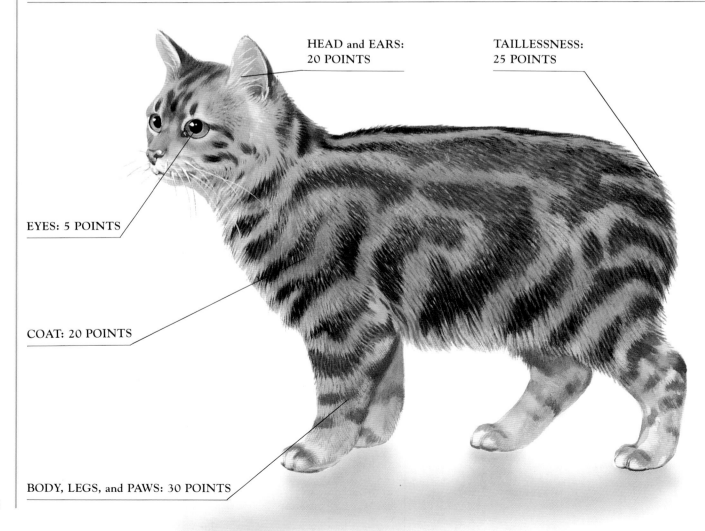

HEAD and EARS: 20 POINTS

TAILLESSNESS: 25 POINTS

EYES: 5 POINTS

COAT: 20 POINTS

BODY, LEGS, and PAWS: 30 POINTS

KEY CHARACTERISTICS

- **CATEGORY** Shorthair.

- **OVERALL BUILD** Medium sized with a general impression of roundness.

- **COAT** *Manx* Short, dense, and double, giving a padded quality due to the comparatively long, open outer coat and the close, cottony undercoat. *Cymric* Of medium length, with close dense undercoat and longer outer coat standing away from the body; full around the neck and on the breeches; tufted ears and toes.

- **HEAD** Round, though slightly longer than it is broad, with a rounded forehead, prominent cheeks, and a jowly appearance. The definite whisker break enhances large, round whisker pads and the muzzle is well-developed.

- **NOSE** In profile there is a gentle nose dip.

- **CHIN** Firm and strong.

- **EYES** Large, round, and full.

- **EARS** Medium size, set wide apart, and turned slightly outward.

- **BODY** Solidly muscled and compact with sturdy bone structure. The chest is broad and the back short, forming a smooth, continuous arch from the shoulders to the rump, where it curves to give the desirable round look.

- **LEGS** The legs and feet are heavily boned. The hind legs are much longer than the forelegs, causing the rump to be higher than the shoulders in the standing cat.

- **PAWS** Neat and round.

- **TAIL** Taillessness is absolute in the perfect Manx, with a definite hollow at the end of the spine where, in a tailed cat, the tail would begin. A rise of bones at the end of the spine is not always penalized, depending on the amount of bone present.

- **COLORS** All colors and patterns are acceptable with the exception of the Himalayan (Siamese) coat pattern.

PENALTIES

The Manx cat is severely penalized in the show ring if the judge is unable to make it stand or walk properly.

DISQUALIFICATION FEATURES

- poor physical condition
- the incorrect number of toes
- color or pattern indicates hybridization

The cat is transferred from the Manx breed class to that for Any Other Varieties if it has long or silky fur, or there is a definite, visible tail joint.

MANX VARIETIES

THE MANX IS accepted in the following color varieties by most American associations. Each of the varieties listed has identical color requirements to its equivalent in the American Shorthair, with the exception of eye color. In American Shorthair varieties with brilliant gold eye color, the Manx should have eyes of brilliant copper.

The accepted varieties are: Black; Blue; Red; Cream; Tortoiseshell; Blue-cream; Calico; Dilute Calico; Chinchilla; Shaded Silver; Black Smoke; Blue Smoke; Classic and Mackerel Tabby in the following colors: Brown Tabby; Blue Tabby; Red Tabby; Cream Tabby; Cameo Tabby; Silver Tabby; Patched Tabby in Brown, and Blue and Silver.

Other Manx Colors

Any other colour or pattern with the exception of those showing hybridization resulting in the the Himalayan pattern. The eye color should be appropriate to the predominant color of the cat.

**TORBIE &
WHITE MANX**
This adorable little Manx kitten has adopted the typical natural stance of the breed. Manx kittens are precocious and very playful and inquisitive, making wonderful pets.

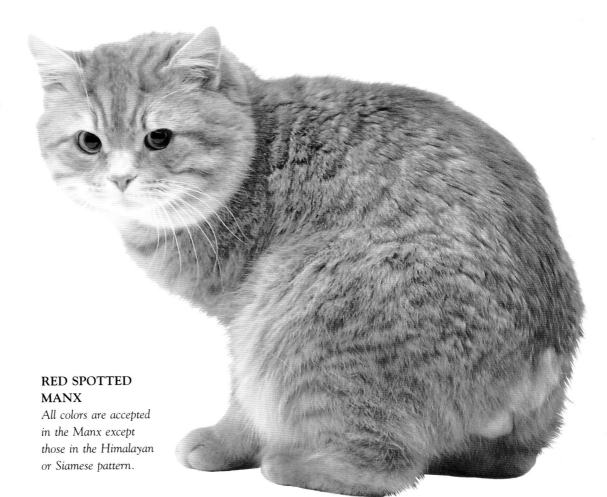

RED SPOTTED MANX
All colors are accepted in the Manx except those in the Himalayan or Siamese pattern.

**BROWN TABBY &
WHITE MANX**
*All tabby patterns are
allowed, including
those with the addition
of white areas.
Taillessness is a high-
scoring feature.*

**BLUE TORTIE &
WHITE MANX**
*The solid compact
body and a short back
makes the typical
Manx a sturdy,
compact cat, and the
hind legs are longer
than the forelegs. The
rump is firm and
rounded.*

CYMRIC

IN THE LATE 1960S breeders of Manx cats in the United States were intrigued to discover that long-coated kittens occasionally appeared in otherwise normal litters from their Manx queens. Although there were no longhaired cats in any of the pedigrees, it is possible that the recessive gene for causing long hair had been inherited from some of the tailed short-haired cats used as outcrosses in past generations. Although the first reaction of the breeders was to let such kittens go as neutered pets, it was decided that the variety could be developed as a separate, very attractive breed in its own right. When choosing a name for the breed, some associations preferred Longhaired Manx, while others accepted Cymric (pronounced koom-rik), the Welsh word for "Welsh." The breed is recognized by some associations, and except for the coat, has the same standard requirements for show purposes as the Manx cat. The coat is of medium length, soft and full, giving a padded, heavy look to the body. The same coat colors and patterns are accepted as for the Manx.

**TORTOISESHELL
CYMRIC**
*The longcoated version
of the Manx cat is not
accepted by all
associations.*

SCOTTISH FOLD

A LITTER OF OTHERWISE normal kittens born on a farm in Scotland contained the first Scottish Fold in 1961. A shepherd, William Ross, noticed the kitten with the quaint, folded ears and expressed an interest in acquiring such a cat. Two years later, the mother cat, Susie, gave birth to two kittens with folded ears, and William Ross was given one. A breeding program was begun in Great Britain, but when it was discovered that a small proportion of cats with folded ears also had thickened tails and limbs, the governing registration body banned Scottish Folds from all shows. The British breeders, who were dedicated to breeding only sound cats, resorted to registering their cats in overseas associations, and the main center of activity for the breed switched to the United States. Today's Scottish Fold cats are bred to British Shorthairs in Britain and to American Shorthairs in the United States, or back to the prick-eared offspring of Folds. The folded ears are due to the action of a single dominant gene, and all Scottish Folds must have at least one fold-eared parent.

Character and Care

The Scottish Fold is a loving, placid, and companionable cat which loves both humans and other pets. The female makes a superb mother, and the kittens are quite precocious.

The short, dense coat is kept in good condition with the minimum of brushing and combing, and the folded ears are kept immacuate by gently cleaning inside the folds with a moistened cotton swab.

BREAKDOWN OF 100 SHOW POINTS

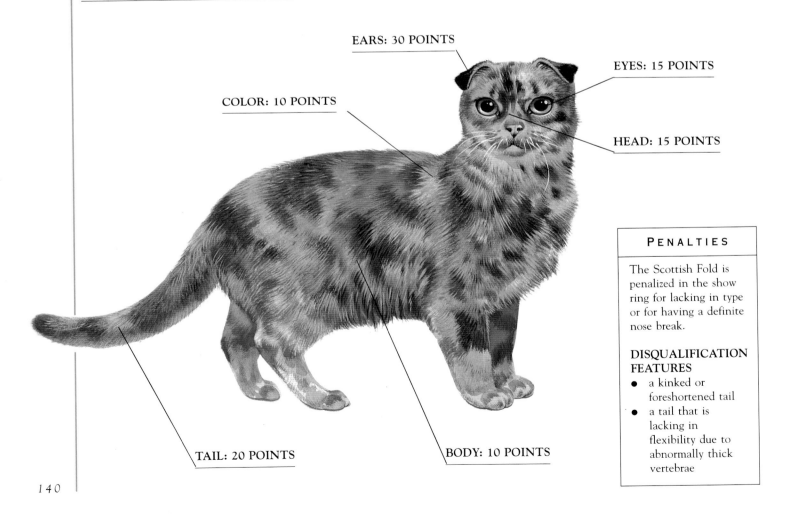

EARS: 30 POINTS

EYES: 15 POINTS

COLOR: 10 POINTS

HEAD: 15 POINTS

TAIL: 20 POINTS

BODY: 10 POINTS

PENALTIES

The Scottish Fold is penalized in the show ring for lacking in type or for having a definite nose break.

DISQUALIFICATION FEATURES

- a kinked or foreshortened tail
- a tail that is lacking in flexibility due to abnormally thick vertebrae

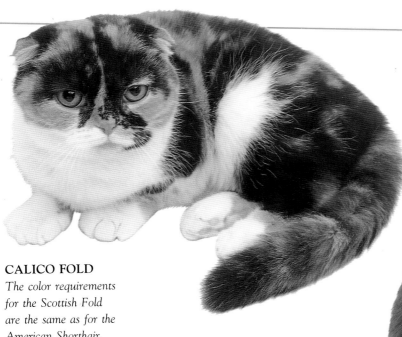

BLACK & WHITE SCOTTISH FOLD

This cat illustrates the caplike attitude of the folded ears in a good example of this breed.

CALICO FOLD

The color requirements for the Scottish Fold are the same as for the American Shorthair.

KEY CHARACTERISTICS

- **CATEGORY** Shorthair.

- **OVERALL BUILD** Medium size, well rounded with medium bone.

- **COAT** Short, dense, and resilient.

- **COLORS** White, black, blue, red, cream, tortoiseshell, calico, dilute calico, blue-cream, chinchilla, shaded silver, shell cameo, shaded cameo, black smoke, blue smoke, cameo smoke, bicolor; Classic and Mackerel Tabby in brown, blue, red, cream, cameo, silver; Patched Tabby in brown, blue, silver; any other color or pattern with the exception of those showing evidence of hybridization resulting in the colors chocolate or lavender, the Himalayan pattern or these combinations with white. The eye color should be appropriate to the coat color. Each variety has identical color requirements to its equivalent variety in the American Shorthair.

- **OTHER FEATURES** Well-rounded head with a firm chin and jaw, and muzzle with well-rounded whisker pads. Short nose with a gentle curve, and with a slight stop at eye level. The ears are small and fold forward and downward, and are set in a caplike fashion to expose a rounded cranium. The ear tips are rounded. The eyes are large and round with a sweet expression. The firm body of medium size has legs of medium bone and neat round paws. The tail is medium to long, flexible and tapering.

A LONGHAIRED VARIETY

This is one of the longcoated cats which have appeared from time to time in litters of Scottish Fold kittens.

PATCHED SILVER TABBY & WHITE

The ears of the Scottish Fold are small and fold forward and downward on the top of the head.

141

EUROPEAN SHORTHAIR

THIS SHOW BREED has been naturally developed from the indigenous cat of continental Europe. Its standard of points is similar to that of the British Shorthair, and it is presumed to be totally free of any admixture of other breeds. The first European Shorthairs were descended from cats introduced to Northern Europe by invading armies of Roman soldiers, who brought their cats with them to keep down vermin in their food storage areas.

Character and Care

The European Shorthair is a placid, good-natured breed which makes an ideal family cat. It also accepts the time it spends in the show ring and the demands of being judged with a quiet, dignified tolerance.

The short dense coat is easy to maintain with a few minutes' daily combing to keep the undercoat in good condition. The eyes and ears should be cleaned regularly with a slightly moistened cotton swab.

BREAKDOWN OF 100 SHOW POINTS

EYE COLOR: 10 POINTS

HEAD: 25 POINTS

BODY: 25 POINTS

COAT: 35 POINTS

*Color, markings, pattern: 25 points
Quality, texture, length: 10 points*

CONDITION: 5 POINTS

KEY CHARACTERISTICS

- **CATEGORY** Shorthair.

- **OVERALL BUILD** Medium to large (not over-large).

- **COAT** Short and dense, tight and glossy, not wooly.

- **HEAD** Fairly large; it appears round, but is a little longer than its breadth; slightly rounded forehead and skull and well-developed cheeks. Neck muscular and of medium length.

- **NOSE** Medium length and straight.

- **CHIN** Firm.

- **EYES** Round and open, widely separated and set slightly obliquely.

- **EARS** Medium size, slightly rounded at the tips, set upright and well apart.

- **BODY** Robust, strong, and muscular with well-developed chest.

- **LEGS** Medium length, strong and sturdy, narrowing gradually to paws.

- **PAWS** Firm and round.

- **TAIL** Medium length, thick at the base, tapering gradually to a rounded tip.

- **COLORS** White with blue, green, yellow, orange or odd eyes; black, blue, red, cream, black torbie, blue torbie; smoke: black, blue, red, cream, black torbie, blue torbie; non-silver tabby: black, blue, red, cream , black torbie, blue torbie (all accepted in Classic, Mackerel, and Spotted); silver tabby: black, blue, red, cream, black torbie, blue torbie (all accepted in Classic, Mackerel, and Spotted); bicolor: black, blue, red, cream, black torbie, blue torbie (all accepted in van, harlequin, and bicolor).

PENALTIES

The European Shorthair is penalized in the show ring for being too large in overall size or being either too cobby or too slender.

DISQUALIFICATION FEATURES

- hanging jowl pouches
- a definite nose stop
- over-long or wooly appearance to coat
- any signs of crossbreeding in its ancestry

EUROPEAN SHORTHAIR VARIETIES

MANY EUROPEAN SHORTHAIRS have British Shorthair ancestors and are found in a similar range of coat colors and patterns. Tabbies are popular, particularly in the silver range, plus the typy reds and creams, and pretty blue-creams.

EUROPEAN WHITE There are three sub-varieties of the European White, and all must have pure white coats without any sign of yellow tingeing or colored hairs. The first sub-variety should have eyes of deep blue; the second may have either green, yellow, or orange eye color; the third, the White Odd-eyed, has one eye of deep blue and the other eye either green, yellow, or orange.

EUROPEAN SOLID The Solid-colored European may be black, blue, red, or cream. All must have a coat color sound to the roots. The eye color may be green, yellow, or orange.

EUROPEAN TORBIE These patched varieties may be either black and red, giving the Black Torbie, or blue and cream, giving the Blue Torbie. For both, the eye color may be green, yellow, or orange.

EUROPEAN SMOKE Cats in this group have a white or silver undercoat, and the six accepted varieties are Black Smoke, Blue Smoke, Red Smoke, Cream Smoke, Black Torbie Smoke, and Blue Torbie Smoke. All may have either green, yellow, or orange eye color.

Tabby Varieties

The non-silver tabby group may have a coat pattern blotched (also known as the Classic tabby), Mackerel, or Spotted. The six accepted varieties are Black Tabby, Blue Tabby, Red Tabby, Cream Tabby, Black Torbie Tabby, and Blue Torbie Tabby. All may have green, yellow, or orange eye color.

In the silver tabby group, the markings are of the main varietal color etched on a base color of pure pale silver. There should be no ticked hairs or brindling in the pattern. The three tabby patterns – Classic, Mackerel, and Spotted – are accepted, and the six accepted varieties are Black Silver Tabby, Blue Silver Tabby, Red Silver Tabby, Cream Silver Tabby, Black Torbie Silver Tabby, and Blue Torbie Silver Tabby. Eye color may be green, yellow, or orange, but green is preferred.

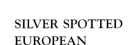

SILVER SPOTTED EUROPEAN
This typical European Shorthair shows the black version of the silver spotted, which is well-marked on the flanks, but with the pattern tending to form mackerel stripes over the ribs.

Non-tabby Bicolor Varieties

Three patterns are accepted, van, harlequin and bicolor. The markings may be black, blue, red, cream, black torbie, or blue torbie.

In van and harlequin, the eye color may be deep blue, green, yellow, or orange; or odd-eyed with one eye deep blue and the other green, yellow, or orange. In the Bicolor pattern, the eyes may be green, yellow, or orange. For judging purposes, the van and harlequin cats are grouped together by eye color.

Van-patterned cats are basically white, with two colored patches on the head, separated by a white blaze down the nose, and a tail colored from rump to tip. The ears may be colored, but white ears with a pink inner surface to the pinna are preferable; the chest and stomach must be white, but up to three small, irregularly distributed color patches on the body and/or legs are tolerated for judging purposes. There must be no white hairs in the colored areas of the coat.

Tabby Van cats have the same basic requirements and may have patches of any of the three basic tabby patterns – all Tabby Van cats are judged in the same class, regardless of pattern. Torbie Van cats also have the same basic requirements, but have torbie markings on the patched areas.

Nose leather may be pink or as expected for the color of the patterned areas. In the Tabby Van, the nose leather should be pink or pinkish-red outlined with the appropriate color for the patterned areas; in the Torbie Van, the nose leather should be patched with pink.

Harlequin-patterned cats are basically white with solid-colored patches over at least one quarter, but not more than one half, of the body surface. The colored parts should consist of various patches surrounded by white, and there must be no single white hairs present in the colored areas. Tabby and Torbie Harlequin cats are also accepted. The nose leather and paw pads are as for the Van pattern.

The bicolored cat is basically white with colored patches, which must be clearly separated from one another. At least one half, but not more than two-thirds, of the cat must be colored; the color must be even and harmoniously distributed over the cat's body. A white blaze down the face and some white on the back are desirable characteristics. There must be no single white hairs in the colored areas.

The Tabby Bicolor may be either Classic (blotched), Mackerel, or Spotted; the Torbie Bicolor should have large, well-defined patches of clear, bright colors. The nose leather and paw pads are as specified for the Van pattern.

CLASSIC TABBY
The Classic tabby pattern consists of a precise set of clearly defined, dense markings on a paler ground color.

MACKEREL TABBY
A beautiful example of a well-marked Mackerel tabby, this red cat has excellent type, matching the European Shorthair standards of points.

AMERICAN SHORTHAIR

AT THE BEGINNING of the twentieth century, an English cat fancier gave a pedigree Red Tabby Shorthair male to a friend in the United States, to be mated with some of the indigenous shorthaired felines. This cat was registered in the name of Belle and was the first pedigree cat to appear in the records of the Cat Fanciers' Association. Other British cats followed, including a male Silver Tabby named Pretty Correct, and the register grew with listings of "home-grown" cats as well as imports. At first, the breed was called the Shorthair, then its name was changed to Domestic Shorthair, and in 1966 it was renamed the American Shorthair. To gain it credence as a natural American breed, registration bodies accepted applications of non-pedigree cats and kittens conforming to the required breed standards, and in 1971 one such cat won the ultimate accolade of the best American Shorthair of the Year in CFA.

Despite the influence of the introduction of the British Shorthair imports in the breeding programs, the American Shorthair has retained its distinctive characteristics.

Character and Care

A cat of very even temperament, the American Shorthair makes an ideal family pet. It is an intelligent and good-natured animal which gets along well with other breeds and with dogs.

Its short, thick coat is quite easy to keep in good condition with a simple grooming routine. Combing keeps the coat neat, and stroking with the hand or a silk scarf imparts a healthy sheen. The eyes and ears are easily cleaned with a cotton swab, and a scratching post helps the indoor cat to trim its claws.

BREAKDOWN OF 100 SHOW POINTS

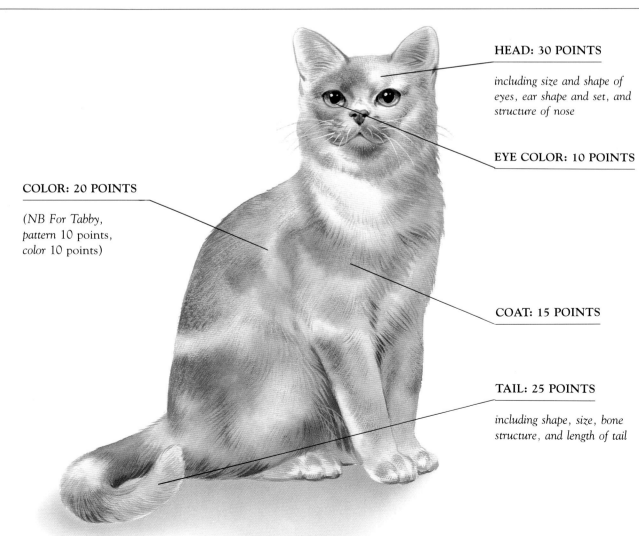

HEAD: 30 POINTS

including size and shape of eyes, ear shape and set, and structure of nose

EYE COLOR: 10 POINTS

COLOR: 20 POINTS

(NB For Tabby, pattern 10 points, color 10 points)

COAT: 15 POINTS

TAIL: 25 POINTS

including shape, size, bone structure, and length of tail

KEY CHARACTERISTICS

- **CATEGORY** Shorthair.

- **OVERALL BUILD** Medium to large, well-knit and powerful, not excessively cobby or rangy.

- **COAT** Short, thick, and even, hard in texture, somewhat heavier and thicker in winter.

- **HEAD** Large, with full cheeks giving an oblong effect, head very slightly longer than it is wide, with square muzzle. Set on a medium-length, muscular neck.

- **NOSE** Medium length.

- **CHIN** Firm and well developed.

- **EYES** Round, wide-set, with a very slight slant to the outer aperture.

- **EARS** Medium size with rounded tips, set wide apart.

- **BODY** Well-knit, powerful body with well-developed chest and heavy shoulders.

- **LEGS** Firm-boned and heavily muscled.

- **PAWS** Firm, full, and rounded paws with heavy pads.

- **TAIL** Medium length, heavy at the base, tapering to an apparently blunt end.

- **COLORS** White, black, blue, red, cream, chinchilla, shaded silver, shell cameo, shaded cameo, black smoke, blue smoke, cameo smoke, tortoiseshell smoke, brown patched tabby, blue patched tabby, silver patched tabby, silver tabby, red tabby, brown tabby, blue tabby, cream tabby, cameo tabby, tortoiseshell, calico, dilute calico, blue-cream, bicolor, van bicolor, van calico, van blue-cream-and-white.

AMERICAN SHORTHAIR VARIETIES

AMERICAN SHORTHAIR

Developed from the American domestic "working" cat, the American Shorthair has been refined and standardized into an attractive and viable breed of show cat in a wide variety of coat colors and patterns.

IN THE CFA STANDARD of points, the American Shorthair is lovingly described. It says that some naturalists believe the breed to be the original domestic cat, which has, for centuries, adapted itself willingly and cheerfully to the needs of man, without allowing itself to become effete, or its natural intelligence to diminish.

The standard goes on: "Its hunting instinct is so strong that it exercises the skill even when well provided with food. This is our only breed of true working cat ... This is a cat lithe enough to stalk its prey, but powerful enough to make the kill easily. Its reflexes are under perfect control. Its legs are long enough to cope with any terrain, and heavy and muscular enough for high leaps. The face is long enough to permit easy grasping by the teeth with jaws so powerful they can close against resistance. Its coat is dense enough to protect from moisture, cold, and superficial skin injuries, but short enough and of sufficiently hard texture to resist matting or entanglement when slipping through heavy vegetation. No part of the anatomy is so exaggerated as to foster weakness. The general effect is that of the trained athlete, with all muscles rippling easily beneath the skin, the flesh lean and hard, and with great latent power held in reserve."

Because the American Shorthair was developed from domestic cats in all colors and coat patterns, which were crossed with show-quality imported British Shorthairs, today's cats are seen in a wide variety of accepted coats.

The best known and most popular of the American Shorthair varieties is undoubtedly the silver tabby, with the Classic, Marbled, or Spotted pattern being the favorites among fanciers. Other tabby colors are also very popular, but each of the accepted varieties has its own following of ardent fans.

TABBY VARIETIES

AMERICAN SHORTHAIR TABBY varieties may have the Classic or Mackerel pattern. In the Classic tabby, markings should be dense and clearly defined, the legs evenly barred with bracelets and the tail evenly ringed; and the cat should have several unbroken necklaces on the neck and upper chest. On the head, frown marks form a letter "M," and an unbroken line runs back from the outer corner of each eye. There are swirl markings on the cheeks, and vertical lines run over the back of the head to the shoulder markings, which resemble a butterfly, with both upper and lower wings distinctly outlined and marked with dots within the outlines. The back is marked with a spine line and a parallel line on each side, with all three lines separated by stripes of the coat's ground color. A large solid blotch on each side of the body should be encircled by one or more unbroken rings, and the side markings should be the same on both sides of the body. A double row of "vest" buttons should run down the chest and under the stomach.

In the Mackerel tabby, markings should be dense and clearly defined and all resemble narrow pencil lines. The legs should be evenly barred with narrow bracelets, and the tail barred. There are several distinct narrow necklaces around the neck. The head is barred, with a distinct "M" on the forehead and unbroken lines running back from the eyes. More lines run back over the head to meet the shoulder markings. Along the spine, the lines run together forming a dark saddle, and fine, pencil-like markings run down each side of the body from the spine.

BLUE TABBY Base color of coat for the blue tabby, including lips and chin, is pale bluish-ivory with very deep blue markings. The whole coat color has warm fawn overtones. Nose leather "old rose" in color; paw pads are rose, and the eye color is brilliant gold.

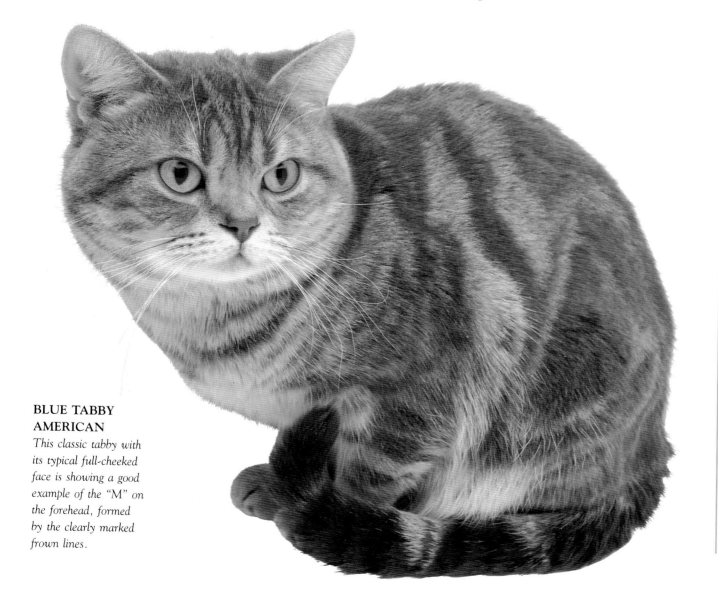

BLUE TABBY AMERICAN

This classic tabby with its typical full-cheeked face is showing a good example of the "M" on the forehead, formed by the clearly marked frown lines.

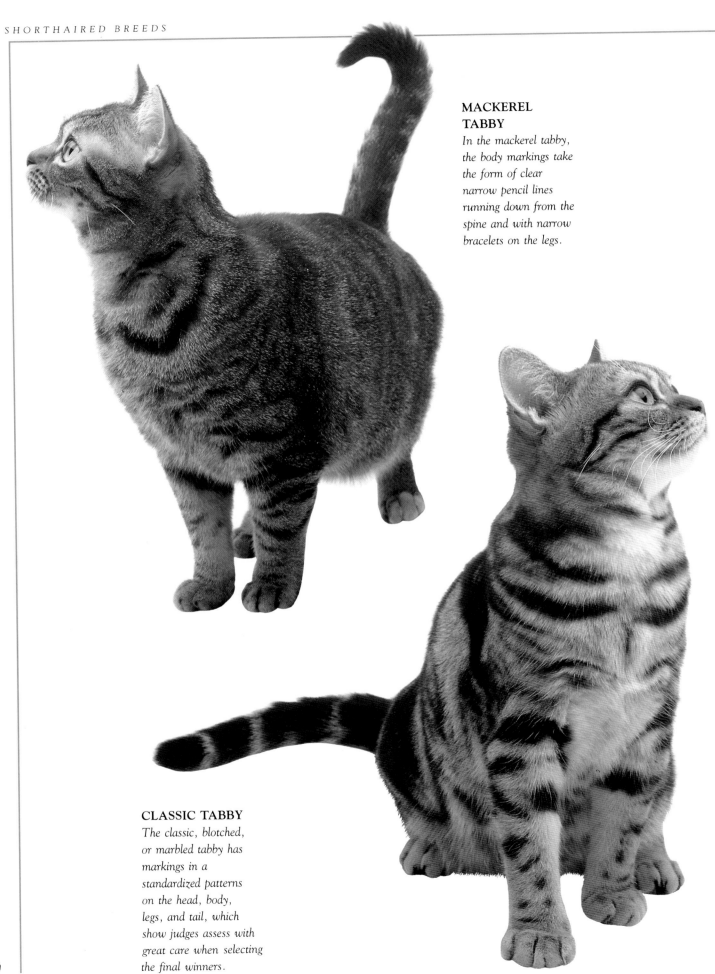

MACKEREL TABBY
In the mackerel tabby, the body markings take the form of clear narrow pencil lines running down from the spine and with narrow bracelets on the legs.

CLASSIC TABBY
The classic, blotched, or marbled tabby has markings in a standardized patterns on the head, body, legs, and tail, which show judges assess with great care when selecting the final winners.

BROWN TABBY Base color of coat is a brilliant coppery brown with dense black markings. Lips and chin should be the same shade as the rings around the eyes, and backs of legs black from paw to heel. Nose leather is brick red; paw pads black or brown. Eye color is brilliant gold.

RED TABBY Base color of coat, including lips and chin, is red with deep rich red markings. Nose leather and paw pads are brick red and the eye color brilliant gold.

CREAM TABBY Base color of coat, including lips and chin, is very pale cream with buff or cream markings sufficiently darker than the base color to afford good contrast. Nose leather and paw pads are pink, and the eye color is brilliant gold.

CAMEO TABBY Base color of coat is off-white with red markings. Nose leather and paw pads are rose-colored, and the eye color is brilliant gold.

RED TABBY

This fine cat is very well-marked in the Classic pattern, and the red color of both the base coat and the markings is correctly defined.

CAMEO TABBY

The Cameo is a soft and delicate color. This Classic tabby exhibits the intricacies of the pattern on the sides and flanks, and shows good contrast between the colors of the base coat and markings.

151

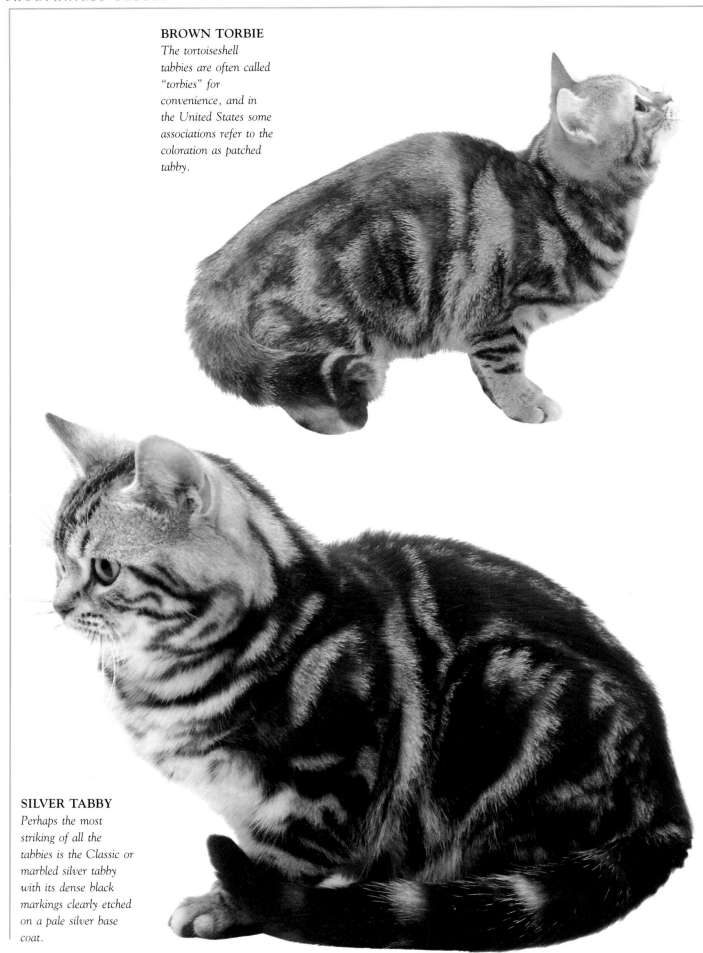

BROWN TORBIE
The tortoiseshell tabbies are often called "torbies" for convenience, and in the United States some associations refer to the coloration as patched tabby.

SILVER TABBY
Perhaps the most striking of all the tabbies is the Classic or marbled silver tabby with its dense black markings clearly etched on a pale silver base coat.

SILVER TABBY Base color, including lips and chin, is pale clear silver with dense black markings. Nose leather brick red, paw pads black, and eye color may be green or hazel.

PATCHED TABBY or TORBIE The Patched Tabby or Torbie is similar to the established varieties of tabby, but with the addition of patches of red and light red, or cream.

BROWN PATCHED TABBY Base color of coat is brilliant coppery brown with Classic or Mackerel markings of dense black and patches of red and/or light red clearly defined on both body and extremities; a blaze of red or light red on the face is desirable. Lips and chin to be the same shade as the rings around the eyes; the eye color is brilliant gold.

BLUE PATCHED TABBY Base color of coat, including lips and chin, is pale bluish-ivory, with Classic or Mackerel markings of very deep blue and patches of cream clearly defined on both body and extremities; a blaze of cream on the face is desirable, and warm fawn overtones suffuse the whole body. The eye color is brilliant gold or hazel.

SILVER PATCHED TABBY Base color, including lips and chin, is pale clear silver with Classic or Mackerel markings of dense black and patches of red and/or light red clearly defined on both body and extremities; a blaze of red and/or light red on the face is desirable. Eye color may be hazel or brilliant gold.

BLUE TORBIE
Still clearly marked, but with paler coloring, the blue patched tabby or torbie is the dilute version of the brown torbie, having blue and cream markings instead of black and red.

153

AMERICAN WIREHAIR

IN VERMONT, IN 1966, one of a litter of farm kittens was born with an unusual sparse and wiry coat. An experienced cat breeder acquired the kitten and one of its plain-coated litter-mates and sent hair samples from both for analysis by a British expert in feline genetics. The coat was of a different type to anything previously encountered in the domestic cat, and a breeding program was soon established to develop the wirehaired trait.

The first wirehaired cat was a red and white male named Adam. He was first mated to his normal-coated litter-mate, and then to other unrelated shorthaired cats, and from these beginnings a new breed was born. All Amer-ican Wirehair cats are descended from Adam, and breeding stock has been very carefully selected over the years to guarantee refinement and viability of the breed. Championship status was granted by the CFA in 1977.

Character and Care

The Wirehair is said by its owners to rule the home and cats of other breeds with an "iron paw," but to make a devoted parent. They are affectionate and playful, with a strongly inde-pendent character.

The unusual wiry coat is easy to maintain in peak condition by correct feeding and needs a minimum of grooming.

BREAKDOWN OF 100 SHOW POINTS

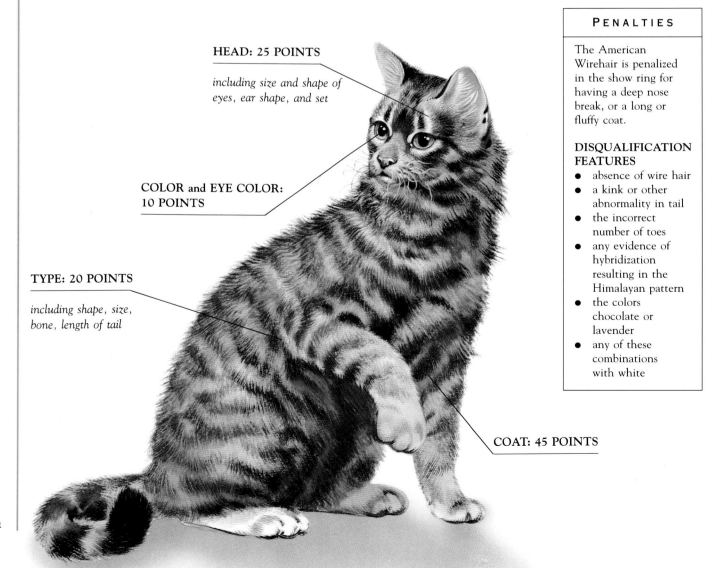

HEAD: 25 POINTS

including size and shape of eyes, ear shape, and set

COLOR and EYE COLOR: 10 POINTS

TYPE: 20 POINTS

including shape, size, bone, length of tail

COAT: 45 POINTS

PENALTIES

The American Wirehair is penalized in the show ring for having a deep nose break, or a long or fluffy coat.

DISQUALIFICATION FEATURES
- absence of wire hair
- a kink or other abnormality in tail
- the incorrect number of toes
- any evidence of hybridization resulting in the Himalayan pattern
- the colors chocolate or lavender
- any of these combinations with white

KEY CHARACTERISTICS

- **CATEGORY** Wirehair.

- **OVERALL BUILD** Medium to large, with medium bone. Males larger than females.

- **COAT** Springy, dense, and resilient, feels coarse and hard. The hairs are crimped and wiry, hooked at the tips. The facial hairs and whiskers are crimped and often set at odd angles.

- **COLORS** Requirements as for the American Shorthair (see pages 146–153). White, black, blue, red, cream, tortoiseshell, calico, blue-cream, dilute calico, chinchilla, shaded silver, shell cameo, shaded cameo, black smoke, blue smoke, cameo smoke, bicolor; Classical or Mackerel tabby in brown, blue, red, cream, cameo, silver.

- **OTHER FEATURES** Round head with prominent cheekbones and a well-developed muzzle with a slight whisker break. Nose shows a gentle, concave curve in profile. The chin is firm, and the eyes are large, round, bright and clear, set wide apart, with a slightly tilted aperture. The ears are medium sized with rounded tips, set wide apart on the head. Body is medium to large with a level back and well-rounded rump. Legs are well muscled and paws oval and compact. Length of tail in proportion to body, tapering from the rump to a rounded tip, neither blunt nor pointed.

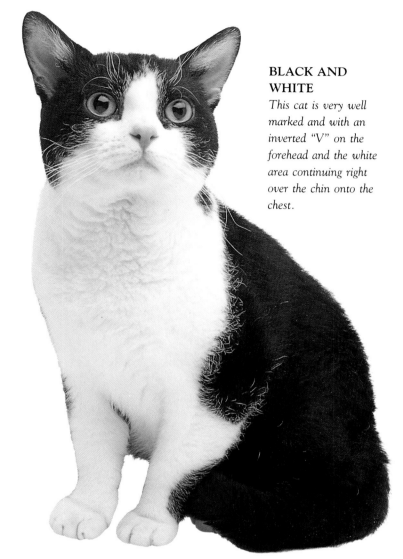

BLACK AND WHITE
This cat is very well marked and with an inverted "V" on the forehead and the white area continuing right over the chin onto the chest.

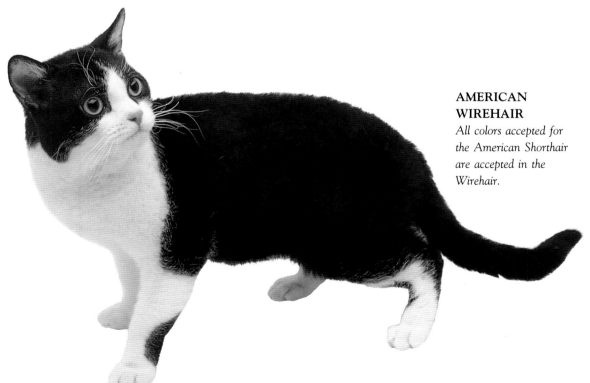

AMERICAN WIREHAIR
All colors accepted for the American Shorthair are accepted in the Wirehair.

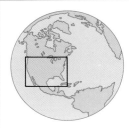

EXOTIC SHORTHAIR

In the development of British and American Shorthairs, and during the introduction of alternative color factors in the Persians, breeders occasionally mated together pedigree cats of longhaired and shorthaired varieties. This was generally done as a single exercise, the offspring being back-crossed to the main breed in successive generations to strengthen the desired traits.

During the 1960s, cats of mixed Shorthair and Persian lineage were, with the approval of the board of the CFA, given the breed name Exotic Shorthair. The breed is, in essence, a short-coated version of the typical Persian, with the conformation of the latter, but the added bonus of a coat that is relatively easy to care for. The coat stands out from the body and is longer than that of the British or American Shorthair cat breeds.

Character and Care

In temperament the Exotic Shorthair is quiet, gentle, and placid. It is an ideal show cat, easy to prepare for the show ring, and enjoys being handled and admired.

The medium-length coat is quite easy to comb through, and being groomed from the tail toward the head encourages the plush fur to stand away from the body. Body condition and shining fur is achieved by correct feeding, and the eyes and ears are kept immaculate by gentle cleaning with a cotton swab.

BREAKDOWN OF 100 SHOW POINTS

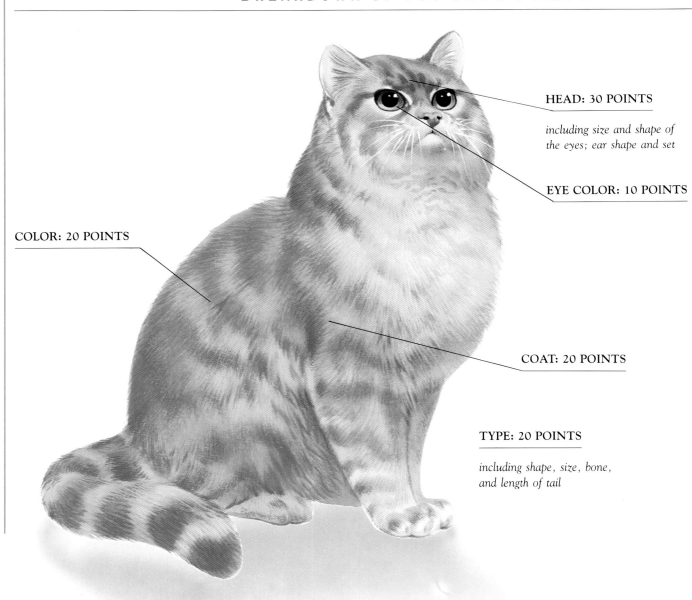

HEAD: 30 POINTS

including size and shape of the eyes; ear shape and set

EYE COLOR: 10 POINTS

COLOR: 20 POINTS

COAT: 20 POINTS

TYPE: 20 POINTS

including shape, size, bone, and length of tail

KEY CHARACTERISTICS

- **CATEGORY** Shorthair.

- **OVERALL BUILD** Medium to large, cobby.

- **COAT** Medium length, dense and plush, soft-textured, standing well away from the body due to its density, never flat or close-lying.

- **HEAD** Round and massive, with great depth of skull, set on a short, thick neck. Round face, full cheeks, broad and powerful jaws.

- **NOSE** Short and stubby with a definite "break."

- **CHIN** Full and well developed.

- **EYES** Large, round, and set wide apart.

- **EARS** Small, round-tipped, set wide and low on the head.

- **BODY** Cobby, with a deep chest, massive shoulders and rump and a level back.

- **LEGS** Short and thick.

- **PAWS** Large and round.

- **TAIL** Short.

- **COLORS** White (blue eyed and orange red), black, blue, chocolate, lilac, red, cream: tabby in Classic or Mackerel pattern: silver, brown, blue chocolate, lilac, red, cream: torbie tabby: black, chocolate, lilac: torbie, blue-cream, chocolate tortie, lilac-cream. Calico, blue calico, chocolate calico, lilac calico; bicolor and Van Bicolor and Tricolor: any recognized color with white; spotted tabby: brown, blue chocolate, lilac, red, cream, silver; smoke: any recognized color with silver-white undercoat; tipped: any recognized color with white undercoat and color restricted to very tips of hair.

PENALTIES

DISQUALIFICATION FEATURES
- undesirable white markings such as a locket
- a kink or other abnormality in the tail
- the incorrect number of toes

SOLID VARIETIES

CREAM EXOTIC
The coat of the Exotic Shorthair is very dense and plush, soft in texture, and stands out and away from the body.

BLUE EXOTIC
The head type of the Exotic Shorthair is almost identical to that of a show-standard Persian.

SELF-COLORED EXOTIC cats are bred to a very exacting standard and are penalized at shows for having incorrect or extremely pale eye colors or for flecks of incorrect color in either of the eyes' irises. Oriental or almond-shaped eyes or those set on a slant are also unacceptable.

WHITE The color is pure, glistening white with pink nose leather and paw pads. Eye color is deep blue or brilliant copper. Odd-eyed Whites should have one blue and one copper eye of equal color intensity.

BLACK The dense coal-black coat should be sound from roots to tips of fur. Nose leather is black and paw pads black or brown. Eye color is brilliant copper.

BLUE An even tone of blue stretches from the nose to the tip of the tail, and is sound to the roots. Lighter shades are preferred. Nose leather and paw pads are blue, and the eye color is brilliant copper.

RED A deep, rich, brilliant red is required, without any shading, markings, or ticking. Lips and chin should be the same color as the coat. The nose leather and paw pads are brick red, and the eye color is brilliant copper.

CREAM One even shade of buff cream throughout should have no shading or markings, with lighter shades preferred. The nose leather and paw pads are pink, and the eye color is brilliant copper.

CHOCOLATE The coat is warm-toned medium to dark chocolate, free from shading or markings. The nose leather and paw pads are chocolate. Eye color is copper or orange.

LILAC The warm-toned lilac coat is sound and even in color. Lilac nose leather and paw pads, and copper or orange eye color.

TABBY AND BICOLOR VARIETIES

THE EXOTIC SHORTHAIR is accepted in the Classic and Mackerel patterns with the following colors allowed: silver, brown, blue, chocolate, lilac, red, and cream. They have identical color requirements to the equivalent varieties in the British Shorthair, except for eye color, which in the Exotic Shorthair is brilliant copper.

Torbie tabbies are accepted in brown, blue, chocolate, and lilac. The Spotted Tabby Exotic, in the same color range as the Classic and Mackeral Tabbies, is very attractive with numerous well-defined round, oval, or rosette-shaped marks clearly etched in distinct color on the lighter base coat.

BICOLOR The coat of the Bicolor is white with unbrindled patches of either black, blue, red, or cream, as seen in the American Shorthair. Nose leather and paw-pad color corresponds with the basic coat color. The eye color is brilliant copper.

VAN BICOLOR The coat of the Van Bi-color is white with unbrindled patches of either black, blue, red, or cream confined to the head, tail and legs, although one or two small colored patches on the body are allowed.

VAN TRICOLOR The coat of the Van Tricolor is white with unbrindled patches of both black and red confined to the head, tail, and legs, although up to three small colored patches on the body are allowed.

VAN BLUE-CREAM-AND-WHITE The coat of this variety is white with unbrindled patches of both blue and cream confined to the head, tail, and legs, although one or two small colored patches on the body are allowed.

BLUE AND WHITE EXOTIC
Bicolored Exotic cats should have clear and well-distributed patches of color, as in this fine blue and white. The face should be patched with color and with white.

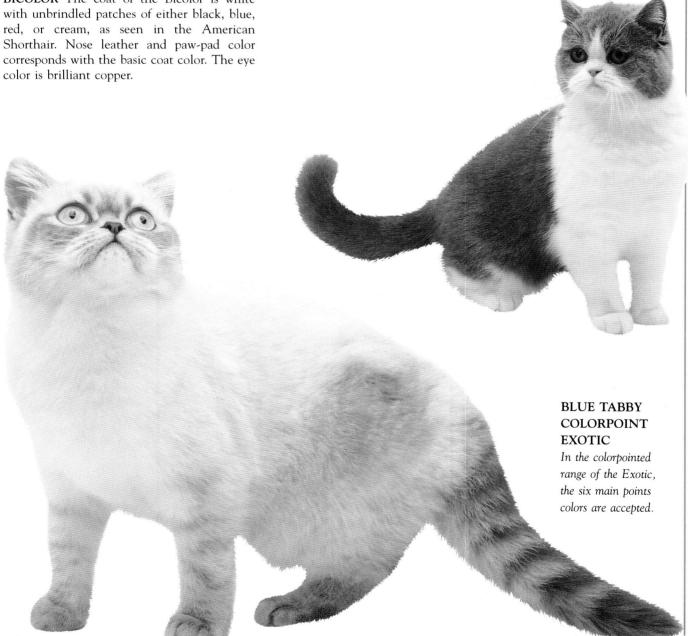

BLUE TABBY COLORPOINT EXOTIC
In the colorpointed range of the Exotic, the six main points colors are accepted.

159

OTHER VARIETIES

BLUE TORTIE AND WHITE EXOTIC

Well-distributed patches of light to medium blue, pale cream, and white form the pattern of this color variety, known as the dilute calico in the USA.

THE EXOTIC SHORTHAIR is the ideal breed for the owner who craves for a cat with true Persian type, but does not have the time necessary to care correctly for the demanding Persian coat. Exotics are indeed a short-coated version of their Persian ancestors, and show standards for the two breeds, apart from the coat, are almost identical

TORTOISESHELL The coat is black with clearly defined, well-broken, unbrindled patches of red and light red on the body and extremities. A red or light red blaze on the face is desirable. Eye color is brilliant copper.

CALICO The coat is white with unbrindled patches of black and red, with white predominant on the underparts. Eye color is brilliant copper.

BLUE-CREAM The coat is blue with clearly defined, well-broken patches of solid cream on the body and the extremities. The eye color is brilliant copper.

BLUE-CREAM-AND-WHITE The coat is white with unbrindled patches of blue and cream, with white predominant on the underparts. Eye color is brilliant copper.

CHINCHILLA The undercoat is pure white. The coat on the back, flanks, head, and tail is sufficiently tipped with black to give a characteristic sparkling silver appearance. The legs may be slightly shaded with tipping. Chin, ear tufts, stomach, and chest are pure white, and the rims of the eyes, lips, and nose are outlined with black. Nose leather brick red, paw pads black, eye color green or blue-green.

SHADED SILVER The undercoat is pure white and the coat heavily shaded with black to form a mantle over the spine, sides, and on the face and tail, gradually shading from very dark on the spine to white on the chin, chest, stomach, and under the tail. Legs are the same tone as the face. The general effect is much darker than the Chinchilla. Rims of the eyes, lips, and nose are outlined with black. Nose leather brick red, paw pads black, eye color green or blue-green.

CHINCHILLA GOLDEN The undercoat is a rich warm cream. The coat on the back, flanks, head, and tail is sufficiently tipped with seal brown to give a golden appearance. The legs may be slightly shaded with tipping. Chin, ear tufts, stomach, and chest are cream, and the rims of the eyes, lips, and nose are outlined with seal brown. Nose leather is deep rose, paw pads are seal brown, and the eye color green or blue-green.

SHADED GOLDEN The undercoat is a rich, warm cream, and the coat is heavily shaded with seal brown to form a mantle over the spine, sides, and on the face and tail, gradually shading from dark on the spine to cream on the chin, chest, stomach, and under the tail.

BROWN TABBY EXOTIC

The head has the frown lines created by the dark "M" marking on the forehead.

SILVER TABBY EXOTIC

The intensity of the dark markings is reduced by the density of the coat when etched on a silver base coat. This cat has the required brick-red nose leather for its variety.

SHADED TORTOISESHELL The undercoat is white, and the coat is heavily shaded with black tipping and clearly defined patches of red and light red tipped hairs as in the pattern of the Tortoiseshell, to form a mantle over the spine, sides, and on the face and tail. The general effect is much darker than the Shell Tortoiseshell. A blaze of red or light red tipping on the face is desirable. The nose leather and paw pads are black, pink, or mottled. The eye color is brilliant copper.

SMOKE EXOTIC The Smoke Exotic may be of any color accepted in the Exotic Group, but instead of being sound in color from the tips to the roots of the coat, the base of each hair is silvery white. There must be no tabby markings, and the contrast between the top coat and the undercoat should be pronounced. The nose leather and paw pads should correspond with the coat color, and the eye color should be copper, orange, or deep gold.

TIPPED EXOTIC The tipping may be of any color accepted in the Persian varieties. The undercoat must be as white as possible and the tips of each hair lightly colored, giving a characteristic sparkling effect. Nose leather in cats with black tipping is brick red, and in all other colors, to correspond with the coat color. Paw pads in black tipped may be either black or seal brown. In other colors, to correspond with the coat color. Paw pads in black tipped may be either black or seal brown. In other colors, to correspond with the coat color.

COLOR POINTED EXOTIC This variety exhibits the Himalayan effect with a pale body and color on the points – face, tail, legs, and paws. There must be good contrast between the body and points color; the points should be free from white hairs, and the body ideally free from shading, which if present should tone with the points. Nose leather and paw pads correspond with individual points' color. Eye color decidedly blue.

BLUE-CREAM SMOKE EXOTIC

The undercoat of the Smoke Exotic is silvery white, but only shows when the dense coat is parted.

SHADED SILVER

The pure white undercoat has a mantle of black tipping and more tipping on the face and tail, producing the characteristically sparkling effect.

164 Abyssinian	**192** Devon Rex
168 Somali	**196** Sphynx
174 Russian Blue	**198** Japanese Bobtail
176 Korat	**200** Burmese
178 Havana Brown	**206** Tiffanie
180 Egyptian Mau	**207** Singapura
182 Ocicat	**208** Tonkinese
184 Bengal	**214** Bombay
188 Cornish Rex	**216** Burmilla

FOREIGN SHORTHAIRED BREEDS

ABYSSINIAN

NO EVIDENCE EXISTS to connect an Abyssinian cat, recorded as having been taken from Ethiopia to England in 1868, with today's pedigree cats. Recognized as a true breed in 1882, the Abyssinian was also known as the Spanish, Russian, Ticked, Hare, or Bunny Cat – it was once thought that it had resulted from a cross between a cat and wild rabbit!

The modern Abyssinian is a well-established breed worldwide. It has been referred to as the Child of the Gods because of its close resemblance to the sacred cats of the Ancient Egyptians. Whatever their color, all Abyssinian cats have unusual ticked coats, known as the agouti, or wild-type pattern. Selective breeding over many generations has resulted in a reduction of the natural tabby bars normally found on the face, neck, tail, and underparts, so that today's show cat has a clear, glowing, ticked coat, rather like that of a Belgian hare.

The Abyssinian is another foreign short-haired breed which is judged by slightly different standards in Europe and North America. The American Abyssinian has a shorter head and a more rounded profile than its European counterpart. In the allocation of show points, the American fancy gives most weight by points to body type, while the European standards place more emphasis on coat color.

BREAKDOWN OF 100 SHOW POINTS

HEAD: 25 POINTS

Muzzle: 6 points
Skull: 6 points
Ears: 7 points
Eye shape: 6 points

BODY: 30 POINTS

Torso: 15 points
Legs and feet: 10 points
Tail: 5 points

COAT: 10 POINTS

Texture: 10 points

COLOR: 35 POINTS

Color: 15 points
Ticking: 15 points
Eye color: 5 points

Character and Care

The Abyssinian cat is typically quiet and gentle. It can be shy and reserved, mistrusting strangers, but it generally gets along well with other cats and adores its owner.

The coat is simple to keep immaculate with the minimum of grooming, and the large ears must be kept clean at all times, by regular use of moistened cotton swabs.

KEY CHARACTERISTICS

- **CATEGORY** Foreign Shorthair.

- **OVERALL BUILD** Medium size, lithe and muscular.

- **COAT** Soft, silky, fine textured; medium in length to accommodate two or three bands of ticking.

- **HEAD** Slightly rounded and wedge shaped with gentle contours, gently curved in profile. The muzzle is neither pointed nor square.

- **NOSE** Medium length.

- **CHIN** Firm.

- **EYES** Almond-shaped, large, brilliant and expressive.

- **EARS** Large and alert.

- **BODY** Long, lithe, and graceful.

- **LEGS** Slim and fine-boned.

- **PAWS** Small and oval.

- **TAIL** Thick at the base, fairly long and tapering.

- **COLORS** Usual, blue, red or sorrel, chocolate, lilac, cream, beige-fawn, torbie in all these colors. (Note that not all varieties are recognized by all associations.)

ABYSSINIAN VARIETIES

THE USUAL OR RUDDY is the normal coat color for the Abyssinian, and is genetically black – the rich golden hairs having two or three bands of black ticking. The Red or Sorrel is produced by the action of the light-brown gene.

RUDDY (USA, Europe) **USUAL** (UK–GCCF) The coat is warm ruddy brown with black ticking; the base color deep apricot or orange. The tail tip, ear tips, and eye rims are black; the nose leather brick red (may be outlined with black). Paw pads, back of feet, and toe tufts are seal brown or black. The eye color is gold or green; rich deep colors are preferred.

BLUE The coat is warm blue-gray with dark, steel blue-gray ticking; the base color pale fawn/cream. The tail tip and ear tips are dark steel blue-gray; the eye rims blue-gray. Nose leather is old rose (may be outlined with blue-gray); paw pads are old rose/blue-gray; backs of feet and toe tufts are deep steel blue-gray. Eye color is as Ruddy Abyssinian.

SORREL or RED The coat is a bright, warm, copper red with chocolate-brown ticking; the base color deep apricot. The tail tip, ear tips, eye rims, backs of feet, and toe tufts are red-brown. Nose leather is pale red (may be outlined with red-brown); paw pads cinnamon to chocolate. Eye color is as Ruddy Abyssinian.

USUAL ABYSSINIAN

The rich golden brown coat ticked with bands of black gives the Usual Abyssinian its unusual appearance. It is known as the Ruddy Abyssinian in Europe and America.

BEIGE-FAWN The coat is dull beige with deep, warm, fawn ticking; the base color pale cream. The tail tip, ear tips, backs of feet, and toe tufts are dark warm cream; the eye rims old rose. Nose leather is pink (may be outlined with old rose); paw pads are pink. Eye color is as Ruddy Abyssinian.

BLACK SILVER The coat is pure silver-white with black ticking; the base color pure silver-white. The tail tip and eye rims are black; the ear tips, paw pads, backs of feet, and toe tufts are black or seal brown. Nose leather is brick red (may be outlined with black). Eye color is as Ruddy Abyssinian.

BLUE SILVER The coat is pure silver-white with dark steel blue-gray ticking; the base color pure silver-white. The tail tip, ear tips, eye rims, backs of feet, and toe tufts are dark steel blue-gray. Nose leather is old rose (may be outlined with dark steel blue-gray); paw pads are old rose or blue-gray. Eye color is as Ruddy Abyssinian.

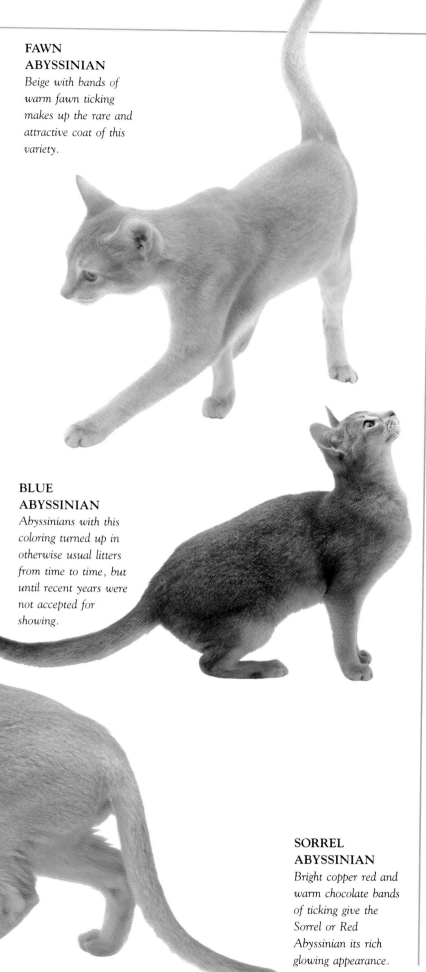

FAWN ABYSSINIAN
Beige with bands of warm fawn ticking makes up the rare and attractive coat of this variety.

BLUE ABYSSINIAN
Abyssinians with this coloring turned up in otherwise usual litters from time to time, but until recent years were not accepted for showing.

SORREL ABYSSINIAN
Bright copper red and warm chocolate bands of ticking give the Sorrel or Red Abyssinian its rich glowing appearance.

SOMALI

THIS BREED IS the longhaired version of the Abyssinian cat, and its coat color is typically Abyssinian. It was thought that the long coat was due to a spontaneous mutation occurring within the Abyssinian breed, but genetic investigation of the history of the Somali showed that the gene for long hair was probably introduced when cats of Abyssinian type and lineage were outcrossed to others in the early days of breeding and showing.

When the first long-coated kittens appeared in otherwise normal litters of Abyssinian kittens, they were discarded and given away as pets, but later, having seen some of these cats at maturity when the full beauty of the ticked longhaired coat was apparent, breeders decided to develop the longhaired Abyssinian as a separate variety. A worldwide network of breeders – in North America, Europe, New Zealand, and Australia – worked together and agreed on Somali as the cats' name. The breed was granted full championship status by the CFA in 1978.

Character and Care

Like the Abyssinian, the Somali is gentle and receptive to quiet handling and affection. It is soft-voiced, playful, and athletic, and makes a perfect companion pet.

The coat, though full, is not wooly and is therefore very easy to groom. The full ruff (frill) and tail need regular combing through, and the large ears must be gently cleaned and kept free from dust.

BREAKDOWN OF 100 SHOW POINTS

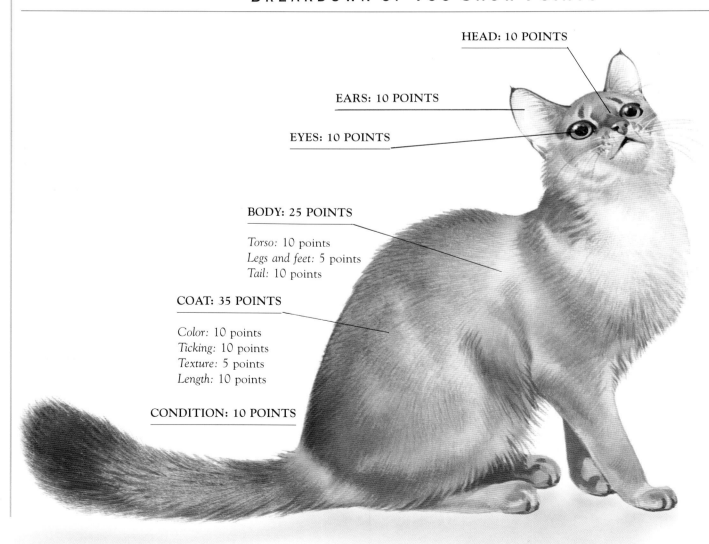

HEAD: 10 POINTS

EARS: 10 POINTS

EYES: 10 POINTS

BODY: 25 POINTS

Torso: 10 points
Legs and feet: 5 points
Tail: 10 points

COAT: 35 POINTS

Color: 10 points
Ticking: 10 points
Texture: 5 points
Length: 10 points

CONDITION: 10 POINTS

KEY CHARACTERISTICS

- **CATEGORY** Foreign Longhair.

- **OVERALL BUILD** Medium to large.

- **COAT** Extremely fine and very dense, of medium length but shorter on the shoulders. A well-developed ruff (frill) and breeches are desirable.

- **HEAD** Wedge-shaped and of medium proportions; wide at the top with soft contours.

- **NOSE** Medium long with a soft curve in profile, with neither a stop nor a straight nose.

- **CHIN** Firm and well developed.

- **EYES** Large, almond-shaped, and set well apart.

- **EARS** Large and broad at the base, slightly rounded at the tips, with lynx-like tufts, set well apart and pricked.

- **BODY** Of medium length. Bone structure firm, lithe, and muscular.

- **LEGS** Long and fine-boned, in proportion to the body.

- **PAWS** Small and oval.

- **TAIL** Fairly long and tapering; broad at the base and well-furred.

- **COLORS** As for the Abyssinian: ruddy, blue, red, or sorrel, beige-fawn, black, silver, blue silver, sorrel silver, beige-fawn silver.
  Note Not all associations recognize all color varieties.

PENALTIES

The Somali is penalized for having a cold gray or sandy tone to the coat color; mottling or speckling in unticked areas; black roots to body hair; incorrect markings; a white locket or white anywhere other than the upper throat, chin or nostrils; incorrect color of paw pads and/or nose leather; Siamese type and a whip tail.

NON-SILVER VARIETIES

ALTHOUGH DIFFERENT CAT associations have their own rules for acceptance of new varieties, the Somali is recognized in most of the regular Abyssinian color varieties by most registering bodies. In the United Kingdom, the Cat Association of Britain accepts all colors, while the GCCF has granted full Championship status to the Usual and Sorrel in the non-Silver group, and has given preliminary status only to the blue, chocolate, lilac, and fawn non-Silvers, and to all the Silver Somali cats in the full range of colors.

LILAC USUAL The coat is rich and glowing golden brown ticked with black. The tail is tipped with black; the ears with black or dark brown. Nose leather is tile red; the paw pads and heels, and toe tufts are black or dark brown.

BLUE Any shade of blue ticked with darker blue is allowed, and the base hair is cream or oatmeal. The ears and tail are tipped with the same color as the ticking. The nose leather is blue-mauve, and the blue-mauve paw pads have deeper blue between the toes and extending up the heels. The toe tufts are deep blue.

CHOCOLATE The coat is rich golden coppery

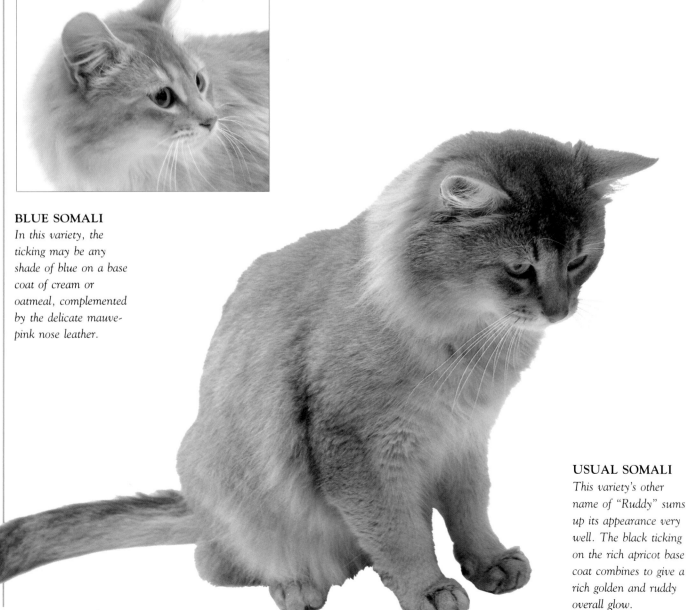

BLUE SOMALI
In this variety, the ticking may be any shade of blue on a base coat of cream or oatmeal, complemented by the delicate mauve-pink nose leather.

USUAL SOMALI
This variety's other name of "Ruddy" sums up its appearance very well. The black ticking on the rich apricot base coat combines to give a rich golden and ruddy overall glow.

CHOCOLATE SOMALI

Somali kittens are slow to mature both in size and in developing the full ticked effect of the typical coat.

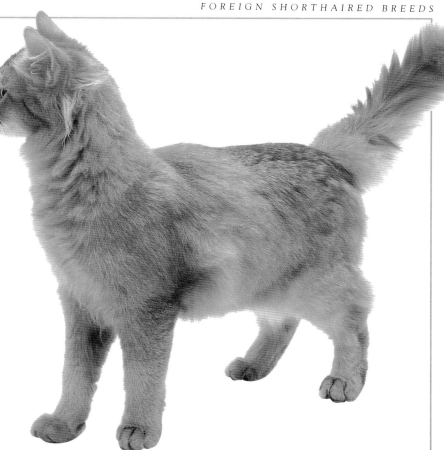

brown ticked with dark chocolate, with paler base hair. The ears and tail are tipped with the same shade as the ticking. The nose leather is pinkish chocolate. The paw pads are chocolate with darker chocolate between the toes and extending up the heels. The toe tufts are dark chocolate.

LILAC The pinkish dove-gray coat is ticked with a deeper shade of the same color and a paler base coat. This variety has a powdered effect to the coat. The ears and tail are tipped with the same color as the ticking. The nose leather is pinkish mauve; the pinkish-mauve paw pads have deeper dove gray between the toes and extending up the heels. The toe tufts are deep dove gray.

SORREL The warm, glowing copper coat is ticked with chocolate and a base coat of deep apricot. The ears and tail are tipped with chocolate. The nose leather is pink; the paw pads are pink with chocolate between the toes and extending up the heels; the toe tufts are chocolate.

FAWN The warm fawn coat is ticked with a deeper shade of the same color and a paler base coat. The ears and tail are tipped with the same color as the ticking. The nose leather is pink; the pinkish-mauve paw pads have deep fawn between the toes and extending up the heels. The toe tufts are deep fawn.

FAWN SOMALI

A diluted version of the red or sorrel, the fawn Somali has an attractive "powdered" effect to its warm fawn coat, ticked with a deeper fawn color. This is an elegant young kitten.

SILVER VARIETIES

A YELLOWISH EFFECT on the body, known as "fawning," is an undesirable trait in the Silver series of Somali cats. It occurs particularly in the usual silver, and in blue silver varieties especially on the face and paws.

USUAL SILVER The white base coat is ticked with black; the tail and ears are tipped with black. The nose leather is light brick red. The paw pads are black or brown with black between the toes and extending up the heels with black toe tufts.

BLUE SILVER The white base coat is ticked with blue, giving an overall sparkling silver-gray effect. The ears and tail are ticked with blue. The nose leather is blue-mauve. The blue-mauve pads have blue between the toes, extending up the heels; the toe tufts are blue.

USUAL SILVER
The coat gives an overall appearance of silver produced by black ticking on a white base coat.

RED SILVER
The Sorrel or Red Silver has a sparkling coat of a silvery peach shade. The ticking is a medium chocolate shade.

CHOCOLATE SILVER The white base coat has dark chocolate ticking, giving an overall sparkling silvery chocolate effect. The nose leather is pinkish chocolate, and the ears and tail are tipped with dark chocolate. The paw pads are chocolate with dark chocolate between the toes and extend up the heels. The ear tufts are dark chocolate.

LILAC SILVER The white base coat is ticked with dove-gray giving an overall sparkling dove-gray effect. The nose leather is pinkish mauve; pinkish-mauve pads have dove gray between the toes and extending up the heels. The toe tufts are dove-gray.

SORREL SILVER The white base coat has chocolate ticking, giving the overall sparkling silvery peach effect. The ears and tail are tipped with chocolate. The nose leather is pink. The pink paw pads have chocolate brown between the toes and extending up the heels. The toe tufts are dark chocolate.

FAWN SILVER The white base coat is ticked with fawn, giving an overall sparkling silvery fawn effect. The ears and tail are tipped with fawn. The nose leather is pink. The pinkish-mauve paw pads have fawn between the toes and extending up the heels. The toe tufts are fawn.

BLUE SILVER

Another striking color in the Silver Somali range, where the white base coat is ticked with blue giving a sparkling silvery blue-gray coat pattern. As in all Somali varieties, the ears and tail color should match that of the ticking.

RUSSIAN BLUE

THE VERY HANDSOME and unique Russian Blue is a natural breed with a unique combination of conformation, color, and coat that make it a striking animal.

The first Russian Blue cats are thought to have originated near the White Sea port of Archangel, just outside the Arctic Circle, and were carried as trade goods by merchant sailors on ships trading with England. The cats were shown extensively in England during the latter part of the nineteenth century, but differed from those of today in having bright orange eyes. The breed was exhibited under a number of names, including the Spanish Blue, the

Archangel, and the Maltese. In the first cat shows, all shorthaired blue cats competed in one class, regardless of type. In 1912, the Russian Blue was given its own classes, but during World War II, the breed almost became extinct, being saved only by outcrossing to Siamese. Cats of foreign type were then shown as Russian Blues, but eventually breeders made a coordinated attempt to return to the prewar characteristics of the breed, and in 1966 the show standard was changed to state specifically that Siamese type was undesirable in the Russian Blue.

BREAKDOWN OF 100 SHOW POINTS

PENALTIES

The Russian Blue is penalized in the show ring for any white or tabby markings, or for having a kinked or abnormal tail.

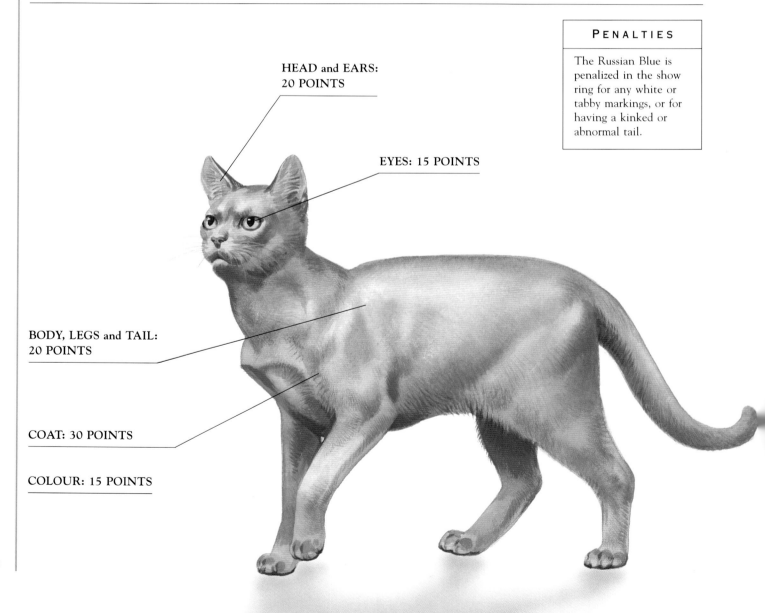

HEAD and EARS:
20 POINTS

EYES: 15 POINTS

BODY, LEGS and TAIL:
20 POINTS

COAT: 30 POINTS

COLOUR: 15 POINTS

Maltese or Russian Blue cats are recorded in the United States as long ago as 1900, but only in 1947 did breeders really start work with these unique cats, and even today the breed is rare in the show rings of the world.

Character and Care

The Russian Blue has a delightful temperament, being quiet-voiced and very affectionate. It does not like to be left alone for long periods and needs the company either of a human being, or other pets.

The unique coat, with its short, thick double fur, should be regularly combed through and may be stroked both ways without exposing the blue skin. The sparsely furred ears must be kept clean at all times.

KEY CHARACTERISTICS
● **CATEGORY** Foreign Shorthair.
● **OVERALL BUILD** Medium in size, lithe and muscular.
● **COAT** Short, fine, and plush, its density causes the double-textured coat to stand out from the body.
● **COLOR** Blue only (some associations in Australia and New Zealand recognize a Black Russian and a White Russian.) A clear, even blue, the guard hairs being silver-tipped giving the cat an overall lustrous silvery sheen. Lighter blue shades are preferred in the United States, and medium blue shades in Britain. Nose leather is slate gray; paw pads, lavender-pink or mauve; eye color, vivid green.
● **OTHER FEATURES** Wedge-shaped head with flat skull, broad at eye level with nose of medium length and level chin. Wide-based ears with very little hair inside or out. In the United States, the ears should be set far apart on the head; in Britain, the ears must be set vertically. Wide-set eyes of vivid green and a rounded aperture in the United States, but almond-shaped in Britain. Fine-boned, long and muscular body with long, slender legs and small paws. The tail should be long and tapered.

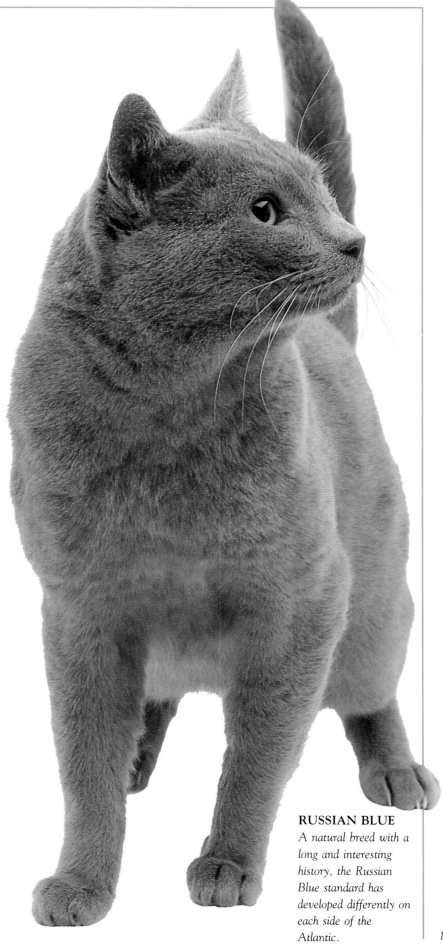

RUSSIAN BLUE

A natural breed with a long and interesting history, the Russian Blue standard has developed differently on each side of the Atlantic.

175

KORAT

THE BREED ORIGINATED in Thailand where it is called Si-Sawat, a descriptive compound word referring to its silver gray coat and luminous, light green eyes. The thirteenth-century *Book of Cat Poems* in the National Library of Bangkok illustrates the breed with the caption: "The cat Mal-ed has a body like Doklao, the hairs are smooth with roots like clouds and tips like silver, the eyes shine like dewdrops on a lotus leaf." *Mal-ed* refers to the seed of the Look Sawat, a silvery gray fruit lightly tinged with green. *Dok* is a flower, and *lao* a plant with silver-tipped flowers. Highly prized in its native land, the Si-Sawat is considered a harbinger of good fortune, and a pair of these cats is a traditional wedding gift, intended to bring longevity, wealth, and happiness to the couple.

First exhibited in London in 1896, the Korat was disqualified, being judged as a Siamese cat and not having the desired fawn coat, dark points, and blue eyes! In 1959 Korat cats arrived in the United States, where they were officially recognized in 1966. The cat fanciers of South Africa and Australia officially accepted the breed in 1968 and 1969 respectively, but Britain's Governing Council of the Cat Fancy delayed recognition until 1975 and then withheld championship status. In 1983, the Cat Association of Britain finally accepted the Korat for full status, and Britain's first champion was chosen by judges from England, Belgium, and Australia.

Character and Care

The Korat is a dainty, quiet-voiced little cat, generally alert, inquisitive, and affectionate.

Its short, dense coat is easily cared for with a weekly brushing and buffing with a silk scarf.

BREAKDOWN OF 100 SHOW POINTS

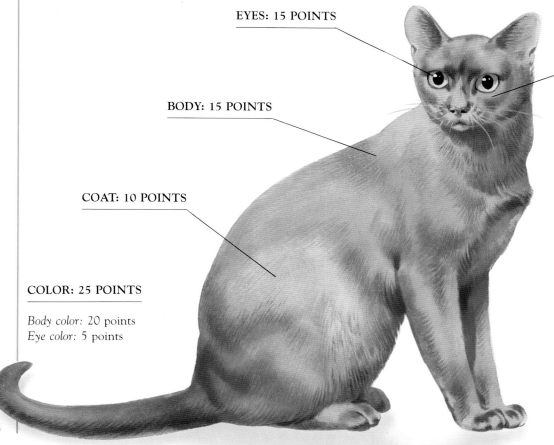

EYES: 15 POINTS

BODY: 15 POINTS

COAT: 10 POINTS

COLOR: 25 POINTS

Body color: 20 points
Eye color: 5 points

HEAD: 20 POINTS

Broad head: 5 points
Profile: 6 points
Breadth between eyes:
4 points
Ear set and placement:
5 points

PENALTIES

The Korat is penalized if it is any color but silver blue; has a visible tail kink; or white spot or locket. Kittens and young cats are not penalized for incorrect eye color; this is not set until maturity in the Korat.

KEY CHARACTERISTICS

- **CATEGORY** Foreign Shorthair.

- **OVERALL BUILD** Small to medium size.

- **COAT** Short to medium length, fine textured and glossy.

- **COLOR** Blue only. Silver blue tipped with silver. Nose leather and lips, dark blue or lavender; paw pads, dark blue ranging to lavender with a pinkish tinge. Eye color, luminous green preferred, amber acceptable.

- **OTHER FEATURES** Heart-shaped head with large, round-tipped ears set high, giving an alert expression. Slight stop in profile of nose and a firm chin, lion-like in profile. The eyes are luminous and oversized for the face, and with an Asian slant when closed. The body is muscular and supple, midway between the Shorthair and the Siamese in type, with females being daintier than males. Well-proportioned legs with neat oval paws, and a tail of medium length heavier at the base and tapering to a rounded tip.

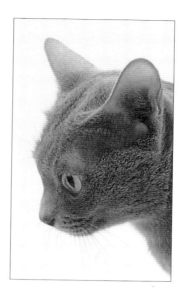

PROFILE

Always blue and with a fine short coat, the Korat is a dainty, quiet little cat.

KORAT

A natural breed discovered in Thailand, the Korat was considered as a good luck charm and often given as a wedding gift.

177

HAVANA BROWN

THIS UNIQUE, MAN-MADE breed came into being when British breeders were working with Russian Blue and Shorthair cross-matings during the early 1950s, and self-colored chocolate brown kittens were occasionally produced. At that time, the science of feline color genetics was in its infancy, but it was soon established that chocolate kittens could only occur when both parents carried the chocolate factor, and when two chocolate cats were mated, chocolate kittens always resulted.

Cats from these early matings were developed in Britain as the Chestnut Brown Foreign Shorthair and were outcrossed to Siamese to establish Oriental type and conformation. Others were sent to the United States to establish a new breed and were bred to a unique standard of points as the Havana Brown.

Character and Care
This breed is highly intelligent, affectionate, and very agile. Less vocal than the Siamese, it is playful and craves human company. It makes a superb pet.

The coat is easy to maintain in good condition with the minimum of grooming. Combing removes any loose hairs, and buffing with the hand or a silk scarf produces a sheen on the glossy brown coat.

BREAKDOWN OF 100 SHOW POINTS

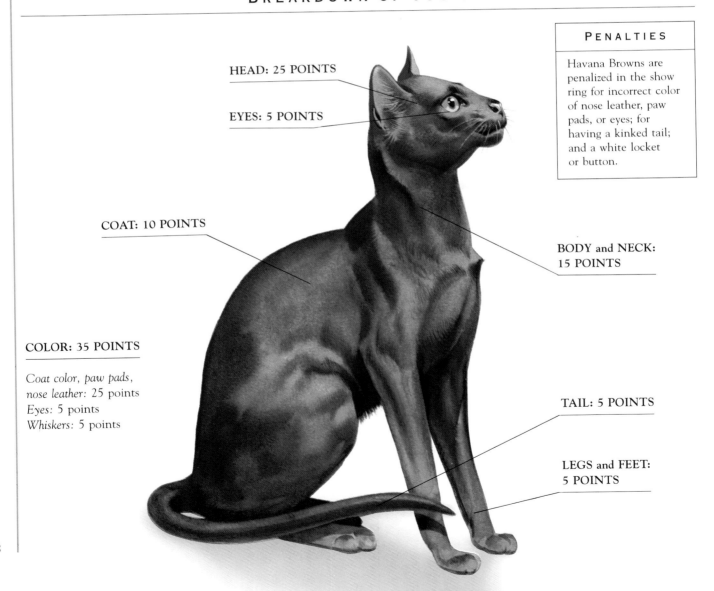

HEAD: 25 POINTS

EYES: 5 POINTS

COAT: 10 POINTS

COLOR: 35 POINTS

Coat color, paw pads, nose leather: 25 points
Eyes: 5 points
Whiskers: 5 points

BODY and NECK: 15 POINTS

TAIL: 5 POINTS

LEGS and FEET: 5 POINTS

PENALTIES

Havana Browns are penalized in the show ring for incorrect color of nose leather, paw pads, or eyes; for having a kinked tail; and a white locket or button.

HAVANA BROWN

The Havana Brown as shown in the United States was developed from early imports of Chestnut Brown Foreign Shorthairs from Britain. It is a unique breed and bears very little resemblance to the Havana, or Oriental Chocolate, found in Europe and Britain.

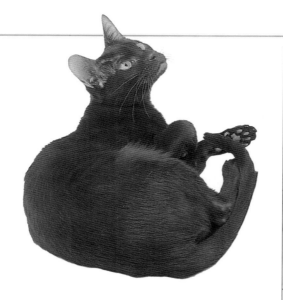

KEY CHARACTERISTICS

- **CATEGORY** Foreign Shorthair.

- **OVERALL BUILD** Medium size, muscular build.

- **COAT** Short to medium length coat, smooth and lustrous.

- **COLOR** Warm brown only. Coat of a rich and even shade of warm brown throughout. Kittens are not penalized for showing ghost tabby markings. The nose leather is brown with a rosy flush; the paw pads must have a rosy tone. The eye color is a vivid green.

- **OTHER FEATURES** Head slightly longer than it is wide, with a distinct change in slope or "stop" at eye level when viewed in profile. The rounded muzzle has a definite break on each side behind the whisker pads, well-developed chin. Large round-tipped ears, wide set but not flaring and slightly pricked forward, giving an alert appearance. Oval eyes of vivid green. Firm muscular body of medium length with legs in proportion, and neat oval paws. A medium length tail, tapering gently to a slightly pointed tip.

HAVANA BROWN

Large pricked ears and vivid green oval eyes give the face of the Havana Brown its typical, sweet expression. The smooth, lustrous coat is evenly colored in warm brown.

EGYPTIAN MAU

NOT TO BE CONFUSED with cats of the same name bred experimentally in Britain during the 1960s and now called Oriental Tabbies. The Egyptian Mau was bred in the United States, and came from foundation stock brought there from Egypt via Rome in 1953. It is a spotted cat, very similar to those pictured in ancient Egyptian scrolls and cartoons. It gained official recognition from the CFF in 1968 and finally from the CFA in 1977.

Character and Care
Rather shy but very loving, the Mau tends to attach its affections to only one or two people. It is naturally active and may be taught one or two tricks.

Although the short coat is easy to keep in good condition, regular combing is required to remove dead hair.

BREAKDOWN OF 100 SHOW POINTS

HEAD: 20 POINTS

Muzzle: 5 points
Skull: 5 points
Ears: 5 points
Eye shape: 5 points

COAT: 5 POINTS

Texture and length: 5 points

PATTERN: 25 POINTS

BODY: 25 POINTS

Torso: 10 points
Legs and feet: 10 points
Tail: 5 points

COLOR: 25 POINTS

Eye color: 10 points
Coat color: 15 points

PENALTIES

Egyptian Mau cats are penalized in the show ring for the following: short or round head; pointed muzzle; small, round or Oriental eyes; cobby or Oriental body type; short or whip tail; incorrect Mau pattern; poor condition; amber cast in eyes of cats over one and a half years of age.

DISQUALIFICATION FEATURES
- lack of spots
- blue eye color
- a kinked or abnormal tail

SILVER MAU

The silver Egyptian Mau has clear markings in dark charcoal on a pale silver ground color. The green eyes complete the rather exotic effect.

BRONZE MAU

The Bronze Egyptian Mau is perhaps the cat that most resembles the color of the cats of the ancient Egyptians. Dark brown markings show up clearly on the light bronze base coat. The whole coat has a warm glowing appearance.

SMOKE MAU

Unusual black markings on a charcoal gray base and with a silver undercoat give this unusually colored cat the appearance of shot silk, the color changing almost imperceptibly as it moves.

KEY CHARACTERISTICS

- **CATEGORY** Foreign Shorthair.

- **OVERALL BUILD** Medium size, long and graceful; muscular strength.

- **COAT** Silky and fine coat, dense and resilient to touch, with a lustrous sheen. Medium length hair, two or more bands of ticking, separated by lighter bands.

- **COLORS**
Silver Pale silver ground color; dark charcoal markings contrasting with ground color. Backs of the ears are grayish pink tipped in black; the nose, lips, and eyes are outlined in black. The upper throat, chin, and around the nostrils is pale clear silver, appearing white. Nose leather is brick red; paw pads are black; eye color is light green. *Bronze* Light bronze ground color with creamy ivory underparts, dark brown markings against the ground color. Backs of the ears are tawny pink tipped in dark brown; the nose, lips, and eyes are outlined in dark brown, with ocher on the bridge of the nose. The upper throat, chin, and around the nostrils are pale creamy white. Nose leather is brick red; paw pads are black or dark brown; eye color is light green. *Smoke* Charcoal gray ground color with silver undercoat, the jet black markings plainly visible. Nose, lips, and eyes outlined in jet black; upper throat, chin, and around the nostrils are lightest in color. Nose leather and pads black: eye color light green.

- **OTHER FEATURES** Slightly rounded wedge head of medium length. Muzzle neither short nor pointed. Medium to large ears alert and slightly pointed. Inner ear delicate shell pink. Ears tufts accepted. Legs in proportion to body, with higher hind legs and small, slightly oval paws. Medium long tail thick at the base, slightly tapered.

OCICAT

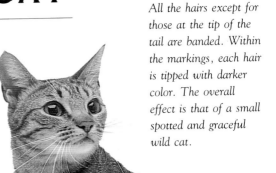

THE FIRST KITTEN of this breed appeared in the litter of an experimentally bred hybrid queen, from an Abyssinian-pointed Siamese breeding program, mated with a chocolate-pointed Siamese male. The kitten, which was called Tonga, reminded its breeder of a baby ocelot, and she decided to produce similar cats, which were eventually recognized as a separate breed called Ocicats.

Apart from the Ocicat itself, outcrosses to Abyssinian, American, and Siamese are allowed in the pedigree. The Ocicat is a rather large, but well-proportioned cat, muscular and agile, with a typically "wild-cat" appearance. It is remarkable for its very clear spotted pattern and its striking golden eyes.

Character and Care

Ocicats are loving and gentle, inquisitive and playful, and make excellent pets.

Their coats are groomed by gentle brushing and combing through on a regular basis to remove dead hair.

TYPICAL OCICAT
All the hairs except for those at the tip of the tail are banded. Within the markings, each hair is tipped with darker color. The overall effect is that of a small spotted and graceful wild cat.

BREAKDOWN OF 100 SHOW POINTS

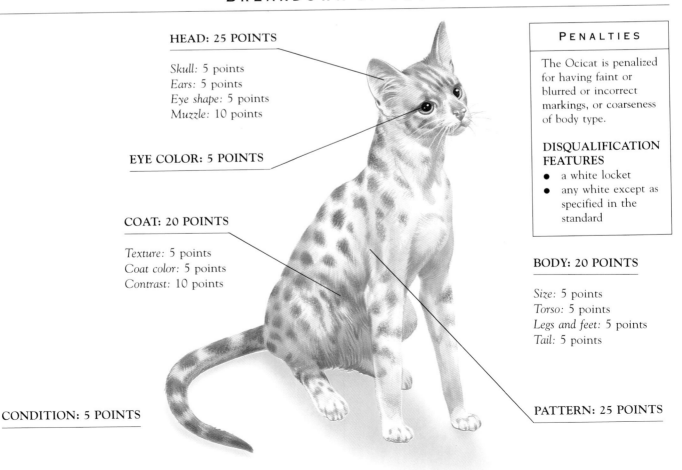

HEAD: 25 POINTS

Skull: 5 points
Ears: 5 points
Eye shape: 5 points
Muzzle: 10 points

EYE COLOR: 5 POINTS

COAT: 20 POINTS

Texture: 5 points
Coat color: 5 points
Contrast: 10 points

PENALTIES

The Ocicat is penalized for having faint or blurred or incorrect markings, or coarseness of body type.

DISQUALIFICATION FEATURES
- a white locket
- any white except as specified in the standard

BODY: 20 POINTS

Size: 5 points
Torso: 5 points
Legs and feet: 5 points
Tail: 5 points

CONDITION: 5 POINTS

PATTERN: 25 POINTS

CHOCOLATE SILVER

In this variety, the tabby markings are in a warm shade of chocolate on a pure silver base coat.

KEY CHARACTERISTICS

- **CATEGORY** Foreign Shorthair.

- **OVERALL BUILD** Medium to large, athletic build.

- **COAT** Short smooth coat, satiny and lustrous, yet long enough to accommodate the necessary bands of color.
  Ticking All hairs except those on the tip of the tail are banded. Within the markings, hairs are tipped with the darker color; hairs in the ground color are tipped with a lighter color.
  Markings Distinctive markings must be clearly seen from any angle. Markings on the face, legs, and tail may be darker than those on the body. The ground color may be darker on the saddle and lighter on the underside, chin, and lower jaw.
  Pattern The pattern is that of a spotted cat. This breed is noted for its powerful, graceful "wild cat" appearance.

- **COLORS** Black spotted; blue spotted; chocolate spotted; lavender spotted; cinnamon spotted; fawn spotted; black silver spotted; blue silver spotted; chocolate silver spotted; lavender silver spotted; cinnamon silver spotted; fawn silver spotted. All colors should be clear. The lightest color is on the face, around the eyes, on the chin, and the lower jaw; the darkest color is at the tip of the tail.

- **OTHER FEATURES** Modified wedge-shaped head with a broad, well-defined muzzle and strong chin. Alert, moderately large ears preferably with ear tufts, set fairly wide apart on the head. Large, almond- shaped eyes. Long solid body, athletic with substantial bone and muscle structure; medium long legs with compact oval paws and a fairly long, slightly tapered tail.

BLUE SPOTTED

Markings on the face, legs, and tail may be darker than those on the body, and the ground color may be darker on the saddle.

BLACK SILVER

This kitten is very well patterned with clear spots the correct head markings and pleasing type.

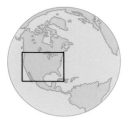

BENGAL

BASED ON CROSSES between Asian leopard cats which live wild in southeastern Asia, and domestic cats, the Bengal was first produced in the United States. It seems to have preserved the self-assurance and confidence of the Asian Leopard Cat in conjunction with the affectionate disposition of the domestic, producing a miniature leopard with a loving nature. The appearance of the Bengal should be as close as possible to that of the first cross, but without the possibility of its being mistaken for an actual Asian leopard cat. The texture of this breed's coat is unique, having the feel of satin or silk, and a glittering appearance as if sprinkled with gold dust or fragments of pearl.

Its cooing or chirruping call is quite different from that of the ordinary domestic cat, which adds to the impression the ideal Bengal gives of being a truly wild cat.

Character and Care
Self-assured and as confident as its leopard cat ancestors, the Bengal has acquired an affectionate disposition and a loving, dependable temperament.

The thick, luxuriant coat is kept in good condition with a well-balanced diet, and regular brushing and combing.

BREAKDOWN OF 100 SHOW POINTS

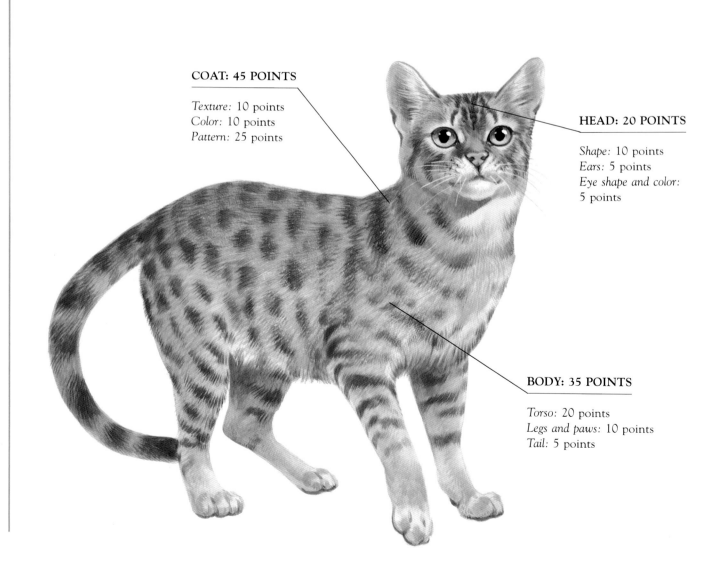

COAT: 45 POINTS

Texture: 10 points
Color: 10 points
Pattern: 25 points

HEAD: 20 POINTS

Shape: 10 points
Ears: 5 points
Eye shape and color: 5 points

BODY: 35 POINTS

Torso: 20 points
Legs and paws: 10 points
Tail: 5 points

KEY CHARACTERISTICS

- **CATEGORY** Foreign Shorthair.

- **OVERALL BUILD** Large, robust, and muscular.

- **COAT** Short to medium length, dense, luxuriant and unusually soft to touch.

- **HEAD** Broad, medium wedge with rounded contours, rather small in proportion to the body. Profile has a gentle curve from the forehead to the bridge of the nose; prominent brow.

- **NOSE** Large, broad nose with a puffed nose leather. Full broad muzzle and pronounced whisker pads.

- **CHIN** Strong.

- **EYES** Oval or slightly almond-shaped, large but not bold, set on the slant toward base of ear.

- **EARS** Medium to small, rather short with a wide base and rounded tips; set as much on the side as the top of the head; pointing forward in profile.

- **BODY** Large and robust with a broad chest. Very muscular, but long and sleek, with hindquarters slightly higher than the shoulders.

- **LEGS** Medium length, strong and muscular.

- **PAWS** Large and rounded.

- **TAIL** Of medium length, thick and even with a rounded tip.

- **COLORS** Leopard spotted or marble markings in brown tabby, blue-eyed snow, or blue.

PENALTIES

The Bengal is penalized for having a long, rough, or coarse coat; a ticked coat; incorrect color of the tail tip or paw pads; a whip tail; an unspotted stomach; and white patches or spots other than the *ocelli* (light spots on the backs of the ears).

DISQUALIFICATION FEATURES

- Aggressive behavior which threatens to harm.

BENGAL VARIETIES

IN BOTH THE Leopard Spotted and Marble Patterned, the spectacles which encircle the eyes should extend into vertical streaks which may be outlined by an "M" on the forehead. Broken streaks in the Marble, and streaks or spots in the Leopard, run over the head on each side of a complex scarab marking, down the neck onto the shoulders. A bold "chinstrap" and "mascara" markings, unbroken or broken necklets, and blotchy horizontal streaks are desirable in the Marble streaks, or spots in the Leopard.

The Marble should have a distinct pattern with large swirled patches or streaks, clearly defined but not symmetrical, giving a marble-like impression, preferably with a horizontal flow. The pattern should be formed of distinct shapes and sharp outlines with sharp contrast between the base coat, and the markings should bear no similarity to that of the Classic Tabby.

The Leopard Spotted should have generally large, well-formed, and randomly distributed spots. Extreme contrast between the ground color and the spots, which should be arrow-shaped, or rosetted in the case of larger spots. The cat's stomach must be spotted, and the legs may show broken horizontal lines and/or spots along its length with a solid dark-colored tip. It is important that the spots do not run vertically into a mackerel tabby pattern.

BROWN TABBY All variations are allowed in both Leopard Spotted and Marble Bengals, but a high degree of reddish-brown yielding a yellow, buff, golden, or orange ground color is preferred. The overall appearance should be of a cat dusted with gold glitter. The markings may be black or various shades of brown, and there may be *ocelli* – light-colored spots on the backs of the ears. The whisker pads and chin must be very pale, and the chest, underbody, and inner legs should be pale compared with the general ground color. The eye rims, lips, and nose leather are outlined in black; the center of the nose leather is brick red. Paw pads and tail tip are black; eye color is gold, green, or hazel, with deep shades preferred.

BROWN SPOTTED BENGAL

This kitten exhibits the arrowhead spots favored in the Leopard Spotted variety of the Bengal cat.

SNOW BENGAL
This variety shows the Burmese/Tonkinese coat pattern, where the most intense color is at the points, but the pattern is still visible on the body and has a special glittering appearance.

MARBLE BENGAL
Striking markings easily identify Bengals with the Marble pattern, with its complex whorls, distinct shapes, and sharp outlines. The pattern bears little or no resemblance to the Classic Tabby.

BLUE-EYED SNOW This variety is of the Himalayan type, with the pattern restricted to the points. The ground color is ivory to cream, with the overall appearance being that of a cat dusted with pearl glitter. The pattern varies in color from charcoal to dark or light brown; there are light-colored spectacles, whisker pads, and chin; and *ocelli* are preferred on each ear. The eye rims, lips, and nose leather are outlined in black; the center of the nose leather is brick red. The paw pads are rosy-toned brown; the tail tip is charcoal or dark brown; the eye color is blue.

BROWN SNOW This variety shows the Burmese/Tonkinese restriction of coat pattern. The ground color is cream to light brown, with the overall appearance being that of a cat dusted with pearl glitter. The clearly visible pattern varies in color from charcoal to light brown; there are light-colored spectacles, whisker pads, and chin; and *ocelli* are preferred on each ear. The eye rims, lips, and nose leather are outlined in black; the center of the nose leather is brick red. The paw pads are rosy-toned brown; the tail tip is charcoal or dark brown; the eye color is gold, green, or blue-green.

BLUE The ground color is pinkish mushroom to warm oatmeal, with the overall appearance being that of a cat dusted with pearl glitter. The clearly visible pattern is pale blue to blue-gray; there are light-colored spectacles, whisker pads, and chin; and *ocelli* are preferred on each ear. The eye rims, lips, and nose leather are outlined in slate gray; the center of the nose leather is dark pink. The paw pads are mauvish pink; the tail tip is dark blue. The eye color is gold, green, or blue-green.

CORNISH REX

IN 1950 A CURLY-COATED kitten was born in an otherwise normal litter at a farm in Cornwall in southwestern England. Microscopic examination by a geneticist of the kitten's hair samples showed they were similar to those of the Rex rabbit. When the kitten, named Kallibunker, matured, he was mated with his mother, and two of the resulting three kittens had Rex coats. The male, Poldhu, eventually sired a stunning Rex female called Lamorna Cove, which was exported to the United States to found the Cornish Rex breed on the other side of the Atlantic. British Shorthairs and Burmese cats were used as foundation stock in the early days of Cornish Rex breeding, and eventually there were enough curly-coated cats to establish an acceptable breed which could be registered. In Britain, the Cornish Rex achieved full breed status in Britain in 1967 and in the United States, in 1979.

Character and Care

The Cornish Rex cat is intelligent, affectionate, and rather extrovert by nature. Playful and mischievous, it makes a wonderful pet.

The unique curled coat does not shed hair, making it extremely easy to groom with hand stroking and the occasional use of a comb.

BREAKDOWN OF 100 SHOW POINTS

COAT: 40 POINTS

Texture: 10 points
Length: 5 points
Wave, extent of wave: 20 points
Close-lying: 5 points

HEAD: 25 POINTS

Size and shape: 5 points
Muzzle and nose: 5 points
Eyes: 5 points
Ears: 5 points
Profile: 5 points

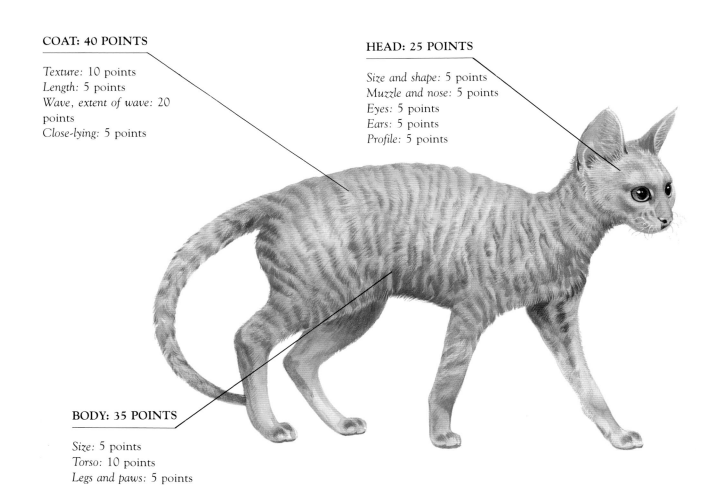

BODY: 35 POINTS

Size: 5 points
Torso: 10 points
Legs and paws: 5 points
Tail: 5 points
Bone: 5 points
Neck: 5 points

KEY CHARACTERISTICS

- **CATEGORY** Foreign Shorthair, curled.

- **OVERALL BUILD** Medium sized, slender build.

- **COAT** Short plush coat without guard hairs. Curls waves or ripples over the body particularly on the back and tail. Whiskers and eyebrows crinkled.

- **HEAD** Medium size, wedge shaped. About one third longer than it is wide.

- **NOSE** Rounded muzzle. In profile, a straight line is seen from the center of the forehead to the end of the nose.

- **CHIN** Strong.

- **EYES** Medium to large, oval shaped.

- **EARS** Large, set high on the head.

- **BODY** Medium length. Slender, hard, and muscular.

- **LEGS** Long and straight.

- **PAWS**

- **TAIL** Long, slender, and tapering.

- **COLORS** Most associations accept virtually all colors and patterns except white markings on Siamese patterned cats.

CORNISH REX VARIETIES

IN ORDER TO widen the gene pool and to insure stamina in the Cornish Rex as a breed, it was necessary for the pioneer breeders to outcross to other breeds having the desired conformation. Foreign breeds were selected in the main, including Havana and Oriental lilac, and Burmese as well as Siamese of various colors. All the offspring of Cornish Rex to non-rexed cats resulted in cats with normal coats, all carrying the recessive gene for the Cornish curly coat, and when such cats matured, and were mated with similar cats, or back to Cornish Rex, curly-coated kittens were produced. The various colors and coat patterns of the cats selected for the original outcrosses resulted in a wide range of color varieties in the Cornish Rex breed, and breeders soon began to show their preferences for certain colors and combinations of colors. Though conformation

BLACK SMOKE & WHITE CORNISH
The tail of the Cornish Rex is long, fine, and tapered, and must be well covered with waved fur.

BLACK SMOKE VAN PATTERN
Virtually all the feline coat colors and patterns are found in the Cornish Rex. Perhaps one of the most unusual is the Van pattern, in which the cat's coat is basically white, with color restricted to the head and tail.

RED CORNISH REX
The Cornish Rex is medium sized, lithe, and muscular, with long slender legs and small oval paws.

CHOCOLATE SMOKE CORNISH REX
The short plush coat is dense and has uniform narrow waves extending from the top of the head across the back, sides, and hips, and continues to the tip of the tail.

WHITE CORNISH REX
The head should be narrow with a flat skull. A straight line can be seen from the center of the forehead to the end of the nose.

CHOCOLATE TORTIE CORNISH REX
The eyes of the Cornish Rex are medium sized and oval, with a full eye's-width between them.

TORTIE SMOKE AND WHITE
The Cornish Rex stands tall, appearing to walk on tiptoe.

DEVON REX

TEN YEARS AFTER the discovery of the first Cornish Rex kitten, another curly-coated kitten was discovered in the neighboring English county of Devon. The kitten, named Kirlee, was eventually mated with some Cornish Rex queens. To everyone's surprise, all the resulting kittens were flat-coated, and it was concluded that Kirlee's curls were caused by a different gene. More breeding tests confirmed this. The gene for the Cornish coat was labeled Rex gene [i]; the gene for the Devon coat Rex gene [ii]. The two rex-coated varieties were developed quite separately and are quite distinct breeds. The Devon Rex would look rather unusual even without its wavy coat, having a quizzical, pixie-like expression and huge bat-like ears.

In Britain, a popular sub-variety of Devon Rex is known unofficially as the Si-Rex. It combines all of the characteristics of the typical Devon Rex with the Siamese coat pattern and colors.

Character and Care

The Devon is said to be the cat for the connoisseur. It is demanding as a pet, constantly craving human attention, loving, playful, and intelligent.

The cat is very easy to groom with hand stroking and occasional combing. It often shows sparse areas on the body, and when it does, the cat needs extra warmth. The large ears need regular cleaning.

BREAKDOWN OF 100 SHOW POINTS

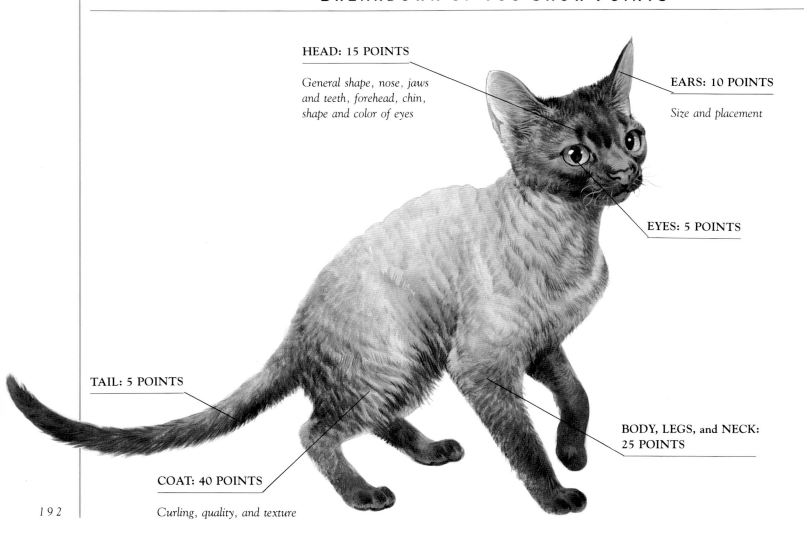

HEAD: 15 POINTS

General shape, nose, jaws and teeth, forehead, chin, shape and color of eyes

EARS: 10 POINTS

Size and placement

EYES: 5 POINTS

TAIL: 5 POINTS

BODY, LEGS, and NECK: 25 POINTS

COAT: 40 POINTS

Curling, quality, and texture

KEY CHARACTERISTICS

- **CATEGORY** Foreign Shorthair, curled.

- **OVERALL BUILD** Medium size, hard and muscular, slender but with a broad chest.

- **COAT** Very short, soft, fine coat without guard hairs; curly or wavy particularly on the body and tail.

- **HEAD** Small, modified wedge shaped with short muzzle and prominent cheekbones.

- **NOSE** No standards set.

- **CHIN** No standards set.

- **EYES** Large, oval and set wide apart, giving a unique "elfin" look.

- **EARS** Large, set low down.

- **BODY** Long and straight with a broad chest.

- **LEGS** Long and slim.

- **PAWS** Small and oval

- **TAIL** Long, fine and tapered.

- **COLORS** All recognized colors or patterns except white markings on Siamese patterned cats.

PENALTIES

Devon Rex cats are penalized in the show ring for having incorrect head type; a short, bare, or bushy tail; a straight or shaggy coat; a cobby body; small ears or ears set high and upright on the head; slack muscles or bare patches (a fault in kittens and a serious fault in cats).

DISQUALIFICATION FEATURES
- baldness
- a kinked or abnormal tail
- a squint
- weak hind legs

DEVON REX VARIETIES

WHATEVER THEIR COLOR or coat pattern, all Devon Rex must conform to the same stringent show standard of points. The coat of the Devon Rex is quite different from that of the Cornish, and in some cats the fur may be sparse and downy on the underparts, often causing the coat color to look indistinct. Like the Cornish Rex, the first Devons were outcrossed to cats of other Foreign breeds in order to widen the gene pool of available breeding stock. Siamese cats were extensively used, and the resulting curled cats were called Si-Rex in the beginning. Si-rex is not now an accepted as correct terminology for the Siamese-patterned Devon Rex, and white markings are not permitted in cats with the Himalayan or Siamese coat pattern, where the color is restricted to the cat's points.

Apart from this requirement, all colors and patterns accepted in the feline standards are recognized in the Devon Rex, with or without white areas.

ODD-EYED WHITE
White Devon Rex cats are accepted with blue eyes, golden eyes, or odd eyes.

CHOCOLATE TORTIE POINT
The Devon Rex appears in a range of Siamese-patterned colors. At one time these cats were called Si-rex.

BLACK SMOKE DEVON REX
The Devon Rex is totally different from the Cornish. It is of similar size, but has a unique head type and unusual bodily conformation.

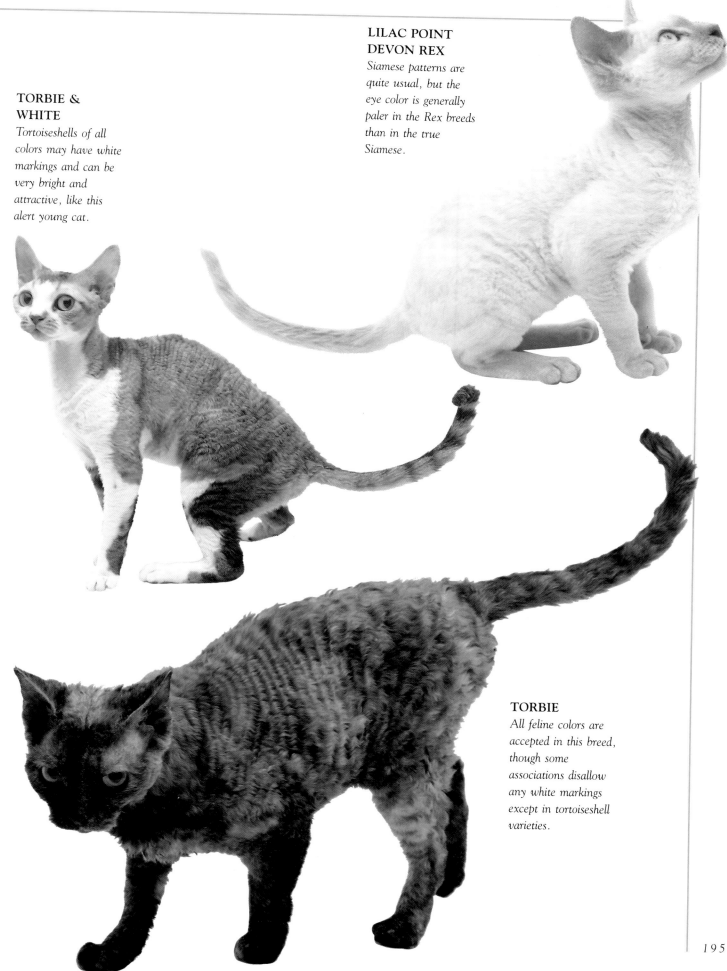

TORBIE & WHITE

Tortoiseshells of all colors may have white markings and can be very bright and attractive, like this alert young cat.

LILAC POINT DEVON REX

Siamese patterns are quite usual, but the eye color is generally paler in the Rex breeds than in the true Siamese.

TORBIE

All feline colors are accepted in this breed, though some associations disallow any white markings except in tortoiseshell varieties.

195

SPHYNX

ALTHOUGH IT APPEARS so, the Sphynx is not truly hairless. The skin has the texture of soft leather and may be covered with a fine down which is almost imperceptible to the eye. A fine covering of hair is sometimes apparent on the ears, muzzle, feet, tail, and scrotum.

The first Sphynx appeared as a spontaneous mutation in a litter born to a black and white domestic cat in Ontario, Canada, in 1966. A breeder of Siamese cats took the hairless kitten, and with other breeders worked on the development of a new breed. The CFA gave the Sphynx provisional status, then revoked it. The CCFF recognized the breed for champion-ship status in 1971, and the first champion was chosen in 1972. Today the Sphynx is accepted only by a few feline associations, and it remains a rare and unique breed.

Character and Care

People-orientated and not fond of other cats, the Sphynx does not like being held or strongly petted. It often stands with one foreleg raised, and resists lying with its body touching the ground, preferring a warm surface.

It never needs brushing, but the suede-like body must be kept in good condition by hand grooming and rubbing down with a soft cloth.

BREAKDOWN OF 100 SHOW POINTS

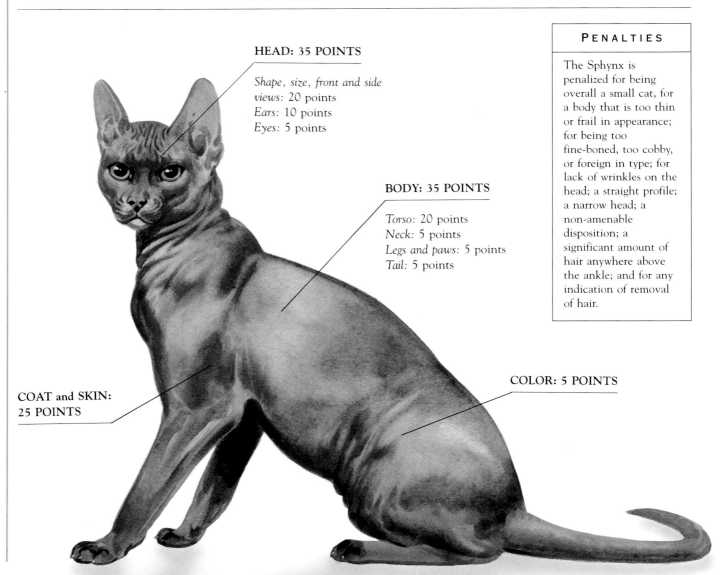

HEAD: 35 POINTS

Shape, size, front and side views: 20 points
Ears: 10 points
Eyes: 5 points

BODY: 35 POINTS

Torso: 20 points
Neck: 5 points
Legs and paws: 5 points
Tail: 5 points

COAT and SKIN: 25 POINTS

COLOR: 5 POINTS

PENALTIES

The Sphynx is penalized for being overall a small cat, for a body that is too thin or frail in appearance; for being too fine-boned, too cobby, or foreign in type; for lack of wrinkles on the head; a straight profile; a narrow head; a non-amenable disposition; a significant amount of hair anywhere above the ankle; and for any indication of removal of hair.

KEY CHARACTERISTICS

- **CATEGORY** Foreign.

- **OVERALL BUILD** Medium size, hard and muscular.

- **COAT** Appears hairless; may be covered with short fine down. Kittens have wrinkled skin; adults should retain some wrinkles.

- **COLORS** All colors and patterns are acceptable; white lockets and buttons are also accepted.

- **OTHER FEATURES** Medium-sized head is a modified wedge with rounded contours, skull is slightly rounded, forehead is flat, cheekbones are prominent. There is a slight stop at the bridge of the nose, and the muzzle is rounded, with a distinct whisker break. Chin is firm; eyes are large and almost round, slanting toward the outer corner of the ear; ears are broad based and very open, set upright on the head, hairless inside and slightly haired on the back. The medium long body has a broad chest and well-rounded abdomen; it is hard and muscular with medium bone. Legs are in proportion to the body and of medium bone; hind legs longer than forelegs, which are widely set and muscular. Paws are medium sized, oval, with long, slender toes and thick paw pads; tail is whip-like, tapering from the body to the tip. A lion tail (with a tuft of hair on the tip) is acceptable.

PROFILE
The head of the Sphynx is a modified wedge with rounded contours.

BLACK & WHITE SPHYNX
The Sphynx may appear to be hairless, but it is usually covered with a very short, fine down.

JAPANESE BOBTAIL

A NATURAL BREED, WHICH has existed in its native Japan for centuries, the Japanese Bobtail is considered to be a symbol of good luck in the home, and the tricolored variety, known as the *mi-ke* (meaning three colors), is particularly favored.

The Bobtail first came to the attention of cat fanciers in the Western world when an American cat show judge visiting Japan became captivated by the breed. Five years later, in 1968, three Bobtails were exported from Japan to the United States. More were to follow, and Bobtails were accepted for provisional status by the CFA in May 1971.

After five years of careful breeding, the Japanese Bobtail became well established in the United States and gained full recognition and Championship Status in the CFA in May 1976. It is also recognized in Britain by the Cat Association.

Character and Care

The Japanese Bobtail has an endearing personality and loves human company. It is a vocal cat, and has a soft melodious voice with a range of sounds. As a house cat, the Bobtail is well-behaved, intelligent, and playful; and as a show cat it is easy to handle.

The silky coat is easy to maintain in perfect condition with gentle brushing and combing, finishing with the hands or a silk scarf. The pompom on the tail is combed into shape, and the wide ears are kept in pristine condition by wiping daily with a cotton swab.

BREAKDOWN OF 100 SHOW POINTS

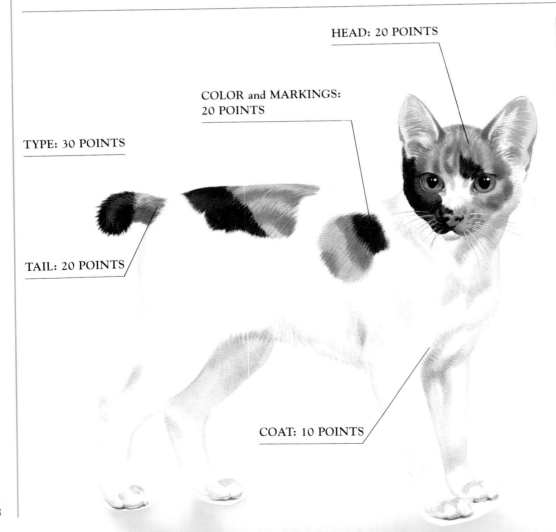

HEAD: 20 POINTS

COLOR and MARKINGS: 20 POINTS

TYPE: 30 POINTS

TAIL: 20 POINTS

COAT: 10 POINTS

PENALTIES

The Bobtail is penalized in the show ring for having a short round head or cobby build.

DISQUALIFICATION FEATURES

- tail bone absent, or extending too far beyond the body
- tail bone lacking a pompom or a fluffy appearance
- the delayed pompom effect, apparent when the pompom is preceded by an inch or two of normal tail with close-lying fur, rather than appearing to start at the base of the spine.

BROWN TABBY & WHITE BOBTAIL

The Japanese Bobtail is loving and talkative, and so makes a perfect pet.

BLUE-EYED VAN

The silky coat is very easy to groom by regular brushing and polishing with a silk scarf.

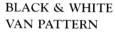

BLACK & WHITE VAN PATTERN

The unique tail of the Bobtail is short and may be straight or bent into one or more curves, with the hair fanning out to create a pompom effect.

KEY CHARACTERISTICS

- **CATEGORY** Shorthair.

- **OVERALL BUILD** Medium size, lean and well-muscled.

- **COAT** Soft and silky, medium length; no noticeable undercoat and relatively little shedding of hair.

- **COLORS** White, black, red, black and white, red and white, *mi-ke* (tricolor – black, red, and white), tortoiseshell. Other colors include any other color or pattern or combination of colors and patterns except coloring that is restricted to the points, such as Himalayan, or unpatterned agouti, such as Abyssinian ticking. Patterned categories include any variety of tabby with or without areas of solid unmarked color, preference being given to bold dramatic markings and rich vivid coloring.

- **OTHER FEATURES** Long fine head forming a perfect equilateral triangle with gentle curving lines, high cheek bones, and a noticeable whisker break. The muzzle is fairly broad, rounding into the whisker break. The ears are large and upright, set wide apart and at right angles to the head, and the eyes are large and oval, wide and alert. The medium-sized body is lean but well-muscled, and the legs are long and slender with neat oval paws. The short tail is said to resemble a bunny tail with the hair fanning out to create a pompom effect. If straightened, the tail bone could be four or five inches in length. It is usually jointed only at the base and may be either straight or composed of one or more curves and angles.

BURMESE

ALL MODERN BURMESE cats can trace their ancestry back to a Siamese hybrid female named Wong Mau, who was taken from Rangoon to the United States in 1930. Wong Mau was almost certainly a cat of the type known as Tonkinese today. At first she was mated with Siamese males; then her offspring were inter-mated, and some back-crossed to Wong Mau herself. From these matings three distinct types of kittens emerged – some identical to Wong Mau, some Siamese, and some much darker than Wong Mau. These cats were the foundation of the Burmese breed, which was officially recognized in 1936 by the Cat Fanciers' Association, and was the first breed of pedigree cats to be developed completely in the United States.

Due to the lack of suitable Burmese cats, out-crosses to Siamese were made from time to time. Because of this, registration was suspended by the CFA from 1947 to 1953, but the breed soon became stabilized, with a strict standard of points ensuring that it maintained its unique physique and character.

Burmese cats were exported to Britain and accepted at shows during the 1950s. Since then, the breed has developed to slightly different standards on opposite sides of the Atlantic.

Character and Care

The Burmese is a highly intelligent, active cat which can be strong-willed, but repays firm, kind handling with affection.

Its short, glossy coat needs very little grooming to keep it in top condition.

BREAKDOWN OF 100 SHOW POINTS

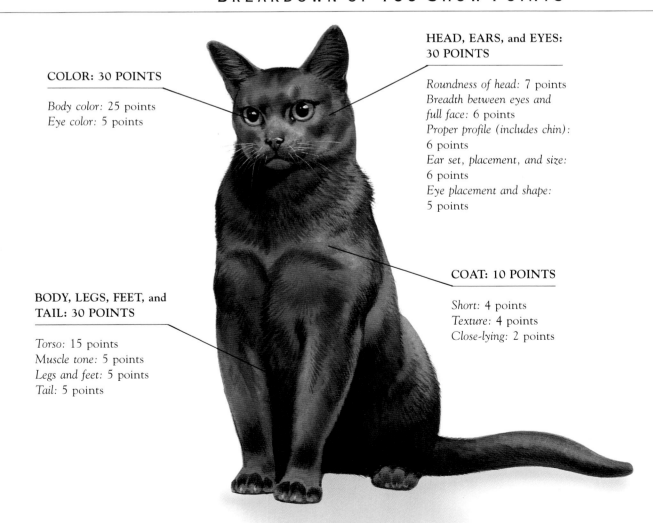

COLOR: 30 POINTS

Body color: 25 points
Eye color: 5 points

HEAD, EARS, and EYES: 30 POINTS

Roundness of head: 7 points
Breadth between eyes and full face: 6 points
Proper profile (includes chin): 6 points
Ear set, placement, and size: 6 points
Eye placement and shape: 5 points

COAT: 10 POINTS

Short: 4 points
Texture: 4 points
Close-lying: 2 points

BODY, LEGS, FEET, and TAIL: 30 POINTS

Torso: 15 points
Muscle tone: 5 points
Legs and feet: 5 points
Tail: 5 points

KEY CHARACTERISTICS

- **CATEGORY** Foreign Shorthair.

- **OVERALL BUILD** Medium size with substantial bone structure and good muscular development. The cat is surprisingly heavy for its size.

- **COAT** Very short and close lying, fine and glossy with a satin-like texture.

- **HEAD** Pleasingly rounded, with no flat planes whether viewed from the front or in profile. The face is full with a broad, short muzzle.

- **NOSE** In profile there is a definite nose break.

- **CHIN** Firm and rounded.

- **EYES** Large, set wide apart, with a rounded aperture.

- **EARS** Medium size, set well apart and tilted slightly forward, giving an alert expression.

- **BODY** Muscular, compact, with strong shoulders and hips.

- **LEGS** Well proportioned.

- **PAWS** Round.

- **TAIL** Medium length and straight.

- **COLORS** *USA* In some US associations, only the sable or brown varieties are classed as Burmese. The blue, champagne or chocolate, platinum or lilac are classed as dilute division Burmese in some associations, and as Malayan in others. *UK* All accepted colors in Burmese and Malayan compete as Burmese.

SOLID VARIETIES

STANDARDS FOR THE ideal Burmese cat differ on each side of the Atlantic Ocean. The American Burmese has a rounder head and a slightly heavier body than its British counterpart. America's Burmese also tend to have better eye color, but as this breed was originally developed in the United States, this is probably to be expected. Eye color is very difficult to assess under the artificial light of a show hall, and judges often take Burmese entrants to a window with natural light if the eye color is at all suspect.

RED The coat is actually a light tangerine color as even as possible, though very slight tabby markings are allowed on the face. Ears are darker than the body. Nose leather and paw pads are pink; eye color is yellow to gold, with deeper shades preferred.

CREAM The coat is pastel cream, with ears slightly darker than the body. Nose leather and paw pads are pink; eye color is yellow to gold, with deeper shapes preferred.

SABLE or BROWN The rich, warm, sable brown coat shades almost imperceptibly to a lighter tone on the underparts, otherwise without any shading, barring, or markings of any kind. Kittens may be ligher in color. The nose leather and paw pads are brown; the eye color ranges from yellow to gold, with the deeper shades preferred.

BLUE The coat is soft silver gray, very slightly darker on the back and tail. There should be a distinct silver sheen on the ears, face, and feet. Nose leather and paw pads are blue-gray; eye color is yellow to gold.

CHOCOLATE or CHAMPAGNE The warm milk chocolate coat should be as even as possible, though the mask and ears may be very slightly deeper in color. Nose leather is chocolate brown; paw pads are cinnamon to chocolate brown; eye color is yellow to gold, with deeper shades preferred.

LILAC or PLATINUM The pale delicate dove-gray coat has a pinkish tone, as even as possible. though the mask and ears may be very slightly deeper in color. Nose leather and paw pads are lavender pink; eye color is yellow to gold, with deeper shades preferred.

RED BURMESE

Tangerine rather than red in color, this variety is bright and very attractive, particularly when it has the desired golden eyes.

SABLE BURMESE
It is interesting to compare this American cat with those raised in Britain, when the slight differences encouraged by the slightly differing show standards become apparent.

BROWN BURMESE
Known as the Sable Burmese in the US where the breed was first developed, this variety has a rich dark brown coat and gold eye color.

CREAM BURMESE
The paler colors in the Burmese often show a very slight Himalayan effect, with darker color on the points – the face, ears, legs, paws, and tail.

LILAC BURMESE
Lilac Burmese appeared in litters when cats which carried both the chocolate and blue color genes were mated together. At first they were considered "poor Blues," but were later accepted as a new variety.

CHOCOLATE BURMESE
With its warm chocolate coat and slightly darker points, this variety is very attractive.

BLUE BURMESE
A simple dilute of the usual brown color, the Blue Burmese was the first additional variety to be recognized and accepted.

TORTOISESHELL VARIETIES

THE ORANGE (RED) gene was first introduced into the Burmese in Britain from three sources, a shorthaired ginger tabby, a red-pointed Siamese, and a calico domestic cat. From these beginnings, a breeding program was set up; and by the mid-1970s, clear-coated red Burmese, cream Burmese, and the invariably female tortoiseshells had been produced in considerable numbers, most of which were of very good Burmese type.

SEAL TORBIE Seal brown, red and/or light red, patched and/or mottled. Nose leather and paw pads are plain or mottled, seal brown and/or pink. The eye color is yellow to gold, with deeper shades preferred.

BLUE-CREAM or BLUE TORBIE Pale tones of blue and cream, patched and/or mottled. Nose leather and paw pads are plain or mottled, pink and/or blue-gray. The eye color is yellow to gold, with deeper shades preferred.

CHOCOLATE TORBIE Milk chocolate, red and/or light red, patched and/or mottled. Nose leather and paw pads are plain or mottled, milk chocolate and/or light red or pink. The eye color is yellow to gold, with the deeper shades preferred.

LILAC-CREAM or LILAC TORBIE Lilac and pale cream, patched and/or mottled. Nose leather and paw pads are plain or mottled, pale pink and/or lavender pink. The eye color is yellow to gold, with deeper shades preferred.

Painted Varieties
The "points" are the mask (face), ears, legs and paws, and the tail. The color of the points is the same as the body color, and show little contrast, but should be as equal in color density as possible.

BLUE TORTIE OR BLUE-CREAM
Tortoiseshells have mixed colors in their coats, the Blue Tortie being blue and cream. There are four colors of Tortie Burmese – brown, blue, chocolate, and lilac.

In all varieties, the body color will be paler on the underparts than on the back and legs.

The eye color is in the yellow/gold range with deeper shades preferred. In non-tabby varieties, allowance is made in kittens and adolescent cats for an overall paler body color, and for faint tabby barring or ghost tabby markings. Tabby markings in adult cats of non-tabby varieties and white hairs are faults.

CHOCOLATE TORTIE BURMESE
After the introduction of the red or orange gene into the breed, a range of tortoiseshell Burmese soon began to appear.

TIFFANIE

TIFFANIE
The Tiffanie is a long-coated cat of Burmese type and is accepted in all colors found in the Burmese and Malayan range.

THIS BREED COMBINES the conformation and coloring of the typical Burmese with an attractive coat of long silky hair. First developed in the United States from long-coated kittens which appeared from time to time in otherwise normal litters of pedigree Burmese, the Tiffanie was later developed as a breed in its own right. The American breeders concentrated on the sable Tiffanie, born a pale *café au lait* color, and gradually developing the long sable coat with maturity. In Britain, long-coated cats of good Burmese conformation came from the Burmilla breeding programs and were refined by back-crosses to Burmese, which resulted in Tiffanie kittens of all colors found in the Burmese and Malayan ranges. At the time of writing (1995), no association officially accepts this breed, and no standard of points is available, including penalties.

Character and Care
Just like its Burmese ancestors, the Tiffanie is playful and affectionate with an extrovert nature, making it a good pet.

The long coat is quite easy to care for with regular grooming.

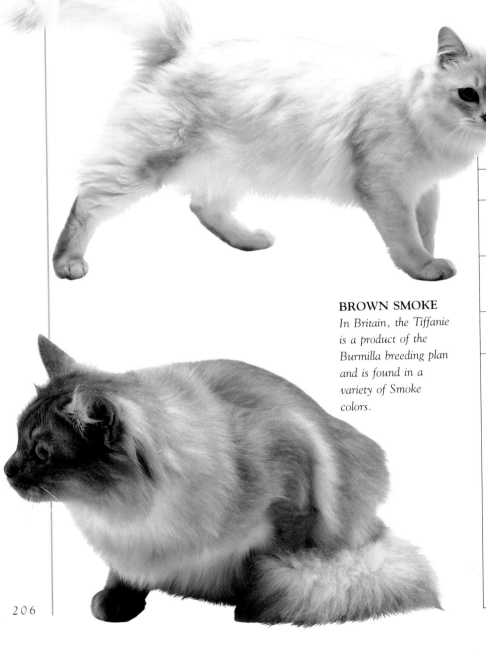

BROWN SMOKE
In Britain, the Tiffanie is a product of the Burmilla breeding plan and is found in a variety of Smoke colors.

KEY CHARACTERISTICS

- **CATEGORY** Semi-longhair.

- **OVERALL BUILD** Medium size with substantial bone; it is surprisingly heavy for its size.

- **COAT** Of medium length, fine and silky, longer at the ruff (frill) and with a flowing plume-like tail.

- **COLORS** USA Sable UK All colors found in the Burmese and Malayan range.

- **OTHER FEATURES** Head is pleasingly rounded with no flat planes; face is full with a broad, short muzzle; nose is short with a break in profile. Chin is strong; eyes large, set wide apart, the top line showing a straight, Oriental slant toward the nose, the lower line rounded. Ears are medium size, broad based with rounded tips, set wide apart with a slight forward tilt. Body is medium length, hard, compact and muscular, with a strong, rounded chest and straight back. Legs are slender, and in proportion to the body; paws small and oval; tail medium length, not thick at the base and tapering only slightly to a rounded tip, well covered with flowing silky hair.

SINGAPURA

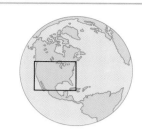

AN AMERICAN CAT breeder, Tommy Meadows, developed the Singapura from cats she discovered in Singapore. She decided to import some into the United States, and drew up a careful programme for the development of the breed. Her work has been rewarded by the production of an attractive, viable feline breed with considerable esthetic appeal. The Singapura has a ticked coat, similar to that of the Abyssinian, and is of moderate Foreign Shorthair bone structure and conformation.

Character and Care

The Singapura is a happy, friendly cat with a playful nature.

The short, fine coat is extremely easy to keep in good condition with very little grooming. A light combing removes dead hairs, and occasional brushing tones the skin. Hand grooming or stroking with a silk scarf imparts a healthy looking sheen to the coat.

KEY CHARACTERISTICS

- **CATEGORY** Foreign Shorthair.

- **OVERALL BUILD** Small to medium in size, moderately stocky and muscular.

- **COAT** Very short and fine; each hair should have at least two bands of dark ticking separated by light bands of colour. Each individual hair is light next to the skin and dark at the tip.

- **COLORS** Sepia Agouti. The ground color is warm ivory; the ticking is dark brown. The muzzle, chin, chest and stomach are the color of unbleached muslin; the ears and bridge of the nose are salmon toned. The nose leather is pale to dark salmon pink, outlined with dark brown; the paw pads are rosy brown; the eye rims are dark brown; the eye color is hazel, green or yellow.

- **OTHER FEATURES** Head is rounded, with a definite whisker break; nose short and blunt; chin well developed; eyes large and almond shaped; ears large and slightly pointed, set fairly wide apart, giving an alert expression. Body is stocky and muscular; legs are heavy; paws small and oval; tail of medium length with a blunt tip.

BROWN TICKED SINGAPURA
With its short, fine, ticked coat and happy, friendly nature, this rare breed makes a perfect pet.

TONKINESE

A HYBRID OF Burmese and Siamese cats, the Tonkinese has physical features of both these breeds. A mating between a Burmese and a Siamese gives all Tonkinese kittens, whereas the mating of two Tonkinese cats produces, on average, two Tonkinese kittens to one Burmese and one Siamese.

Tonkinese cats have dark points which merge gradually into the body color, which is intermediate between the typical pale Siamese and the dark Burmese coloring. Tonkinese eye color is blue-green or turquoise, never Siamese blue or Burmese gold.

Character and Care

The Tonkinese is a friendly and affectionate cat, with a strong sense of mischief. Extrovert and intelligent, it is generally good with other cats, as well as with dogs and children. It is less vocal than the Siamese.

The coat is very easy to keep in good condition with very little grooming. Regular combing to remove dead hair, and buffing with a silk scarf or grooming mitten imparts a healthy sheen.

BREAKDOWN OF 100 SHOW POINTS

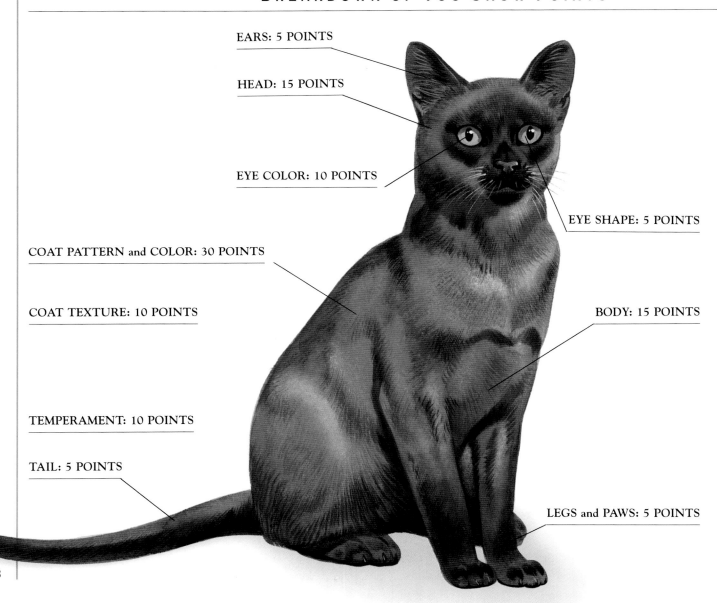

EARS: 5 POINTS

HEAD: 15 POINTS

EYE COLOR: 10 POINTS

EYE SHAPE: 5 POINTS

COAT PATTERN and COLOR: 30 POINTS

COAT TEXTURE: 10 POINTS

BODY: 15 POINTS

TEMPERAMENT: 10 POINTS

TAIL: 5 POINTS

LEGS and PAWS: 5 POINTS

KEY CHARACTERISTICS

- **CATEGORY** Foreign Shorthair.

- **OVERALL BUILD** Medium size, muscular and surprisingly heavy for its size.

- **COAT** Short, fine and close-lying with a soft, fur-like texture.

- **HEAD** Modified wedge shape, longer than it is wide, with high, gently planed cheekbones and strong contours to the brow, cheek and profile. In profile there should be a slight stop at eye level; a definite break is undesirable. The muzzle is blunt, with a definite whisker break.

- **NOSE** No standards available.

- **CHIN** Firm but not massive.

- **EYES** Almond shaped, slanted along cheekbone toward outer edge of ear.

- **EARS** Medium size with oval tips, set wide apart and tilted slightly forward. The hair on the ears is very short.

- **BODY** Medium length, muscular but not coarse, with tight abdomen.

- **LEGS** Slim.

- **PAWS** More oval than round.

- **TAIL** Medium to long, tapering.

- **COLORS** Natural mink, blue, champagne mink, platinum mink, red, cream, natural mink torbie, blue torbie, champagne mink torbie, platinum mink torbie.

PENALTIES

Tonkinese cats are penalized in the show ring for having a palpable tail fault.

DISQUALIFICATION FEATURES
- yellow eyes
- a white locket or button
- a visible kink in the tail

MINK VARIETIES

THE TONKINESE IS bred from Burmese and Siamese, and as would be expected, is intermediate to those breeds in both conformation and coloring. As a pet it suits those people who find the show-type Siamese to be too extreme, but do not favour the typical chunkiness and almost uniform coloration of the Burmese. Indeed, a typical Tonkinese is very similar to the "old-fashioned" type of Siamese cat that many people today desire as pets.

NATURAL MINK A medium-brown coat shades to a lighter tone on the underparts. The points and nose leather are dark brown; the paw pads are medium to dark brown; the eye color is blue-green.

BLUE A soft gray-blue color shades to a lighter tone on the underparts. The points are slate blue (distinctly darker than the body color). Nose leather and paw pads are blue-gray; eye color is blue-green.

CHAMPAGNE MINK The buff-cream body has medium brown points. Nose leather is cinnamon-brown; paw pads are cinnamon-pink to cinnamon-brown; eye color is blue-green.

RED The golden cream coat has apricot underparts. The points are light to medium ruddy brown; the nose leather and paw pads are caramel-pink; the eye color is blue-green.

PLATINUM MINK The pale silvery gray coat has warm overtones (not white or cream). The points are pewter gray – distinctly darker than the body color; nose leather is lavender pink to lavender gray; paw pads are lavender pink; eye color is blue-green.

Pointed Varieties

The "points" are the mask (face) ears, legs and paws, and the tail. The points are densely marked, but gradually merge into the body color. The color of the points is the same as the body color, but denser and darker.

The body color in the adult cat should be rich and even, and shade almost imperceptibly into a slightly lighter color on the underparts. There is a distinct contrast between the points and body color whatever the color variety. The eye color is blue-green (aquamarine), with depth, clarity and brilliance.

N.B. Allowance is made for lighter body color in kittens and adolescent cats, and for slight barring in the coat; colors darken with maturity – full coloration may take up to 16 months to develop, particularly in the dilute color varieties.

BROWN TONKINESE

The darkest color variety with a medium brown coat. As in other Tonkinese varieties, the eye color is blue–green.

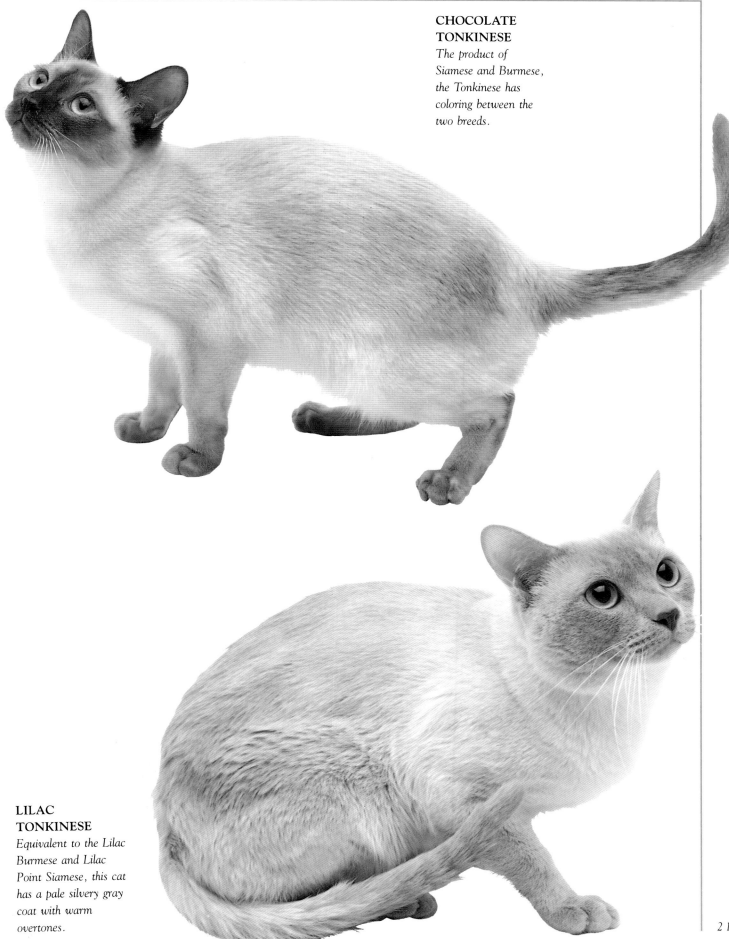

**CHOCOLATE
TONKINESE**
*The product of
Siamese and Burmese,
the Tonkinese has
coloring between the
two breeds.*

**LILAC
TONKINESE**
*Equivalent to the Lilac
Burmese and Lilac
Point Siamese, this cat
has a pale silvery gray
coat with warm
overtones.*

211

NEW VARIETIES

MEMBERS OF THE Cat Association of Britain, working with new colors in Burmese and Siamese cats, decided to introduce these into the Tonkinese, and the breeding programs were provisionally accepted by CA prior to its becoming the British member of FIFe in 1990. The Cat Association of Britain therefore offers special awards for Tonkinese in the following color varieties: seal, blue, chocolate, cinnamon, lilac, fawn, caramel, beige, red, cream, apricot, indigo, and all these colors as tortoiseshell, tabby, and torbie.

CREAM TONKINESE
This cat should be a rich warm cream with slightly darker points, except for the legs which may be paler than in other colors.

RED TONKINESE
Red and Cream Tonkinese are often quite similar and can be difficult to tell apart as kittens.

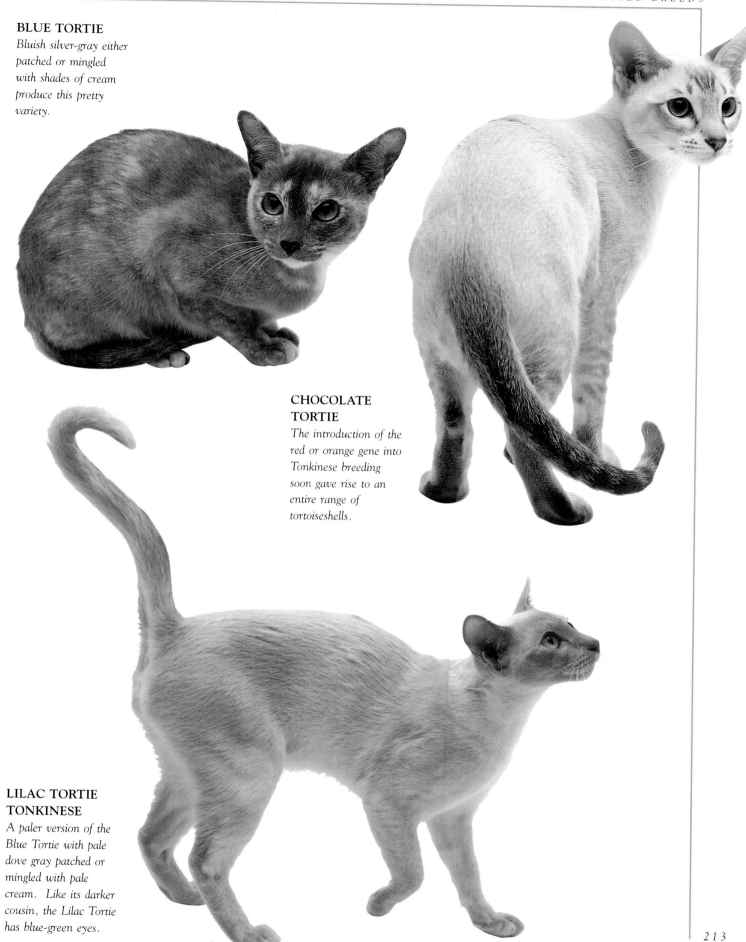

BLUE TORTIE

Bluish silver-gray either patched or mingled with shades of cream produce this pretty variety.

CHOCOLATE TORTIE

The introduction of the red or orange gene into Tonkinese breeding soon gave rise to an entire range of tortoiseshells.

LILAC TORTIE TONKINESE

A paler version of the Blue Tortie with pale dove gray patched or mingled with pale cream. Like its darker cousin, the Lilac Tortie has blue-green eyes.

BOMBAY

BECAUSE OF ITS looks, the Bombay cat has been referred to as the "patent-leather kid with new-penny eyes," an apt description for this shining jet-black feline. Developed from outstanding specimens of black American Shorthair and sable Burmese, the desired type was quickly achieved, and Bombays were found to breed true. Full recognition and championship status was granted by the CFA in 1976.

Although the cat looks like a black American-style Burmese, the early pioneers of the breed thought it looked like a miniature version of the Indian (Asian) black panther and so, after much deliberation, chose Bombay as the breed name.

Character and Care

The Bombay has a very even temperament. It is generally strong and healthy, affectionate and playful, making it a good pet.

The coat is easy to maintain with a balanced diet and minimal grooming. Buffing with a silk scarf or velvet grooming mitt enhances the typical patent-leather gloss.

BREAKDOWN OF 100 SHOW POINTS

HEAD and EARS: 25 POINTS

Roundness of head: 7 points
Full face and proper profile: 7 points
Ears: 7 points
Chin: 4 points

EYES: 5 POINTS

Placement and shape: 5 points

COAT: 20 POINTS

Shortness: 10 points
Texture: 5 points
Close lying: 5 points

BODY: 20 POINTS

Body: 15 points
Tail: 5 points

COLOR: 30 POINTS

Body color: 20 points
Eye color: 10 points

PENALTIES

Bombay cats are penalized in the show ring for excessive cobbiness or ranginess.

DISQUALIFICATION FEATURES
- incorrect color of nose leather, paw pads, or eyes
- incorrect dentition
- kinked or abnormal tail
- a white locket or spots
- an extreme nose break interfering with normal breathing or tear production

BOMBAY

The true Bombay from the United States was produced from Sable Burmese and American Shorthairs, and is a unique, shiny jet black cat with large golden eyes.

BOMBAY (ASIAN BLACK)

In Britain, the black Asian, a product of Burmese and Shorthair, is known as the Bombay.

KEY CHARACTERISTICS

- **CATEGORY** Foreign Shorthair.

- **OVERALL BUILD** Medium size, muscular, surprisingly heavy for size.

- **COAT** Fine and short with satin-like texture, close lying and with a sheen like patent leather.

- **COLOR** Black only. Coat-jet black to the roots with a patent-leather sheen. Nose leather and paw pads, black. Eye color, gold to copper; deeper shades preferred.

- **OTHER FEATURES** Pleasingly round head with no sharp angles, full face with good width between the eyes, tapering to a short, strong muzzle. In profile there is a visible nose break. Medium sized ears with slightly rounded tips set wide apart and tilting slightly forward giving an alert expression. Muscular, medium sized body with legs in proportion, round paws, and a straight, medium length tail.

BURMILLA

AN ACCIDENTAL MATING between a lilac Burmese female and a Chinchilla Silver male in 1981 resulted in the birth of four black-shaded silver female kittens. All were of foreign conformation, and had short dense coats. They looked so spectacular and caused so much interest that similar matings were carried out. In 1983, the Cat Association of Britain accepted breeding programs and a standard of points for the breed to be known as Burmilla, to be developed as a shorthaired silver cat of medium foreign type, showing a striking con-trast between the pure silver undercoat and the shaded or tipped markings. FIFe granted inter-national breed status to the Burmilla in 1994.

This elegant cat is of medium foreign type with a muscular body, long sturdy legs, and a moderately thick, long tail. The head is a medium wedge, with large ears, a short nose, and large expressive eyes. Its most impressive feature, however, is the sparkling shaded or tipped ("shell") coat. The ground color is pure silver white, with shading or tipping in any of the recognized solid or tortoiseshell colors,

BREAKDOWN OF 100 SHOW POINTS

NB Annotated points are those set in Europe.

HEAD: 50 POINTS

Shape, nose and chin:
20 points
Ear placement and shape:
10 points
Eye placement, shape and colour: 20 points

BODY: 25 POINTS

Shape and structure; legs and paws; tail shape and length

COAT: 20 POINTS

Length and texture: 10 points
Evenness of shading/tipping:
10 points

CONDITION: 5 POINTS

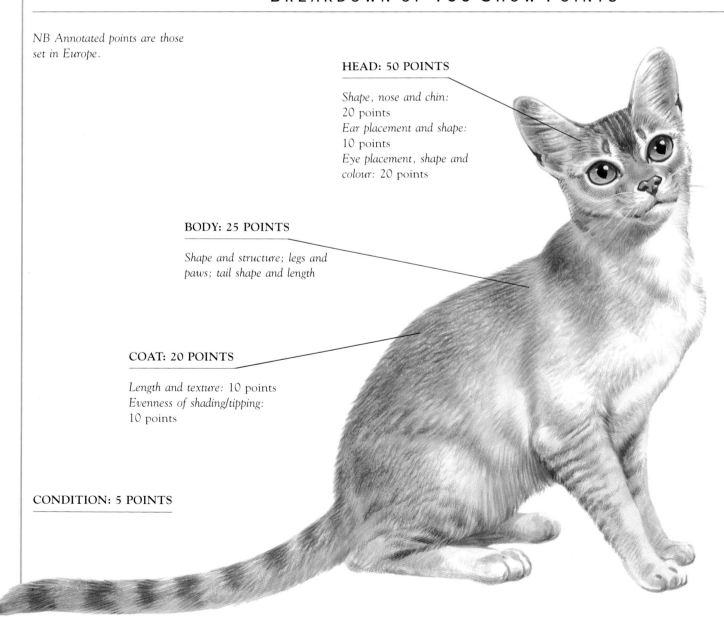

which must be uniformly distributed. The eyelids, lips, and nose leather are rimmed with the basic color, and delicate tracings of tabby markings are present on the points, which are more clearly defined on the shaded Burmilla than on the tipped varieties.

Character and Care

The Burmilla is easy-going and relaxed, has a playful nature, and is very affectionate.

The dense coat is best groomed with a rubber brush to loosen dead hairs before being given a thorough combing.

PENALTIES

The Burmilla is penalized for having a weak chin; incorrect eye color in adults; a cobby or oriental type body in adults; and a coat that is too long or shaggy.

KEY CHARACTERISTICS

- **CATEGORY** Foreign Shorthair.

- **OVERALL BUILD** Medium size and build.

- **COAT** Short and dense with a silky texture; with enough undercoat to give a slight lift to the coat.

- **HEAD** Gently rounded at the top with medium width between the ears; wide at eye level and tapering to a short, blunt wedge.

- **NOSE** The profile shows a gentle nose break.

- **CHIN** Firm, level with the tip of the nose.

- **EYES** Large, set well apart and slightly oblique, luminous and expressive.

- **EARS** Medium to large, broad-based and with rounded tips. Set with a slightly forward tilt.

- **BODY** Medium length, with a straight back and rounded chest.

- **LEGS** Slender, with strong bone; the hind legs are slightly longer than forelegs.

- **PAWS** Neat and oval.

- **TAIL** Medium to long, fairly thick at the base and tapering slightly to a rounded tip.

- **COLORS** Shaded or tipped in the following colors: black, blue, brown, chocolate, lilac, red, cream, red tortoiseshell, blue tortoiseshell, brown tortoiseshell, chocolate tortoiseshell, lilac tortoiseshell.

BURMILLA VARIETIES

BLACK TIPPED
The pure silver white coat of the Burmilla is lightly tipped with black in this variety.

ELEGANT CATS OF medium foreign conformation, the Burmilla male is larger and more stocky than the dainty female. Any tendency to the fine bone of the Siamese, or the cobby type of the Shorthair, is regarded as a fault.

BLACK SHADED or TIPPED The coat is pure silver white, shaded or tipped with black. The nose leather is brick red; the paw pads and soles are black; the eye color is green.

BLUE SHADED or TIPPED The coat is pure silver white, shaded or tipped with blue-gray. The nose leather is brick red; the paw pads and soles are blue-gray; the eye color is green.

BROWN SHADED or TIPPED The coat is pure silver white, shaded or tipped with dark brown. The nose leather is brick red; the paw pads and soles are dark brown; the eye color is green.

CHOCOLATE SHADED or TIPPED The coat is pure silver white, shaded or tipped with milk chocolate. The nose leather is brick red; the paw pads are chocolate tinged with pink; the soles are chocolate; the eye color is green.

CHOCOLATE TIPPED BURMILLA
In the Chocolate Tipped, the pure silver undercoat is tipped with milk chocolate at the ends of each hair.

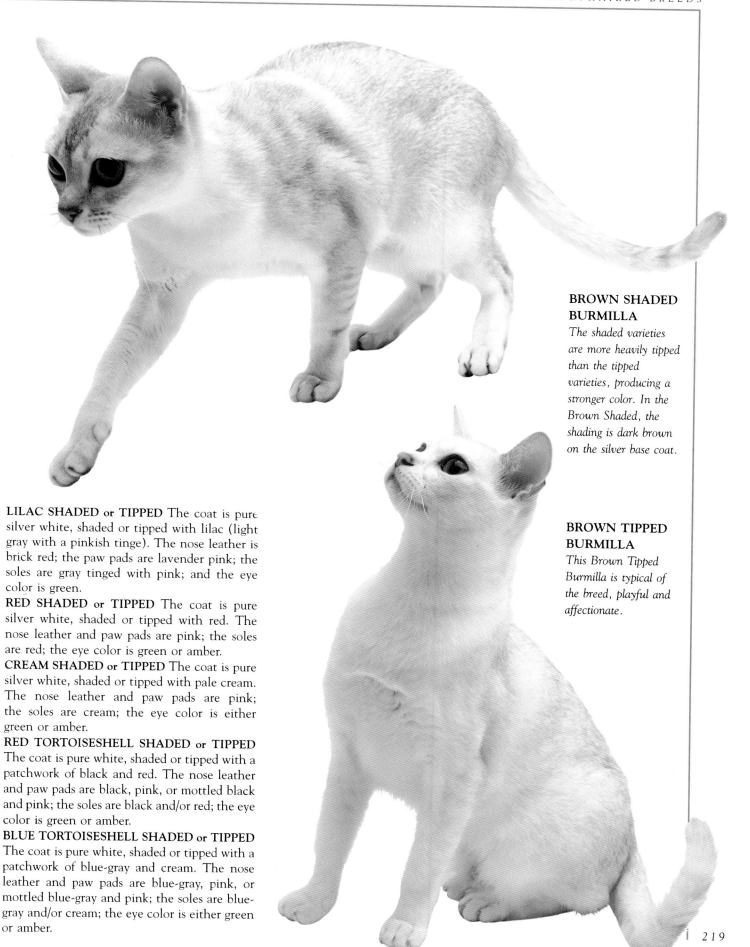

BROWN SHADED BURMILLA
The shaded varieties are more heavily tipped than the tipped varieties, producing a stronger color. In the Brown Shaded, the shading is dark brown on the silver base coat.

BROWN TIPPED BURMILLA
This Brown Tipped Burmilla is typical of the breed, playful and affectionate.

LILAC SHADED or TIPPED The coat is pure silver white, shaded or tipped with lilac (light gray with a pinkish tinge). The nose leather is brick red; the paw pads are lavender pink; the soles are gray tinged with pink; and the eye color is green.

RED SHADED or TIPPED The coat is pure silver white, shaded or tipped with red. The nose leather and paw pads are pink; the soles are red; the eye color is green or amber.

CREAM SHADED or TIPPED The coat is pure silver white, shaded or tipped with pale cream. The nose leather and paw pads are pink; the soles are cream; the eye color is either green or amber.

RED TORTOISESHELL SHADED or TIPPED The coat is pure white, shaded or tipped with a patchwork of black and red. The nose leather and paw pads are black, pink, or mottled black and pink; the soles are black and/or red; the eye color is green or amber.

BLUE TORTOISESHELL SHADED or TIPPED The coat is pure white, shaded or tipped with a patchwork of blue-gray and cream. The nose leather and paw pads are blue-gray, pink, or mottled blue-gray and pink; the soles are blue-gray and/or cream; the eye color is either green or amber.

219

BLUE SHADED BURMILLA

A silver white coat shaded with blue-gray, set off by a brick red nose and large, luminous green eyes.

BROWN TORTOISESHELL SHADED or TIPPED The coat is pure white, shaded or tipped with a patchwork of dark brown and red or light red. The nose leather and paw pads are dark brown, pink, or mottled dark brown and pink; the soles are dark brown and/or red; the eye color is green or amber.

CHOCOLATE TORTOISESHELL SHADED or TIPPED The coat is pure white, shaded or tipped with a patchwork of milk chocolate and light red. The nose leather and paw pads are chocolate, pink, or mottled chocolate and pink; the soles are chocolate and/or light red; the eye color is green or amber.

LILAC TORTOISESHELL SHADED or TIPPED The coat is pure white, shaded or tipped with a patchwork of lilac (light gray with a pinkish tinge) and cream. The nose leather and paw pads are lavender pink, pink, or mottled lavender pink and pink; the soles are gray tinged with pink; the eye color is either green or amber.

Note In all colors, the Tipped Burmilla is lighter overall than the Shaded Burmilla.

BLACK SHADED BURMILLA

As in all Burmilla cats, the paw pads and soles (the area from the paw to the hock) match the color of the shading or tipping on the silver coat.

ASIAN

THE BURMILLA IS just one variety in a larger family of cats known as the Asian Group. All of the variants are of Burmese type and basic conformation, but do not have the Burmese coat color or slight restriction of color to the "points" area as found in the usual Burmese cat.

TICKED TABBY
Each hair of the coat is ticked with two or three bands of color which produces the effect commonly seen in a wild rabbit. All ticked tabby Asian cats should have clear tabby bars marking the legs and tail.

Rather the cats of the Asian Group bear the same relationship to Burmese as the Orientals do to Siamese. Within the Asian Group are found a range of cats with unusual and very attractive coats for color pattern and texture. It includes the Burmilla, Asian Smoke, Asian Tabby, Bombay, and Tiffanie. The Burmilla is by far the most successful in terms of numbers and popularity, and, in fact, most of the other Asians have arisen as off-shoots of the carefully controlled programs designed to breed the Burmilla in a wide variety of colors, and with the creation of a broad and viable base from which to select second and third generation crosses.

ASIAN EYES
All varieties of Asian cats have characteristically large, full, and expressive eyes which are set well apart. They are slightly Oriental in setting, but are neither Oriental nor round in shape.

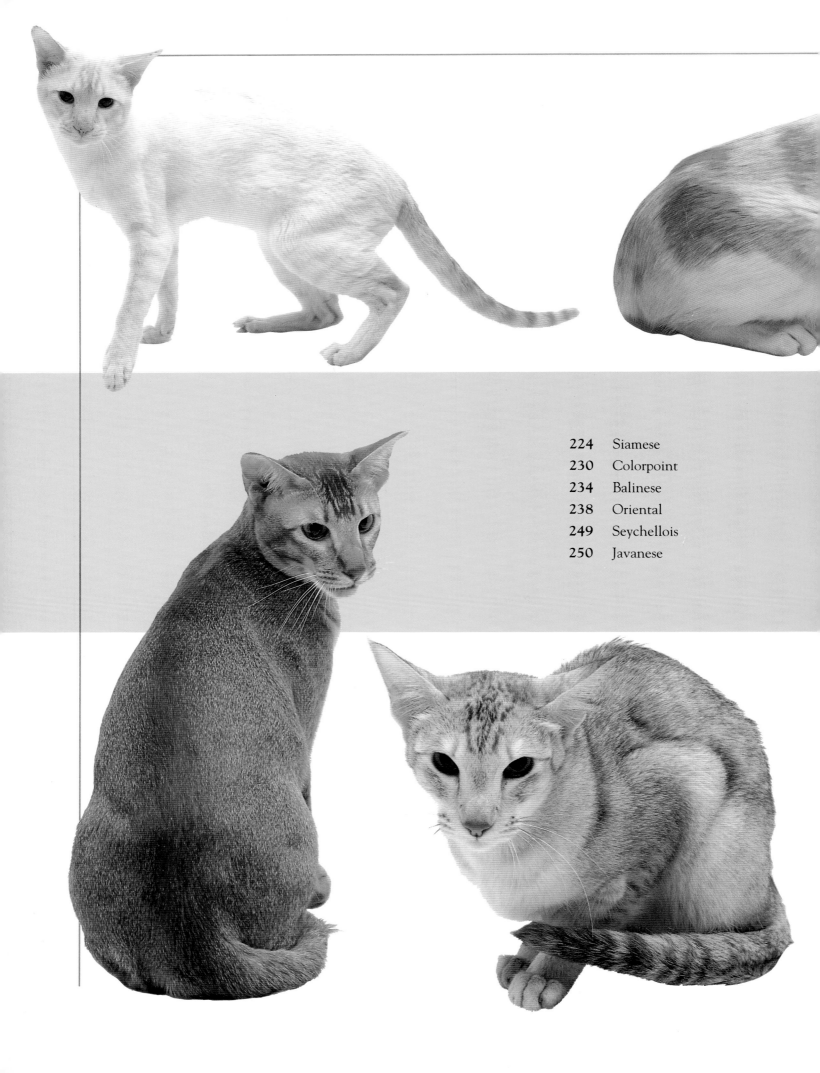

224   Siamese
230   Colorpoint
234   Balinese
238   Oriental
249   Seychellois
250   Javanese

ORIENTAL BREEDS

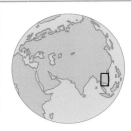

SIAMESE

PROBABLY THE BEST KNOWN of all pedigree breeds, the Siamese cat of today is quite different from that seen in the early 1900s, though it still retains its points, caused by the Himalayan factor, the gene which restricts the true coloring to the animal's face, ears, legs, paws, and tail.

Seal-pointed cats were presented by the Royal Court of Siam to British and American diplomats toward the end of the nineteenth century, and the breed gained public interest which has continued to grow.

Although the original Royal Cats of Siam were seal-pointed, some had lighter brown points and were eventually recognized as being a separate color variety which was called Chocolate Point. A naturally occurring dilute factor also became apparent when the almost black coloration of the seal point gave rise to

cats with slate-gray extremities. These were eventually accepted as the color variety Blue Point.

With increasing knowledge of feline color genetics, breeders of Siamese cats realized that they could increase the range of color varieties by first making judicious outcrosses, then back-breeding the offspring to Siamese of excellent type. The red series of points colors was added by outcrossing to red, red tabby, and tortoise-shell cats, and a range of colors in tabby-pointed cats was developed from out-crosses with tabbies.

Britain's GCCF and the CA recognize all short-coated pointed cats of Oriental type as Siamese, as do some foreign associations, in particular FIFe. Others such as America's CFA accept only the four original, naturally occur-ring colors as Siamese, and register the red

BREAKDOWN OF 100 SHOW POINTS

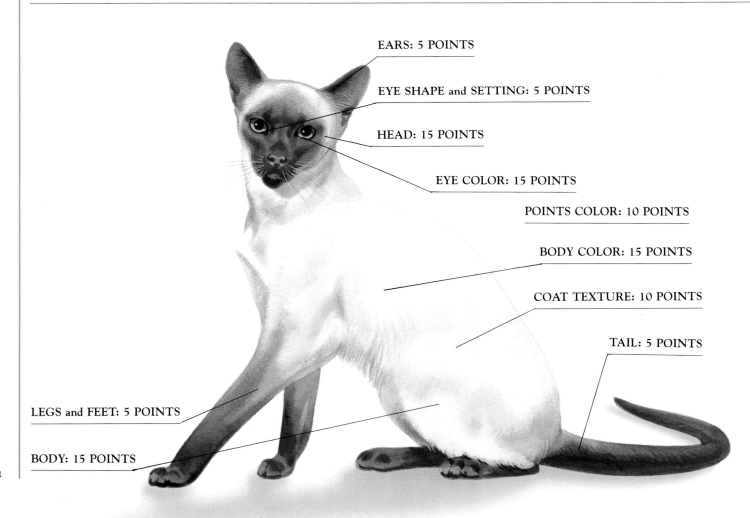

EARS: 5 POINTS

EYE SHAPE and SETTING: 5 POINTS

HEAD: 15 POINTS

EYE COLOR: 15 POINTS

POINTS COLOR: 10 POINTS

BODY COLOR: 15 POINTS

COAT TEXTURE: 10 POINTS

TAIL: 5 POINTS

LEGS and FEET: 5 POINTS

BODY: 15 POINTS

series and the tabby (or lynx point) series as Colorpoint Shorthairs.

Character and Care

The typical Siamese cat has an extrovert personality. It is very affectionate with people and pets that it likes, is lively and intelligent, and can be very vocal. Siamese cats do not like being left alone for long periods, and do better as pets when kept in pairs or small groups. They are naturally fastidiously clean and make perfect house pets.

The short fine coat is kept in good condition by stroking with clean hands or buffing with a silk scarf. The large ears need regular cleaning, and Siamese should be provided with a scratching post and lots of toys.

PENALTIES

The Siamese is penalized for having belly spots or spots on the flanks; white or lighter colored hairs, or ticked hairs in the points; bars and stripes in the points, except in Tabby-pointed varieties; insufficient contrast in color between the body color and the points; white patches or white toes; any eye color other than blue; a kinked tail; and malocclusion resulting in either an undershot or overshot jaw.

KEY CHARACTERISTICS

- **CATEGORY** Foreign Shorthair.

- **OVERALL BUILD** Medium size, long and svelte.

- **COAT** Very short and fine, glossy, silky and close-lying.

- **HEAD** Medium sized in proportion to the body; wedge-shaped with straight lines, the wedge starting at the nose and gradually increasing in width in straight lines on each side to the ears. No whisker break.

- **NOSE** Long and straight without any break.

- **CHIN** Medium size, the tip forming a vertical line with the tip of the nose.

- **EYES** Medium size and almond shaped, set slightly slanting toward the nose in harmony with the lines of the wedge.

- **EARS** Large and pointed, wide at the base, placed to continue the line of the wedge.

- **BODY** Long and svelte, well muscled but still dainty and elegant. The shoulders should not be wider than the hips.

- **LEGS** Long and fine, in proportion to the body.

- **PAWS** Small and oval.

- **TAIL** Very long, thin at the base and tapering to a fine point.

- **COLORS** Seal point, blue point, chocolate point, lilac point, red point, cream point, seal torbie point, blue torbie point, chocolate torbie point, lilac torbie point, seal tabby point, blue tabby point, chocolate tabby point, lilac tabby point, red tabby point, cream tabby point, seal torbie tabby point, blue torbie tabby point, chocolate torbie tabby point, lilac torbie tabby point (lilac (frost) torbie point).

SIAMESE VARIETIES

THE BODY MUST be even in color with subtle shading when allowed in the color variety. The points – mask, ears, legs, feet, and tail – must be all of the same shade and clearly defined. The mask should cover the entire face including the whisker pads and be connected to the ears by traced markings. There should be no ticking or white hairs in the points. The eye color of all the following varieties is deep, vivid blue.

SEAL POINT The body color is beige to cream or pale fawn; the points color dark seal brown. The nose leather and paw pads are dark seal brown; the eye color is deep, vivid blue.

RED POINT The body color is creamy white; the points color bright, warm orange. Nose leather pink; paw pads pink and/or red.

BLUE POINT The body color is bluish-white of a glacial tone; the points color blue-gray. The nose leather and paw pads are blue-gray.

CHOCOLATE POINT The body color is ivory;

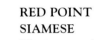

RED POINT SIAMESE

This is a cat of extreme show type with its large flared ears following the lines of the wedge-shaped head. The body is creamy white, and the matching points are a warm orange.

SEAL POINT SIAMESE

The original color, once known as the Royal Cat of Siam. This cat has a pale fawn body and dark seal-brown points, which may appear to be black.

226

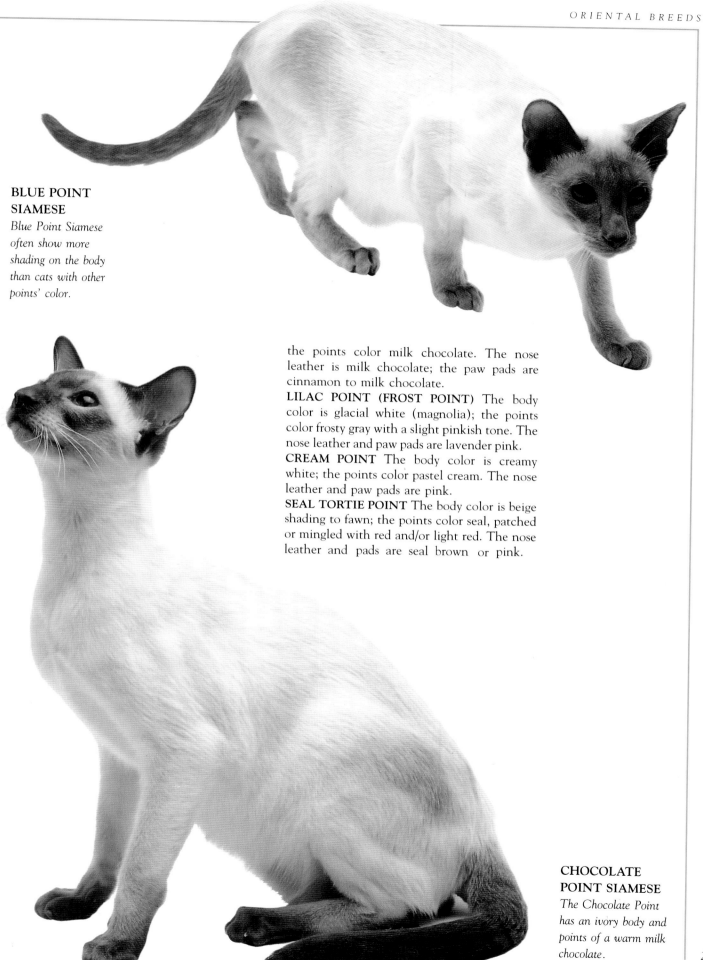

BLUE POINT SIAMESE
Blue Point Siamese often show more shading on the body than cats with other points' color.

the points color milk chocolate. The nose leather is milk chocolate; the paw pads are cinnamon to milk chocolate.

LILAC POINT (FROST POINT) The body color is glacial white (magnolia); the points color frosty gray with a slight pinkish tone. The nose leather and paw pads are lavender pink.

CREAM POINT The body color is creamy white; the points color pastel cream. The nose leather and paw pads are pink.

SEAL TORTIE POINT The body color is beige shading to fawn; the points color seal, patched or mingled with red and/or light red. The nose leather and pads are seal brown or pink.

CHOCOLATE POINT SIAMESE
The Chocolate Point has an ivory body and points of a warm milk chocolate.

LILAC POINT SIAMESE

This is the palest of the Siamese, with a magnolia-colored coat and points of a pink-toned frosty gray. It is known as the Frost Point in some cat associations.

BLUE TORTIE POINT The body color is bluish-white; the points color blue-gray patched or mingled with pastel cream. The nose leather and paw pads are blue-gray and/or pink.

CHOCOLATE TORTIE POINT The body color is ivory; the points color milk chocolate patched or mingled with red and/or light red. The nose leather is milk chocolate and/or pink; paw pads are cinnamon to milk chocolate and/or pink.

FROST TORTIE POINT The body color is glacial white (magnolia); the points color frosty gray with a pinkish tone patched or mingled with pale cream. Nose leather and paw pads lavender pink and/or pale pink.

SEAL TABBY POINT The body color is beige; the points color dark seal tabby; the rims around the eyes and nose are seal brown. The nose leather is brick red, pink or seal brown; the paw pads are seal brown.

BLUE TABBY POINT The body color is bluish white; the points color blue-gray tabby; the rims around the eyes and nose are blue-gray. The nose leather is old rose or blue-gray; the paw pads are blue-gray.

CHOCOLATE TABBY POINT The body color is ivory; the points color milk chocolate tabby; the rims around the eyes and nose are milk chocolate. The nose leather is light red, pink, or milk chocolate; the paw pads are cinnamon to milk chocolate.

FROST TABBY POINT The body color is glacial white (magnolia); the points color lilac tabby – frosty gray with slightly pinkish-toned tabby markings – the rims around the eyes and nose are lavender pink. The nose leather is lavender pink or pink; the paw pads are lavender pink.

RED TABBY POINT The body color is off-

CREAM POINT SIAMESE

The creamy white body of this variety is accented by points of a delicate pastel cream.

white with a slight red tinge; the points color warm orange tabby; the rims around the eyes and nose are dark pink. The nose leather is brick red or pink; the paw pads are pink.

CREAM TABBY POINT The body color is creamy white; the points color cream tabby with a cold tone; the rims around the eyes and nose are dark pink. The nose leather and paw pads are pink.

SEAL TORBIE POINT The body color is beige; the points color has seal tabby markings patched or mingled with red or light red torbie markings. The nose rims are seal; the nose leather and paw pads are seal, brick red, or pink, or seal mottled with brick red and/or pink.

BLUE TORBIE POINT The body color is bluish white; the points color has blue tabby markings, patched or mingled with cream torbie markings. The nose rims are blue-gray; the nose leather is blue-gray, old rose, or pink, or blue-gray mottled with old rose and/or pink; the paw pads are blue-gray and/or pink.

CHOCOLATE TORBIE POINT The body color is ivory; the points color has milk chocolate tabby markings, patched or mingled with red or light red torbie markings. The nose rims are chocolate; the nose leather milk chocolate, pale red, or pink, or milk chocolate mottled with pale red or pink; the paw pads are cinnamon to milk chocolate and/or pink.

FROST TORBIE POINT The body color is glacial white (magnolia); the points color has lilac tabby – frosty gray with slightly pinkish toned tabby markings – patched or mingled with pale cream torbie markings. The nose rims are lavender pink; the nose leather and paw pads are lavender pink, pale pink, or lavender pink mottled with pale pink.

BLUE TABBY POINT SIAMESE
Originally called Lynx Points, Tabby Point Siamese were produced by breeders entranced by a litter of kittens which resulted from a mismating.

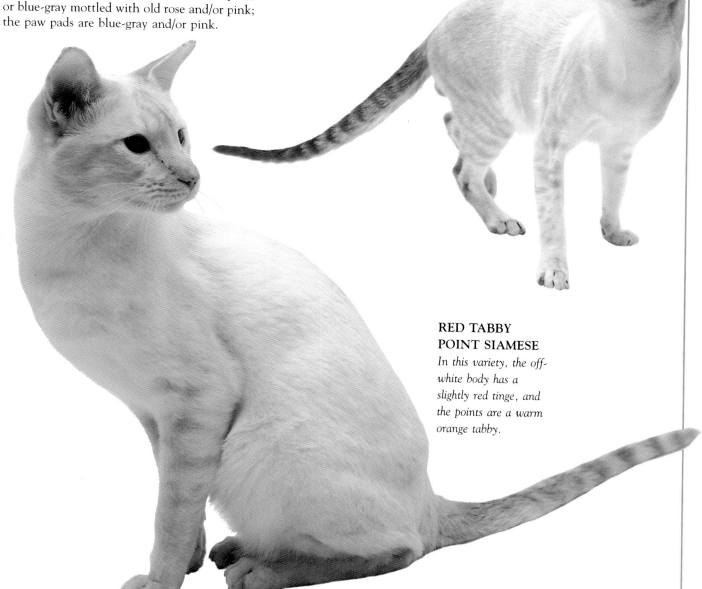

RED TABBY POINT SIAMESE
In this variety, the off-white body has a slightly red tinge, and the points are a warm orange tabby.

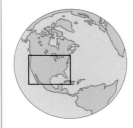

COLORPOINT SHORTHAIR

WHEN SIAMESE CATS were mated with cats of other varieties, such as the tabby shorthair, in order to achieve new colors and patterns, the Colorpoint Shorthair was the result. As the gene which restricts the color to the points in Siamese is recessive, the resulting kittens were colored all over.

When these cross-bred cats were mated back to high-quality Siamese, however, Siamese patterned offspring were produced, and successive back-crossing to Siamese upgraded the "new" Siamese to conform to the rigorous standards set by various associations. In Britain, the new colors were gradually accepted as additions to the Siamese varieties, but in the United States, some associations decided to accept such cats as Colorpoint Shorthairs.

Character and Care

Siamese in everything but name, the Colorpoint Shorthair is a delightfully intelligent, agile, and affectionate pet.

It is very easy to maintain in top condition by feeding a good diet and needs minimal grooming, just combing through to remove any dead hair and buffing the fine coat either with the hands or a silk scarf.

BREAKDOWN OF 100 SHOW POINTS

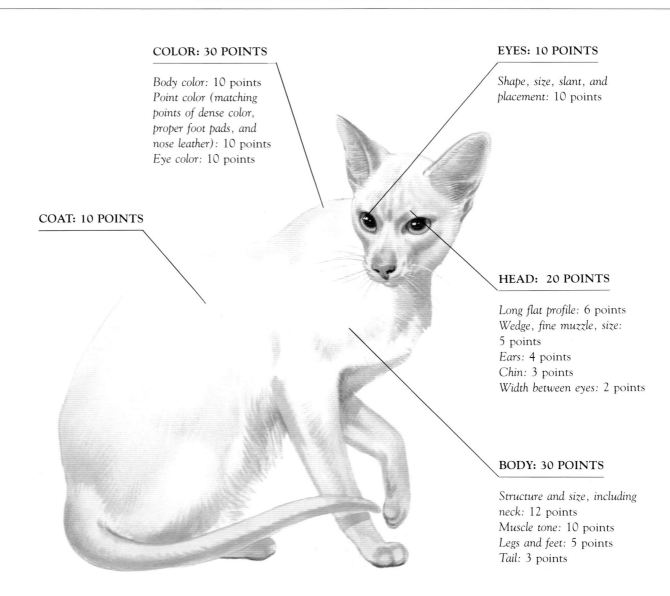

COLOR: 30 POINTS

Body color: 10 points
Point color (matching points of dense color, proper foot pads, and nose leather): 10 points
Eye color: 10 points

COAT: 10 POINTS

EYES: 10 POINTS

Shape, size, slant, and placement: 10 points

HEAD: 20 POINTS

Long flat profile: 6 points
Wedge, fine muzzle, size: 5 points
Ears: 4 points
Chin: 3 points
Width between eyes: 2 points

BODY: 30 POINTS

Structure and size, including neck: 12 points
Muscle tone: 10 points
Legs and feet: 5 points
Tail: 3 points

KEY CHARACTERISTICS

- **CATEGORY** Foreign Shorthair.

- **OVERALL BUILD** Medium size, svelte and dainty.

- **COAT** Short, fine-textured, glossy and close-lying.

- **HEAD** Long, tapering, and wedge-shaped, with a fine muzzle.

- **NOSE** Long and straight.

- **CHIN** Tip of chin lines up with tip of nose.

- **EYES** Medium sized and almond shaped, slanting toward the nose.

- **EARS** Strikingly large and pointed, continuing the line of the wedge-shaped head.

- **BODY** Long and slender, with fine bones, firm muscles, and a tight abdomen. Slim shoulders and hips.

- **LEGS** Long and slim.

- **PAWS** Small and oval.

- **TAIL** Long and thin, tapering to a fine point.

- **COLORS** Red point, cream point, seal lynx point, blue lynx point, chocolate lynx point, lilac lynx point, red lynx point, seal torbie point, chocolate torbie point, blue-cream point, lilac-cream point.

PENALTIES

The Colorpoint Shorthair is penalized for lack of pigment in the nose leather.

DISQUALIFICATION FEATURES
- any evidence of poor health
- weak hind legs
- a visible tail kink
- incorrect eye color
- white toes

COLORPOINT VARIETIES

SIAMESE CATS UNDER a different title in some American associations, the Colorpoint Short-hair group embraces all the Siamese varieties produced by outcrossing to others breeds to introduce the orange (red) and tabby genes.

RED POINT The body is clear white, with any shading toning with the points, which should be bright apricot to deep red. Deeper shades are preferred, with no barring. Nose leather and paw pads are flesh or coral pink; and the eye color a deep, vivid blue.

CREAM POINT The body is clear white, with any shading toning with the points, which should be pale buff to light, pinkish cream with no barring. Nose leather and paw pads are flesh or coral pink; eye color a deep vivid blue.

SEAL LYNX POINT The body is cream or pale fawn, shading to a lighter color on the stomach and chest. Ghost striping is allowed as body shading. The points are distinct seal brown bars, separated by the lighter background color. Ears are seal brown with a paler thumb-print in the center. Nose leather is seal brown, or pink edged in seal brown; paw pads are seal brown; eye color a deep, vivid blue.

BLUE LYNX POINT The body is bluish-white to platinum gray, cold in tone, shading to a lighter color on the stomach and chest. Ghost striping is allowed as body shading. The points

are distinct deep blue-gray bars, separated by the lighter background color. Ears are deep blue-gray with a paler thumb-print in the center. Nose leather is slate-colored or pink-edged in slate; paw pads are slate; eye color a deep, vivid blue.

CHOCOLATE LYNX POINT The body is ivory. Ghost striping is allowed as body shading. The points are distinct warm milk chocolate bars, separated by the lighter background color. Ears are warm milk chocolate with a paler thumb-print in the center. Nose leather is cinnamon, or pink edged in cinnamon; paw pads are cinnamon; eye color is deep blue.

LILAC LYNX POINT The body is glacial white. Ghost striping is allowed as body shading. The points are frosty gray with distinct pinkish-toned bars, separated by the lighter background color. Ears are frosty gray with a paler thumb-print in the center. Nose leather is lavender pink or gray edged with lavender pink; paw pads are lavender pink; eye color is a deep, vivid blue.

RED LYNX POINT The body is white. Ghost striping is allowed as body shading. The points are distinct deep red bars, separated by the lighter background color. Ears are deep red with a paler thumb-print in the center. Nose leather and paw pads are flesh or coral pink; eye color is a deep, vivid blue.

SEAL TORTIE POINT The body is pale fawn to cream, shading to a lighter color on the stomach and chest. It may be mottled with cream in older cats. The points are seal brown-uniformly mottled with red and light red. A blaze is desirable. Nose leather is seal brown; flesh or coral pink mottling is permitted where there is a facial blaze. Paw pads are seal brown; flesh or coral mottling is permitted where the points' color mottling extends into the paw pads. Eye color is a deep, vivid blue.

CHOCOLATE TORTIE POINT The body is ivory and may be mottled in older cats. The points are warm milk chocolate uniformly mottled with red and/or light red. A blaze is desirable. Nose leather is cinnamon; flesh or coral mottling is permitted where there is a facial blaze. Paw pads are cinnamon; flesh or coral mottling is permitted where the points' color mottling extends into the paw pads. Eye color is a deep, vivid blue.

BLUE-CREAM POINT The body is bluish white to platinum gray, cold in tone, shading to a lighter color on the stomach and chest. The body color is mottled in older cats. The points are deep blue-gray, uniformly mottled with cream. A blaze is desirable. Nose leather is

CHOCOLATE TORTIE POINT SIAMESE

Tortie Point Siamese are found in a full range of colors and appeal to those who like to have a completely unique cat – no two tortie points have the same markings.

SEAL TABBY POINT SIAMESE

The body is often shaded with ghost tabby markings. The points are patterned with tabby bars and stripes of the main color. In the Seal Tabby, the markings are deep seal brown.

slate; flesh or coral pink mottling is permitted where there is a facial blaze. Paw pads are slate; flesh or coral mottling is permitted where the points' color mottling extends into the paw pads. Eye color is a deep, vivid blue.

LILAC-CREAM POINT The body is glacial white and may be mottled in older cats. The points are frosty gray with a pinkish tone uniformly mottled with pale cream. A blaze is desirable. Nose leather is lavender pink; flesh or coral pink mottling is permitted where there is a facial blaze. Paw pads are lavender pink; flesh or coral mottling is permitted where the points' color mottling extends into the paw pads. Eye color is a deep, vivid blue.

SEAL TORTIE POINT

In the Seal Tortie Point, the points are patterned in a mixture of black and red or light red, and the cat, like this one, may have a red or light red blaze down the face.

233

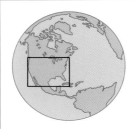

BALINESE

THE LONG-COATED kittens that appeared from time to time in otherwise normal litters of Siamese cats were developed into the Balinese. At first such kittens were quickly discarded and sold as pets, but in the 1940s two breeders in New York and California began to work toward the development of a separate breed. The name was chosen because of the cats' gracefulness and svelte lines, reminiscent of the dancers on the island of Bali. The breed soon gained a lot of admirers, but it was not until 1970 that the CFA first recognized it and granted it championship status. The long coat is nothing like that of the Persian. It has no wooly undercoat and lies flat against the body.

Character and Care

As might be expected from their ancestry, Balinese are very similar to Siamese in character – affectionate, demanding of attention, extremely active, and inquisitive.

The coat is relatively easy to care for with regular gentle combing, and brushing of the ruff (frill) and plumed tail.

BREAKDOWN OF 100 SHOW POINTS

COLOR and COAT:
50 POINTS

Eye color: 15 points
Points color: 10 points
Body color: 10 points
Coat Texture and Length:
15 points

TYPE: 50 POINTS

Head: 15 points
Ears: 5 points
Eye shape: 5 points

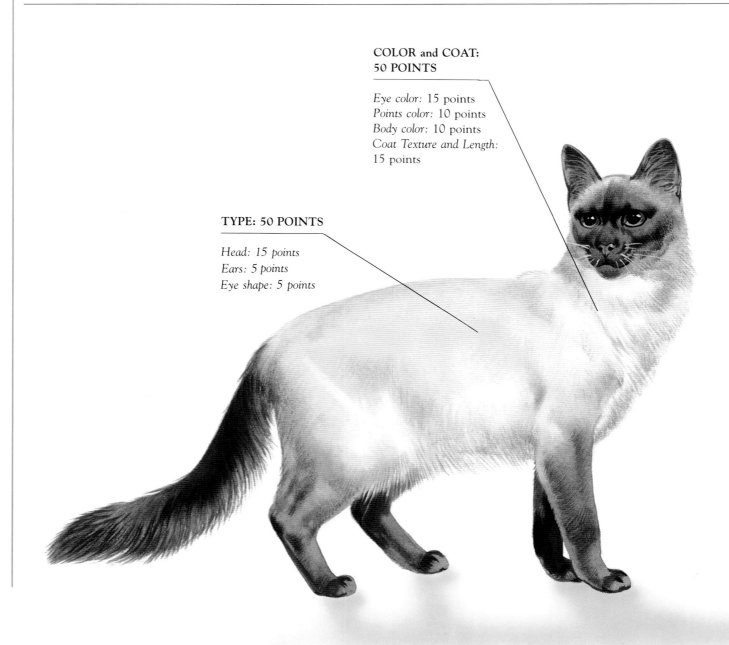

KEY CHARACTERISTICS

- **CATEGORY** Longhair.

- **OVERALL BUILD** Medium size, svelte and elegant.

- **COAT** Fine and silky.

- **HEAD** Medium size, a long tapering wedge shape which starts at the nose and gradually increases in width in straight lines on each side, as far as the ears. No whisker break.

- **NOSE** Long and straight, continuing the line from the forehead without any break.

- **CHIN** Medium size, the tip forming a vertical line with the tip of the nose.

- **EYES** Medium size and almond shaped, set slightly slanted toward the nose.

- **EARS** Large and pointed, wide-based, placed to continue the lines of the wedge.

- **BODY** Long, svelte, well-muscled but dainty. The shoulders should be no wider than the hips.

- **LEGS** Long and fine, in proportion to the body.

- **PAWS** Small, dainty, and oval.

- **TAIL** Very long and thin, tapering to a fine point; the tail hair spreads out like a plume.

- **COLORS** All the colors found in the Siamese (and Colorpoints): Seal point, blue point, chocolate point, lilac (frost) point, red point, cream point, seal tortie point, blue tortie point, chocolate tortie point, lilac (frost) tortie point, seal tabby point, blue tabby point, chocolate tabby point, lilac (frost) tabby point, red tabby point, cream tabby point, seal tortie tabby point (seal torbie point), blue tortie tabby point (blue torbie point), chocolate tortie tabby point (chocolate torbie point), lilac (frost) tortie tabby point (lilac (frost) torbie point). Some associations accept only seal point, blue point, chocolate point, and lilac (frost) point.

PENALTIES

The Balinese is penalized for lack of pigment in the nose leather or paw pads; and for having crossed eyes.

DISQUALIFICATION FEATURES
- any evidence of poor health
- weak hind legs
- mouth breathing due to nasal obstruction
- kinked tail
- eye color other than blue
- white toes and/or feet
- downy undercoat

BALINESE VARIETIES

CREAM BALINESE

The Balinese is a long-coated version of the Siamese. It is accepted in the same range of points' colors.

THE BODY MUST be even in color with subtle shading when allowed in the color variety. The points – mask, ears, legs, feet, and tail – must be all the same shade and clearly defined. The mask should cover the entire face, including the whisker pads, and be connected to the ears by traced markings. There should be no ticking or white hairs in the points. Eye color for all varieties is deep, vivid blue.

SEAL POINT The body color is beige to cream or pale fawn; the points color dark seal brown. The nose leather and paw pads are dark seal brown.

BLUE POINT The body color is bluish-white of a glacial tone; the points color blue-gray. The nose leather and paw pads are blue-gray.

CHOCOLATE POINT The body color is ivory; the points color milk chocolate. The nose leather is milk chocolate; the paw pads are cinnamon to milk chocolate.

LILAC POINT The body color is glacial white (magnolia); the points color frosty gray with a slight pinkish tone. The nose leather and paw pads are pink.

RED POINT The body color is creamy white; the points color bright, warm orange. The nose leather is pink; the paw pads pink or red.

CREAM POINT The body color is creamy white; the points color pastel cream. The nose leather and paw pads are pink.

SEAL TORTIE POINT The body color is beige shading to fawn; the points color seal, patched or mingled with red and/or light red. The nose leather and paw pads are seal brown and/or pink.

BLUE TORTIE POINT The body color is bluish white; the points color blue-gray patched or mingled with pastel cream. The nose leather and paw pads are blue-gray and/or pink.

CHOCOLATE TORTIE POINT The body color is ivory; the points color milk chocolate patched or mingled with red and/or light red. The nose leather is milk chocolate and/or pink; the paw pads are cinnamon to milk chocolate and/or pink.

LILAC TORTIE POINT The body color is glacial white; the points color frosty gray with a slight pinkish tone patched or mingled with pale cream. The nose leather and paw pads are lavender pink and/or pale pink.

SEAL TABBY POINT The body color is beige; the points color dark seal tabby; the rims around the eyes and nose are seal brown. The nose leather is brick red, pink, or seal brown;

BLUE POINT BALINESE

As only top quality Siamese cats were used in the breeding programs for Balinese, most of today's Balinese cats are of outstanding type.

the paw pads are seal brown.

BLUE TABBY POINT The body color is bluish white; the points color blue-gray tabby; the rims around the eyes and nose are blue-gray. The nose leather is old rose or blue-gray; the paw pads are blue-gray.

CHOCOLATE TABBY POINT Body color is ivory; the points color milk chocolate tabby; the rims around the eyes and nose are milk chocolate. The nose leather is light red, pink, or milk chocolate; the paw pads are cinnamon to milk chocolate.

LILAC TABBY POINT The body color is glacial white; the points color lilac tabby – frosty gray with slightly pinkish-toned tabby markings – the rims around the eyes and nose are lavender pink. The nose leather is lavender pink or pink; the paw pads are lavender pink.

RED TABBY POINT The body color is off-white with a slight red tinge; the points color warm orange tabby; the rims around the eyes and nose are dark pink. The nose leather is brick red or pink; the paw pads are pink.

CREAM TABBY POINT The body color is creamy white; the points color cream tabby with a cold tone; the rims around the eyes and nose are dark pink. The nose leather and paw pads are pink.

SEAL TORBIE POINT The body color is beige; the points color has seal tabby markings patched or mingled with red or light red tortie markings. The nose rims are seal; the nose leather and paw pads are seal, brick red, or pink, or seal mottled with brick red and/or pink.

BLUE TORBIE POINT The body color is bluish-white; the points color has blue tabby markings, patched or mingled with cream tortie markings. The nose rims are blue-gray; the nose leather is blue-gray, old rose or pink, or blue-gray mottled with old rose and/or pink; the paw pads are blue-gray and/or pink.

CHOCOLATE TORBIE POINT The body color is ivory; the points color has milk chocolate tabby markings, patched or mingled with red or light red tortie markings. The nose rims are chocolate; the nose leather milk chocolate, pale red or pink, or milk chocolate mottled with pale red or pink; the paw pads are cinnamon to milk chocolate and/or pink.

CHOCOLATE TORTIE POINT BALINESE

Patched or mingled points of milk chocolate and light red allied with an ivory coat make this an unusual and attractive variety.

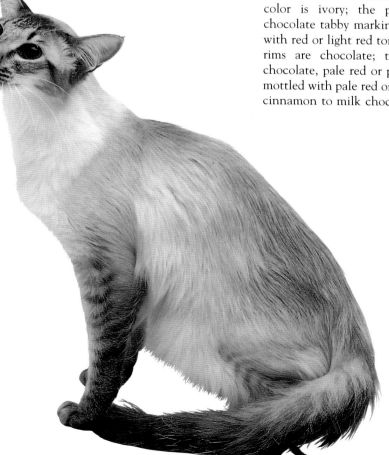

SEAL TABBY POINT BALINESE

This cat epitomizes the Balinese breed, conforming almost exactly to the standard of points.

ORIENTAL

CATS OF THE DISTINCTIVE Siamese body conformation, but without having the true color restricted to the points, are recognized by some associations as Orientals.

In the main, the Oriental is identical to the Siamese in all respects except for not having its color restricted to the points and not having blue eyes. It has a slightly quieter voice than the Siamese, but is equally talkative. Oriental cats have been known for many years, but first became popular in the early 1960s when a small number of fanciers began to breed them in a wide variety of colors, some individuals specializing in just one or two colors or patterns, but each taking extreme care with the selection of their foundation stock to give strength, stamina, and good temperament in their cats, as well as beauty. Some Orientals were produced as offshoots to the breeding programs for the red-, tortie- and tabby- or lynx-pointed Siamese, and others were developed after much genetic research.

A light-brown gene was recognized and gave rise to a whole new series of attractive feline colors, and a pure white Oriental, in fact a Siamese with white masking its points, entranced show visitors with its sapphire eyes. Britain's GCCF designates the self-colored cats of Siamese type "Foreign," and so they are known as the Foreign White, Foreign Black, Foreign Blue, Foreign Lilac, and so on, yet the "Foreign Chocolate" is called the Havana, the name having been changed from Chestnut Brown Foreign in the 1950s. Europe's FIFe and its British member, the Cat Association of Britain, recognize the entire group as Oriental, as does the largest of the American associations, the CFA.

Color terminology varies, too, black being called ebony, chocolate chestnut, lilac lavender, and there is some controversy over the cinnamon, caramel, and fawn colors. The showing system in the CFA proved the most helpful to breeders of Orientals, dividing the

BREAKDOWN OF 100 SHOW POINTS

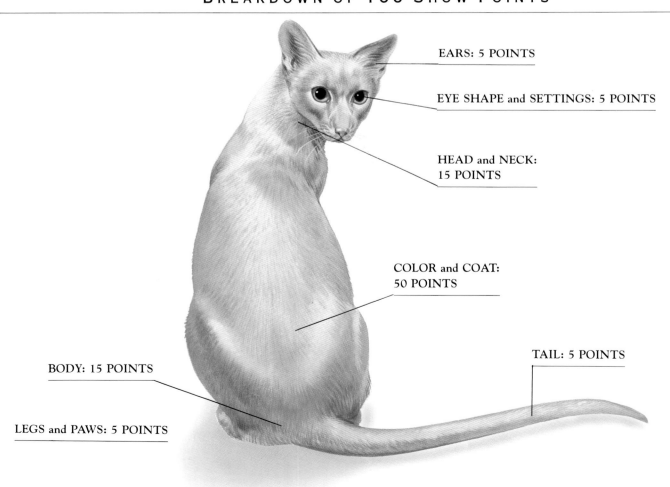

EARS: 5 POINTS

EYE SHAPE and SETTINGS: 5 POINTS

HEAD and NECK:
15 POINTS

COLOR and COAT:
50 POINTS

TAIL: 5 POINTS

BODY: 15 POINTS

LEGS and PAWS: 5 POINTS

breed into five groups: solid colors; shaded; smokes; tabbies, and particolors. In this way the Orientals reached championship status level in 1977, and the following year a number of Orientals featured among the CFA's top twenty. In Britain, each color variety had to work separately toward a breed number, and in 1995 their status as a group is still in confusion in the GCCF.

Character and Care

The Oriental is extroverted, intelligent, and very affectionate with its own family and friends. It is active and playful, and hates being left alone for long periods.

They are naturally very clean cats, and the very short, fine coat can be kept in good condition with daily hand grooming and buffing with a silk scarf. The large ears need regular cleaning, and Orientals should be provided with a scratching post and plenty of toys to play with.

PENALTIES

The Oriental is penalized for any evidence of ill health; weak hind legs; mouth breathing due to nasal obstruction; a visible kink in the tail; miniaturization; a white locket or button; and tabby barring or striping in non-agouti varieties.

KEY CHARACTERISTICS

- **CATEGORY** Foreign Shorthair.

- **OVERALL BUILD** Medium size, long and svelte.

- **COAT** Very short and fine, glossy, silky and close-lying.

- **HEAD** Medium sized in proportion to the body; wedge-shaped with straight lines, the wedge starting at the nose and gradually increasing in width in straight lines on each side to the ears. No whisker break.

- **NOSE** Long and straight without any break.

- **CHIN** Medium size, the tip forming a vertical line with the tip of the nose.

- **EYES** Medium size and almond shaped, set slightly slanting toward the nose in harmony with the lines of the wedge.

- **EARS** Large and pointed, wide at the base, placed to continue the line of the wedge.

- **BODY** Long and svelte, well muscled but still dainty and elegant. The shoulders should not be wider than the hips.

- **LEGS** Long and fine, in proportion to the body.

- **PAWS** Small and oval.

- **TAIL** Very long and thin, thin at the base, and tapering to a fine point.

- **COLORS** Black, white, blue, havana chocolate, lilac, cinnamon, caramel, fawn, red self, cream, black tortie, blue tortie, chocolate tortie, lilac tortie, cinnamon tortie, caramel tortie, fawn tortie, black smoke, blue smoke, chocolate smoke, lilac smoke, cinnamon smoke, caramel smoke, fawn smoke, red smoke, black tortie smoke, blue tortie smoke, chocolate tortie smoke, lilac tortie smoke, cinamon tortie smoke, caramel tortie smoke, black shaded, blue shaded, chocolate shaded, lilac shaded, cameo, black tabby, blue tabby, chocolate tabby, lilac tabby, red tabby, cream tabby, cinnamon tabby, fawn tabby, silver tabby. Tipped: all recognized colors.

SOLID VARIETIES

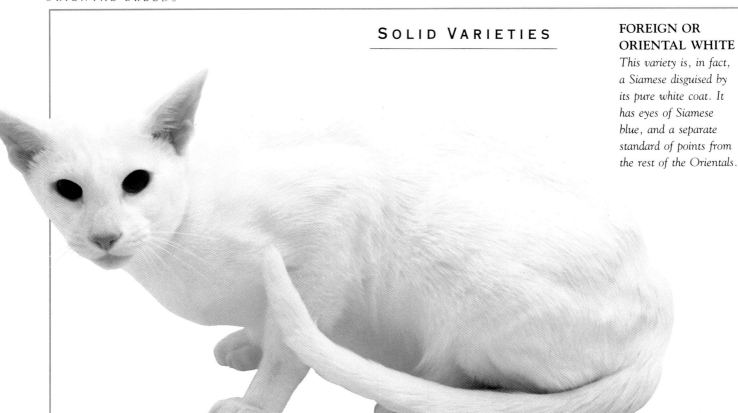

**FOREIGN OR
ORIENTAL WHITE**
*This variety is, in fact,
a Siamese disguised by
its pure white coat. It
has eyes of Siamese
blue, and a separate
standard of points from
the rest of the Orientals.*

As SIAMESE CATS without the gene which restricts the color to the points; the first Orientals to appear in half-Siamese litters were blacks and blues. Later, the elusive chocolate gene produced the Chestnut Brown Foreign, a self chocolate-colored cat, which is now known as the Havana in the UK, and the Oriental Chestnut elsewhere. Some of the early Chestnut Browns were exported to the US, where they formed the nucleus of a totally different breed with its own characteristic features known as the Havana Brown. When the gene for dilution was also present in the cats used for breeding, chocolate, lilac, or lavender kittens began to appear.

ORIENTAL WHITE, FOREIGN WHITE, SIAMESE WHITE The coat color is pure white without markings or shadings of any kind. The nose leather and paw pads are pink; the eye color is deep, vivid blue.
Note: In the CFA, the Oriental White should have green eyes. Blue eye color is also accepted, but odd-eyed cats are not.
BLACK The coat color is dense coal black, sound from the roots to the tips of the hair, free from any rusty tinge, and without any white hairs or other markings. There should be no gray undercoat. The nose leather is black; the paw pads are black or seal brown; the eye color is vivid, intense green.
BLUE The coat color is any shade of blue-gray, but lighter shades are preferred. The color must be sound and even throughout, without any white hairs, shadings, or other markings. Nose leather and paw pads are blue-gray; eye color is vivid, intense green.

ORIENTAL BLUE
*Any shade of blue is
permitted in this
variety, but lighter
shades are preferred.*

CHOCOLATE (CHESTNUT) The coat color is any shade of warm chocolate (chestnut) brown, sound and even throughout without any white hairs, shadings, or other markings. There should be no gray undercoat. The nose leather is milk chocolate; the paw pads are cinnamon to milk chocolate; the eye color is vivid, intense green.

LILAC The coat color is faded lilac with a slight pinkish tinge, sound and even throughout without any white hairs, shadings, or other markings. The nose leather and paw pads are lavender pink or faded lilac; the eye color is vivid, intense green.

CINNAMON The coat color is warm cinnamon brown, sound and even throughout without any white hairs, shadings, or markings. The nose leather is cinnamon brown; the paw pads are cinnamon brown to pink; the eye color is vivid, intense green.

CARAMEL The coat color is a cool-toned bluish fawn, sound and even throughout without any white hairs, shadings, or markings. Nose leather and paw pads are bluish fawn; the eye color is vivid, intense green.

ORIENTAL CINNAMON

This beautiful, unusual color variety excited geneticists when it first appeared in recent years.

HAVANA BROWN

The name Havana was originally chosen to describe the rich tobacco-brown color of this breed's coat, likened to that used for making the best of the Havana cigars. It is far more descriptive than other names used for the warm brown coat.

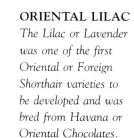

ORIENTAL LILAC

The Lilac or Lavender was one of the first Oriental or Foreign Shorthair varieties to be developed and was bred from Havana or Oriental Chocolates.

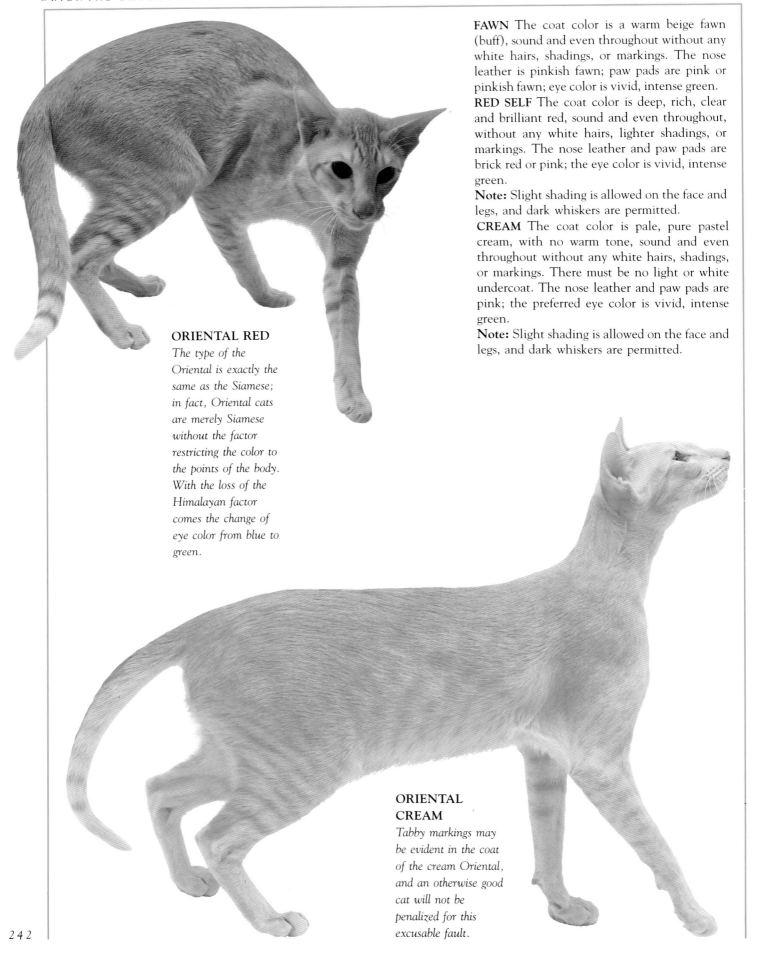

FAWN The coat color is a warm beige fawn (buff), sound and even throughout without any white hairs, shadings, or markings. The nose leather is pinkish fawn; paw pads are pink or pinkish fawn; eye color is vivid, intense green.

RED SELF The coat color is deep, rich, clear and brilliant red, sound and even throughout, without any white hairs, lighter shadings, or markings. The nose leather and paw pads are brick red or pink; the eye color is vivid, intense green.

Note: Slight shading is allowed on the face and legs, and dark whiskers are permitted.

CREAM The coat color is pale, pure pastel cream, with no warm tone, sound and even throughout without any white hairs, shadings, or markings. There must be no light or white undercoat. The nose leather and paw pads are pink; the preferred eye color is vivid, intense green.

Note: Slight shading is allowed on the face and legs, and dark whiskers are permitted.

ORIENTAL RED

The type of the Oriental is exactly the same as the Siamese; in fact, Oriental cats are merely Siamese without the factor restricting the color to the points of the body. With the loss of the Himalayan factor comes the change of eye color from blue to green.

ORIENTAL CREAM

Tabby markings may be evident in the coat of the cream Oriental, and an otherwise good cat will not be penalized for this excusable fault.

TORTOISESHELL VARIETIES

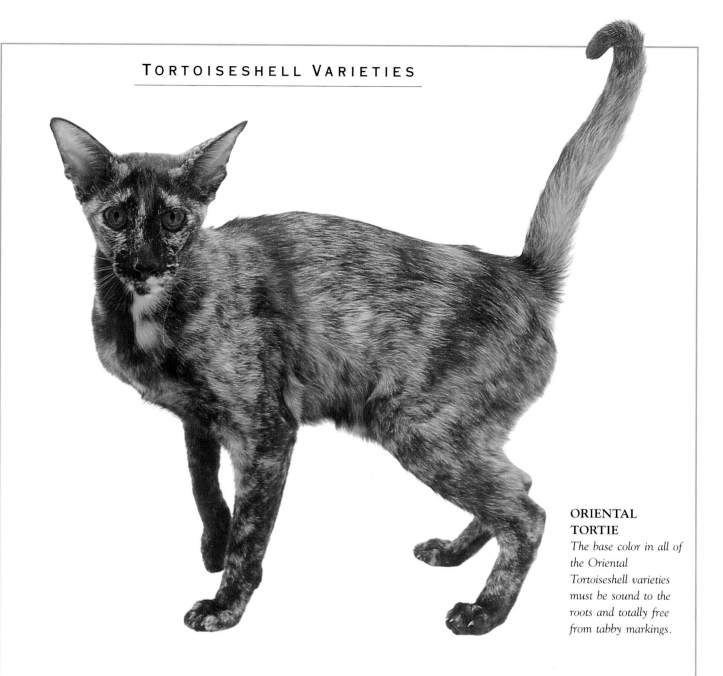

ORIENTAL TORTIE
The base color in all of the Oriental Tortoiseshell varieties must be sound to the roots and totally free from tabby markings.

WITH THE INTRODUCTION of the sex-linked gene which produced the red and the cream, litters included female kittens of various combinations of colors in the pattern called tortoiseshell.

BLACK TORTIE The coat color is black patched or mingled with red and/or light red. The nose leather and the paw pads are black, brick red or pink, or black mottled with brick red and/or pink.

BLUE TORTIE The coat color is light blue-gray patched or mingled with pale cream. The nose leather and paw pads are blue-gray or pink, or blue-gray with pink.

CHOCOLATE TORTIE The coat color is milk chocolate patched or mingled with red or light red. The nose leather is milk chocolate, pale red, or pink, or milk chocolate mottled with pale red and/or pink; the paw pads are cinna-mon to milk chocolate, pale red, or pink, or cinnamon to milk chocolate mottled with pale red and/or pink.

LILAC TORTIE (LAVENDER-CREAM) The coat color is faded lilac with a slight pinkish tinge, patched or mingled with pale cream. The nose leather and paw pads are lavender pale pink, or lavender pink mottled with pale pink.

CINNAMON TORTIE The coat color is warm cinnamon brown patched or mingled with red or light red. The nose leather and paw pads are cinnamon brown, pinkish red or pink, or cinnamon brown mottled with pinkish red and/or pink.

CARAMEL TORTIE The coat color is cool-toned bluish fawn patched or mingled with rich beige and/or cream. The nose leather and paw pads are bluish fawn or pink; or bluish fawn mottled with pink.

TABBY

CARAMEL SPOTTED TABBY

A young Oriental tabby with a nicely spotted coat pattern, good overall type, and a lovely color.

ORIENTAL TABBY CATS may have any of the following four tabby patterns – Classic, Mackerel, Spotted, or Ticked. In the Classic, there should be dense and clearly defined broad markings; the legs should be evenly barred with bracelets coming up to join the body markings. The tail should be evenly ringed; and there should be several unbroken necklaces on the neck and upper chest. Frown marks on the forehead form a letter "M." In Mackerel tabbies, there should be dense and clearly defined stripes like narrow pencil marks; the legs should be evenly barred with narrow bracelets coming up to join the body markings. The tail should be barred; and there should be distinct chain-like necklaces on the neck and

chest. The head should be barred, with an "M" on the forehead. For the Spotted, the spots on the body may vary in size and shape, but those that are round and evenly distributed are preferred. They must not run together to form a broken mackerel pattern. A dorsal stripe runs the length of the body to the tip of the tail and is ideally composed of spots.

The body hairs are clearly ticked, and there are no other spots, bars, or stripes on the body. Typical tabby markings including the forehead "M" are found on the face, and thumb prints on the backs of the ears.

BLACK TABBY (EBONY TABBY) The base coat is brilliant coppery brown; the markings are dense black. The lips and chin should be the same color as the rings around the eyes. The backs of the legs from paw to heel are black; the nose leather is black or brick red rimmed with black; the paw pads are black or seal brown; the eyes are green.

BLUE TABBY The base coat, including the lips and chin, is pale bluish-ivory, or warm gray in the ticked tabby, with markings any shade of blue-gray affording a good contrast with the base color. The backs of the legs from paw to heel are a darker shade of blue-gray; the nose leather is blue or old rose rimmed with blue; the paw pads are blue-gray or rose; the eyes are green.

CHOCOLATE TABBY (CHESTNUT TABBY) The base coat, including the lips and chin, is warm fawn, or sandy beige in the ticked tabby, with markings a rich chocolate brown. The

CHOCOLATE CLASSIC TABBY

The classic tabby pattern is shown to perfection by this superbly marked Oriental cat.

CHOCOLATE SPOTTED TABBY

Although all the tabby markings are correct on the head, legs, and tail, this cat needs to develop better spotting on the body.

backs of the legs from paw to heel are chocolate brown; the nose leather is chocolate or pale red rimmed with chocolate; the paw pads are cinnamon to chocolate; the eyes are green.

LILAC TABBY (LAVENDER TABBY) The base coat is off-white to palest lilac, with markings rich lilac (lilac gray with a pinkish tinge) or lavender, affording a good contrast with the base color. The backs of the legs from paw to heel are a darker shade of lilac; the nose leather is lavender or pink rimmed with lavender; the paw pads are lavender pink; the eyes are green.

RED TABBY The base coat is red, with markings a deep rich red. The backs of the legs from paw to heel are dark red; the nose leather is brick red or pink; the paw pads are pink (Europe); brick red (USA), the eyes are any shade of copper to green, green preferred.

CREAM TABBY The base coat, including the lips and chin, is very pale cream, with markings buff or cream, affording a good contrast with the base color. The backs of the legs from paw to heel are dark cream; the nose leather and paw pads are pink, the eyes are any shade of copper to green, green preferred.

CHOCOLATE TICKED ORIENTAL

The ticked Orientals have two or three bands of ticking on each hair. The basic color also shows at the heels of the hind legs and at the tip of the tail.

245

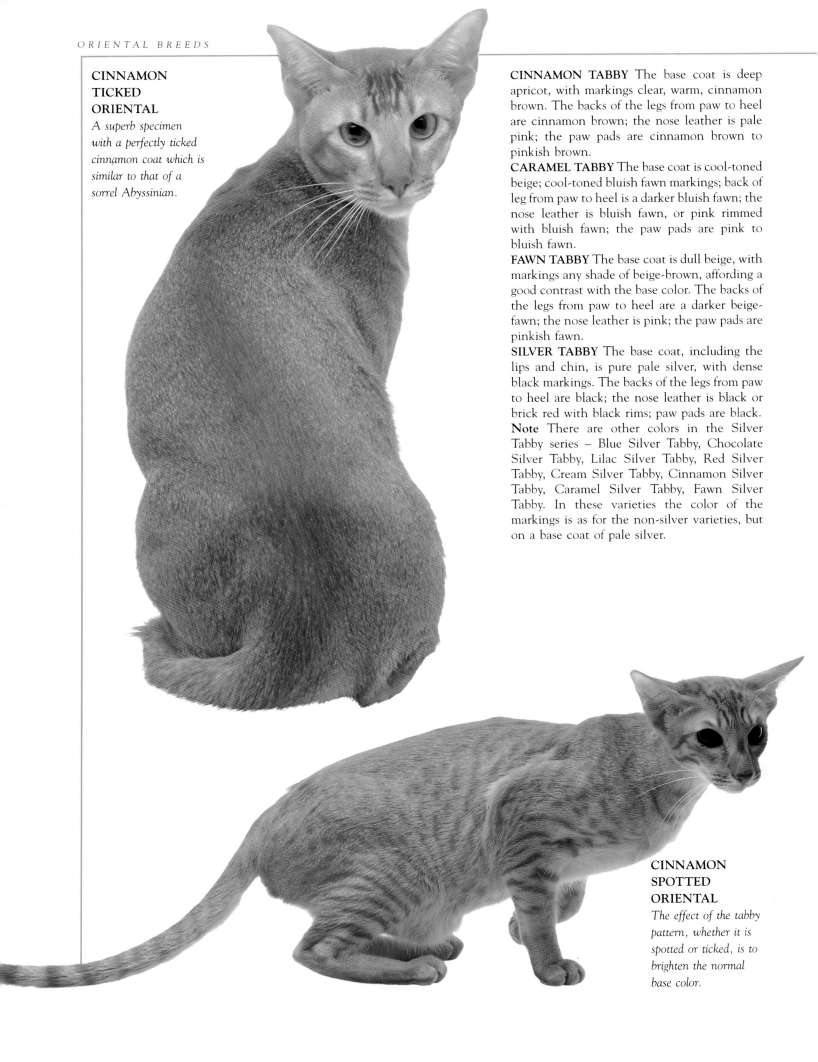

CINNAMON TICKED ORIENTAL

A superb specimen with a perfectly ticked cinnamon coat which is similar to that of a sorrel Abyssinian.

CINNAMON TABBY The base coat is deep apricot, with markings clear, warm, cinnamon brown. The backs of the legs from paw to heel are cinnamon brown; the nose leather is pale pink; the paw pads are cinnamon brown to pinkish brown.

CARAMEL TABBY The base coat is cool-toned beige; cool-toned bluish fawn markings; back of leg from paw to heel is a darker bluish fawn; the nose leather is bluish fawn, or pink rimmed with bluish fawn; the paw pads are pink to bluish fawn.

FAWN TABBY The base coat is dull beige, with markings any shade of beige-brown, affording a good contrast with the base color. The backs of the legs from paw to heel are a darker beige-fawn; the nose leather is pink; the paw pads are pinkish fawn.

SILVER TABBY The base coat, including the lips and chin, is pure pale silver, with dense black markings. The backs of the legs from paw to heel are black; the nose leather is black or brick red with black rims; paw pads are black.

Note There are other colors in the Silver Tabby series – Blue Silver Tabby, Chocolate Silver Tabby, Lilac Silver Tabby, Red Silver Tabby, Cream Silver Tabby, Cinnamon Silver Tabby, Caramel Silver Tabby, Fawn Silver Tabby. In these varieties the color of the markings is as for the non-silver varieties, but on a base coat of pale silver.

CINNAMON SPOTTED ORIENTAL

The effect of the tabby pattern, whether it is spotted or ticked, is to brighten the normal base color.

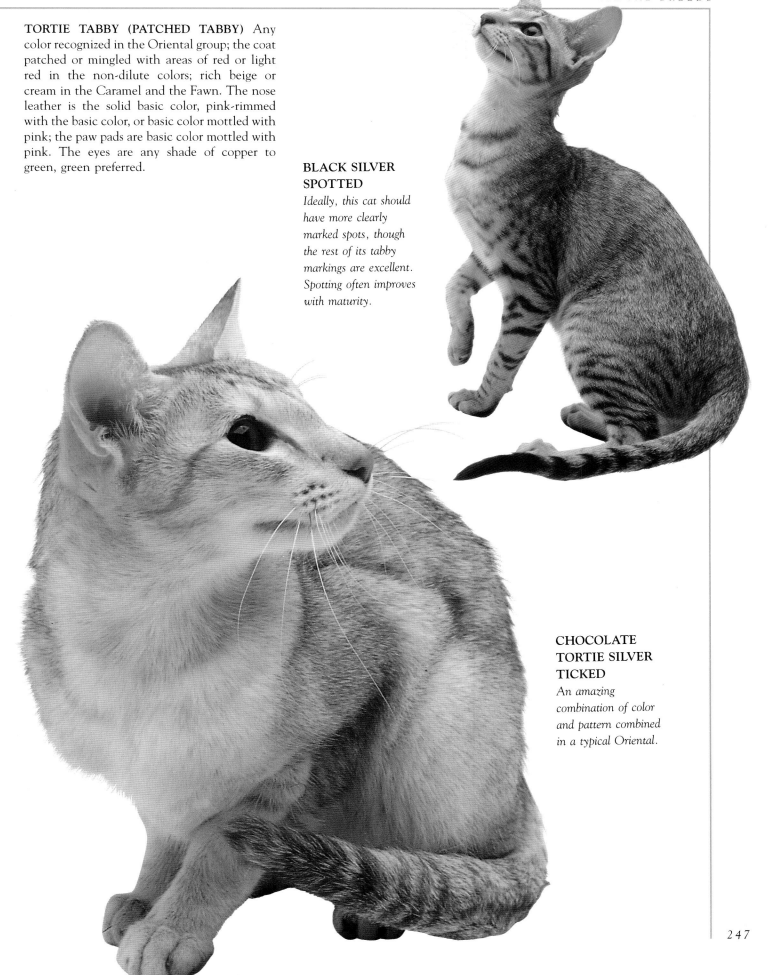

TORTIE TABBY (PATCHED TABBY) Any color recognized in the Oriental group; the coat patched or mingled with areas of red or light red in the non-dilute colors; rich beige or cream in the Caramel and the Fawn. The nose leather is the solid basic color, pink-rimmed with the basic color, or basic color mottled with pink; the paw pads are basic color mottled with pink. The eyes are any shade of copper to green, green preferred.

BLACK SILVER SPOTTED
Ideally, this cat should have more clearly marked spots, though the rest of its tabby markings are excellent. Spotting often improves with maturity.

CHOCOLATE TORTIE SILVER TICKED
An amazing combination of color and pattern combined in a typical Oriental.

SMOKE, SHADED, AND TIPPED VARIETIES

CHOCOLATE SILVER SHADED ORIENTAL
This variety has chocolate markings on a paler, silvery chocolate ground.

BLACK SMOKE ORIENTAL
Looking like a black in repose, the smoke undercoat becomes apparent as the cat moves.

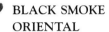

THE INTRODUCTION OF silver to the Oriental breeding programs excited many Oriental fanciers, and before long, cats with short, fine silvery-white coats were bred with various amounts of colored tipping. The most heavily tipped are the smokes, the lightest tipped are just called "tipped," and the intermediates are known as "shaded."

In the Smoke, the hairs are tipped with the appropriate color and have a narrow silver-white band at the roots which can only be seen when the hair is parted. The undercoat is silver-white. In repose, the cat appears to be of solid color, but in motion the silver-white undercoat is clearly visible. In the Shaded, the hair is tipped to about one-third of its length and the undercoat is white, producing the characteristic sparkling appearance of this color group. The face and legs may be shaded with tipping. In the Tipped, the hair is tipped just at its extremity, and the tipping is evenly distributed over the cat's body. The face and legs may be shaded, but in adults, ghost tabby markings are considered a serious fault. The tipped cat is considerably lighter in overall color than the shaded.

SEYCHELLOIS

FOLLOWING A BREEDING program approved by the Cat Association of Britain, the Seychellois was developed by a small group of breeders interested in Oriental cats. It is of medium size and typical Oriental conformation, with a long svelte body, slim legs, and dainty paws. The head is wedge-shaped with very large pointed ears and almond-shaped eyes. It is unusual in having a predominantly white coat, with splashes of color on the head, legs, and body, and a colored tail. Seychellois markings are classified into three groups. The Seychellois Longhair is identical in every respect to the Shorthair except in its coat, which is of medium length, soft and silky in texture, and longer on the frill or ruff. It has ear tufts and a full, plume-like tail.

SEYCHELLOIS NEUVIÈME Almost entirely white with a colored tail and a few tiny colored markings on the head.

SEYCHELLOIS HUITIÈME Mainly white with a colored tail and splashes of color on the head and legs.

SEYCHELLOIS SEPTIÈME White with a colored tail and splashes of color on the head, legs and, body.

KEY CHARACTERISTICS
● **CATEGORY** Foreign Shorthair (Oriental).
● **OVERALL BUILD** Medium size, long and svelte.
● **COAT** *Shorthair* Very short and fine, glossy, silky and close-lying. *Longhair* Of medium length, fine, silky and longer on the ruff (frill) and tail.
● **COLORS** Any color or combination of colors is allowed.
● **OTHER FEATURES** Head medium sized, in proportion to body, wedge shaped with straight lines starting at nose and gradually increasing in width to ears, no whisker break. Nose is long and straight; chin medium sized, the tip forming a vertical line with tip of nose; eyes are medium sized, almond shaped, and set slightly slanting toward nose to follow lines of wedge; ears are large and pointed, wide at base and placed to continue lines of wedge. Body is long and svelte, well muscled but dainty and elegant; shoulders should not be wider than hips. Legs are long and fine boned, in proportion to body; paws small and oval; tail very long and thin, tapering to a fine point. *Longhair* Tail hair spreads out like a plume.

SEYCHELLOIS SHORTHAIR
This rare breed is of Oriental type and is a predominantly white cat with splashes of color on the head, tail, and body.

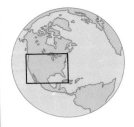

JAVANESE

THE LONGHAIRED ORIENTAL, now known as the Javanese, was selectively bred from Oriental cats and long-coated cats of exceptional Oriental type. In the CFA, the name Javanese was given to Balinese cats not conforming to the four main Siamese colors (seal point, blue point, chocolate point and lilac point). These were the red- and tabby-based colors which in the short-coated varieties are termed Colorpoints by the CFA. In New Zealand, where the red- and tabby-, or lynx-pointed cats with long coats are accepted, along with the four main Siamese colors, as Balinese, it is the spotted and self-coated varieties which are called Javanese. In the UK, the CA, as a member of FIFe, accepts all long-coated colors of Orientals as Javanese.

Medium long on the body, and without an undercoat, the coat of the Javanese cat is fine, with a silky texture. It flows over the body and forms a ruff around the shoulders and chest. The cat has a full, plume-like tail.

Character and Care
Active, always alert, and very inquisitive, the Javanese has an extrovert personality, and is intelligent and quite vocal. It is a very affectionate cat and loves human company, hating to be left alone for long periods.

Regular gentle brushing keeps the coat in good condition; the ruff (frill), underparts and tail can be combed gently with a broad-toothed comb.

BREAKDOWN OF 100 SHOW POINTS

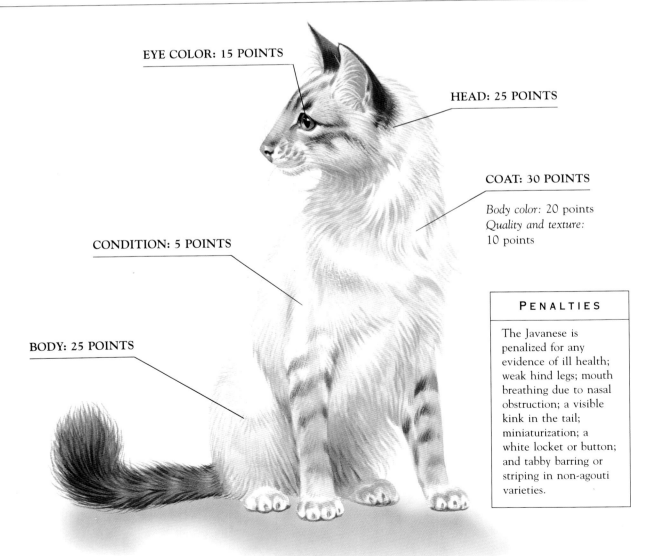

EYE COLOR: 15 POINTS

HEAD: 25 POINTS

COAT: 30 POINTS

Body color: 20 points
Quality and texture: 10 points

CONDITION: 5 POINTS

BODY: 25 POINTS

PENALTIES

The Javanese is penalized for any evidence of ill health; weak hind legs; mouth breathing due to nasal obstruction; a visible kink in the tail; miniaturization; a white locket or button; and tabby barring or striping in non-agouti varieties.

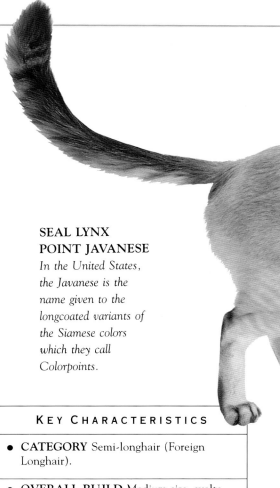

SEAL LYNX POINT JAVANESE

In the United States, the Javanese is the name given to the longcoated variants of the Siamese colors which they call Colorpoints.

KEY CHARACTERISTICS

- **CATEGORY** Semi-longhair (Foreign Longhair).

- **OVERALL BUILD** Medium size, svelte and elegant.

- **COAT** Fine and silky.

- **COLORS** (*UK and Europe*) As for the Oriental Shorthair – black, blue, chocolate, lilac, red, cream, cinnamon, fawn, tortoiseshell (all colors), smoke (all colors), tabby (all colors), tabby-tortoiseshell or torbie (all colors). The eye color for all color varieties is vivid, intense green.

- **OTHER FEATURES** Medium-sized head, a long, tapering wedge which starts at the nose and gradually increases in width in straight lines on each side to the ears, with no whisker break in these lines. Long, straight nose, continuing the line from the forehead without a break; medium-sized chin, its tip lining up with the nose in the same vertical plane; medium-sized eyes, almond shaped, and set slightly slanted toward the nose; ears are wide-based, large and pointed, placed to continue the lines of the wedge; body is long, svelte, well muscled but dainty, with the shoulders no wider than the hips. Legs are long and fine, in proportion to the body, ending in small, dainty, oval paws; tail is very long and thin, tapering to a fine point, with the hair spreading out like a plume.

BLUE LYNX POINT JAVANESE

The Javanese has the same type and conformation as Siamese and Orientals, and is long and svelte with fine bones. The coat is fine and silky, and very easy to care for.

251

INDEX

Page numbers in *Italic* refer to illustrations and captions

A

Abyssinian, 8, 14, *15*, *24*, 164–7, *164*
　Beige-Fawn, 167, *167*
　Black SIlver, 167
　Blue, 166, *167*
　Blue Silver, 167
　Sorrel (Red), 166, *167*
　Usual (Ruddy), 166, *166*
ACA *see* American Cat Association
ACC *see* American Cat Council
ACFA *see* American Cat Fanciers' Association
American Cat Association (ACA), 44
American Cat Council (ACC), 44
American Cat Fanciers' Association (ACFA), 45
American Curl, 40
American Shorthair, 146–7, *146*
American Wirehair, *22*, *31*, 154–5, *154*
Angora, 58, 60, 63, 94, 112–15, *112*
　Bi-color, 114–15
　Black, 114, *115*
　Black Smoke, 115
　Blue, 114
　Blue Smoke, 115
　Blue Tabby, 115
　Blue-cream, 114
　Brown Tabby, 115
　Calico, 114
　Cream, 114
　Odd-eyed White, *114*
　Red, 114
　Red Tabby, 115
　Silver Tabby, 115
　Tortoiseshell, 114
　Turkish, 88, 112
　White, 114, *114*
anthelmintics, 46
anus, *49*
Asian Black, *215*
Asian Group, *221*
　Ticked Tabby, *221*
Asian Smoke, 221
Asian Tabby, 221

B

Balinese, 234–48, *234*
　Blue Point, 236, *236*
　Blue Tabby Point, 237
　Blue Tortie Point, 236
　Blue Torbie Point, 237

Chocolate Point, 236
Chocolate Tabby Point, 237
Chocolate Tortie Point, 236, *237*
Chocolate Torbie Point, 237
Cream Point, 236, *237*
Cream Tabby Point, 237
Lilac Point, 236
Lilac Tabby Point, 237
Lilac Tortie Point, 236
Red Point, 236
Red Tabby Point, 237
Seal Point, 236
Seal Tabby Point, 236–7, *237*
Seal Tortie Point, 236
Seal Torbie Point, 237
Bast (cat goddess), 10, 11, *11*, 13
beckoning cat, 13, *13*
behavior, 8, 26–31
　communication, 30–31, *30*, *31*
　hunting, 8, 26–7
　sexual, 32–4, *32*, *33*, *34*
　sleeping, 28, *28*
　washing, 29, *29*
Bengal, 184–7, *184*
　blue-eyed Sonw, 187
　Brown Snow, 187
　Brown Spotted, *186*
　Brown Tabby, 186
　Leopard Spotted, 186
　Marble-Patterned, 186, *187*
　Snow, *187*
Birman, *15*, 88–93, *88*
　Blue Point, 90, *90*, 92
　Blue Tabby Point, 92, *92*
　Blue Tortie Point, 93
　Blue Torbie Point, 93
　Chocolate Point, 90, *91*, 92
　Chocolate Tabby Point, 92
　Chocolate Tortie Point, 93
　Chcolate Torbie Point, 93
　Cream Point, 91
　Cream Tabby Point, 92
　Lilac Point, 91, *91*, 92
　Lilac Tabby Point, 92
　Lilac Tortie Point, 93
　Lilac Torbie Point, 93
　Red Point, 91
　Red Tabby Point, 92, *93*
　Seal Point, 90, *90*, 92
　Seal Tabby Point, 92, *93*
　Seal Tortie Point, 92, *92*
　Seal Torbie Point, 92
Blue Persian Society, 64
body language, 30
body shape, 16–25
Bombay, 214–15, *214*, *215*, 221
breeding, 38–41
　gestation chart, 39
　selective, 11, *11*, 40, *40*
　starting out, 38, 40
　symbolizing genes, 41, *41*
Burmese, *15*, 25, 30, 88, 200–205, *200*
　Blue, 202, *204*
　Blue-cream (Blue Tortie), 205, *205*
　Chocolate (Champagne), 202, *204*

Chocolate Tortie, 205, *205*
Cream, 202, *203*
Lilac (Platinum), 202, *204*
Lilac-cream (Lilac Tortie), 205
Pointed varieties, 205
Red, 202, *203*
Sable (Brown), 202, *203*
Seal Tortie, 205
Burmilla, 27, 216–20, *216*
　Black Shaded (or Tipped), 218, *218*, 220
　Blue Shaded (or Tipped), 218, *420*
　Blue Tortoiseshell Shaded (or Tipped), 219
　Brown Shaded (or Tipped), 218, *219*
　Brown Tortoiseshell Shaded (or Tipped), 220
　Chocolate Shaded (or Tipped), 218, *219*
　Chocolate Tortoiseshell Shaded (or Tipped), 220
　Cream Shaded (or Tipped), 219
　Lilac Shaded (or Tipped), 219
　Lilac Tortoiseshell Shaded (or Tipped), 220
　Red Shaded (or Tipped), 219
　Red Tortoiseshell Shaded (or Tipped), 219

C

CA *see* Cat Association of Britain
calicivirus, 46
Calico cat *see* Persian, Tortoisehell and White
Canadian Cat Association (CCA), 44
cat care, 46–8, *46*, *47*, *48*
carbohydrates, 53
castration, *37*
Cat Association of Britain (CA), 44, 45
Cat Fanciers' Association (CFA), 44
Cat Fanciers' Fedderation (CFF), 44
cat fights, 32–3, *33*
cat 'flu, 46
cat shows, 42–3, *42*, *43*
cats
　behavior *see* behavior
　breeding *see* breeding
　domestication of, 11
　feeding, 52–3, *52*, *53*
　female, *32*, 34, *34*
　lifespan, 47
　male, 32–3, *32*
　stud, 40
CCA *see* Canadian Cat Association

CCFF *see* Crown Cat Fanciers' Federation
Central Maine Coon Cat Club, 94
CFA *see* Cat Fanciers' Association
CFF *see* Cat Fanciers' Federation
character, 8
Chartreux, 134–5, *134*
China, 13
Chinchilla, *15*, *42*
Chintz cat *see* Persian, Tortoiseshell and White
claws, 20, *20*, *50*
coat
　colors and patterns, 23–5
　　Abyssinian, *24*
　　colored tips, 24
　　Himalayan, *24*
　　multiple colors, *25*
　　solids, *23*
　　tabby colors, *23*
　　tabby markings, *23*
　　Tonkinese, *25*
　types, 22, *22*
Colorpoint Longhair, 78–9, 78–81, *78*
　Blue Point, 80, *80*
　Blue-cream Point, 81
　Chocolate Point, 80
　Cream Point, 81, *81*
　Lilac Point, 80–81
　Red Point, 81, *81*
　Seal Point, 80, *80*
　Tortie Point, 81
Colorpoint Persians, 78–9, *78*, 82
Colorpoint Shorthair, 230–33, *230*
　Blue Lynx Point, 232
　Blue-cream Point, 232–3
　Chocolate Lynx Point, 232
　Chocolate Tortie Point, 232, *232*
　Cream Point, 232
　Lilac Lynx Point, 232
　Lilac-cream Point, 233
　Red Lynx Point, 232
　Red Point, 232
　Seal Lynx Point, 232
　Seal Tabby Point, 233
　Seal Tortie Point, 232, *233*
communication, 30–31, *30*, *31*
Cornish Rex, 14, *22*, 188–91, *188*
　Black Smoke Van Pattern, *190*
　Black Smoke and White, *190*
　Chocolate Smoke, *191*
　Choclate Tortie, *191*
　Red, *190*
　Tortie Smoke and White, *191*
　White, *191*
Crown Cat Fanciers' Federation (CCFF), 44
Cymric, 139
　Tortoiseshell, *139*

D

deafness, 60
declawing, 20
descent of the modern cat, *12*
Devon Rex, *22*, 192–5, *192*,
    194, 195
    Black Smoke Devon Rex,
        194
    Chocolate Tortie Point, *194*
    Lilac Point, *195*
    Odd-eyed White, *194*
    Tortie Tabby, *195*
    Tortie Tabby and White, *195*
diet *see* feeding
Dinictis, 10
diseases, 46

E

ears, 19, *19, 49*
Egypt, ancient, 11, 13
Egyptian Mau, 180–81, *180*
    Bronze, *181*
    Silver, *181*
    Smoke, *181*
Estrus, 34, *34, 40*
eyes, 18, *18, 21, 49*

F

facial expressions, *31*
falling, *17*
fats, 53
Federation Internationale Feline
    (FIFe), 44, 45
feeding, 46, 52–3, *52, 53*
Felidae, 11
feline associations and
    governing bodies, 44–5
feline leukaemia virus, 46
Felis catus, 41
Felis chaus, 11
Felis domesticus, 11
Felis lunensis, 11
Felis lybica, 11
FIFe *see* Federation
    Internationale Feline
fleas, 46, 49
Flehmen Reaction, 18, *18*
Foreign Shorthairs, 17, 21, *21*,
    164–221
    Abyssinian, 8, 164–7, *164*
    Asian, 221, *221*
    Bengal, 184–7, *184, 187*
    Bombay, 214–15, *214, 215*,
        221
    Burmese, 88, 200–205, *200*,
        202, 203, 204, 205
    Burmilla, 216–20; *216, 218*,
        219, 220

Colorpoint, 224–5, 230–33,
    230, 232, 233
Cornish Rex, 188–91, *188*,
    190, 191
Deveon Rex, 192–5, *192*,
    194, 195
Egyptian Mau, 180–81, *180*,
    181
Havan Brown, 178–9, *178*,
    179
Japanese Bobtail, 198–9, *198*,
    199
Korat, 176–7, *176, 177*
Ocicat, 182–3, *182, 183*
Russian Blue, 174–5, *174*,
    175
Seychellois, 249, *249*
Siamese, 88, 174, 224–9
Singapura, 207, *207*
Somali, 168–73, *168*
Sphynx, 196–7, *196, 197*
Tiffanie, 206, *206, 221*
Tonkinese, 208–13, *208, 210*,
    211, 212, 213

G

GCCF *see* Governing Council
    of the Cat Fancy
genes, 41
gestation chart, 39
Governing Council of the Cat
    Fancy (GCCF), 43, 44, 45
grooming, 48, *48*

H

Havana Brown, 178–9, *178*,
    179
head, 21, *21*
health, 49–54
    regime of care, 54
    signs of ill health, 50, *51*
    watching out for problems, 49
hearing, 19, *19*
Himalayan, *24, 88*
    see also Colorpoint Longhair
hunting, 8, 26–7, *27*

I

India, 13
infectious enteritis, 46
International Society for the
    Preservation of the Maine
    Coon, 95

J

James, Mrs H.V., 66
Japan, 13
Japanese Bobtail, 25, 198–9,
    198
    Black and White Van
        Pattern, *199*
    Blue-eyed Van, *199*
    Brown Tabby and White, *199*
    Javanese 250–51, *250*
    Blue Lynx Point, *251*
    Seal Lynx Point, *251*
Javanese (Oriental), 114

K

Kashmir, 84, *84*
kittens
    birth, 35–6, *35*
    development, 36, *36, 37*
    and sexual behaviour, 32, *33*
    sexual differences, 32
Korat, 176–7, *176, 177*

L

lifespan, *47*
lion-cats, 13
litter tray, 36, 46, *47, 49, 50*
Longhairs, 58–85, *58, 88, 89*,
    112, 156
    Balinese *see* Balinese
    Bi-color, 70–71
    Black, 60, 61, *61*
    Black Smoke, 66, *67*
    Black and White Bi-color, 70,
        70
    Blue, 60, 64, *64*
    Blue Point Counterpoint, 80,
        80
    Blue Smoke, 67, *67*
    Blue Tabby, 73, *74*
    Blue Tabby Point, 82–3
    Blue Tortie, 65
    Blue Tortie Tabby, *74*
    Blue Tortie and White, *75*
    Blue and White Bi-color, 70,
        71
    Blue-cream, 65, *65, 75*
    Blue-cream Cameo, *69*
    Blue-cream Point Colorpoint,
        81, *83*
    Blue-cream Smoke, *68*
    Blue-eyed White, 60, *60*
    Brown, 62
    Brown Tabby, 72, 73, *73*
    Brown Tortie Tabby, *74*
    Cameo, 69, *69*
    Cameo Tasbby, *73*
    Chinchilla, 76

Chinchilla Golden, 76, *77*
Chinchilla Silver, 76, *76*
Chocolate, 84, *84*
Chocolate Point Colorpoint,
    80
Chocolate Smoke, 67, *68*
Chocolate Tabby Point, *83*
Chocolate Tortie, *75*
Chocolate Tortie Colorpoint,
    83
Chocolate Tortie tabby, *74*
Colorpoint *see* Coloupoint
    Longhair
Cream, 62, 63, *63*
Cream Point Colorpoint, 81,
    81
Cream Smoke, 6
Cream Tabby, *73*
Cream and White Bi-color,
    70, *71*
Dilute Calico, *75*
grooming, *48*
Himalaya *see* Colorpont
    Longhair
Javanese *see* Javanese
Lilac, 84, *85*
Lilac Point Colorpoint,
    80–81
Lilac Smoke, *67*
Lilac Tabby Point, *83*
Lilac Tortie Smoke, *68*
Lilac-cream, *85*
Mackerel Tabby, *72*
Odd-eyed White, 60, *60*
Orange, 62
Orange Self, 62
Orange Tabby, 62
Orange-eyed White, 60, *60*
Persian *see* Persian
Pewter, *77*
Red, 62, *62*
Red Chinchilla, *69*
Red Point Colorpoint, 81, *81*
Red Shaded, *69*
Red Shell, *69*
Red Smoke, 67, *68*
Red Tabby, 62, 72, 73, *73*
Red Tabby Point, *82*
Red and White Bi-color, 70,
    70
Seal Point Colorpoint, 80, *80*
Seal Tabby Point, 82, *82*
Seychellois *see* Seychellois
Shaded Cameo (Red
    Shaded), *69*
Shaded Golden, *77*
Shaded Silver, 76–7, *77*
Shell Cameo (Red
    Chinchilla), *69*
Shell Tortoiseshell, *69*
Silver Tabby, *15*, 72, *72*
Silver Tortie Tabby, *74*
Smoke, 66–7, *69*
Smoke Cameo, *69*
Smoke Tortoiseshell, *68*
Solid Points, 80–81
Tabby, 72–74
Tabby Points, 82–3
Tortie Point Colorpoint, *81*
Tortie Tabby, *73*
Tortoiseshell, 69, 75, *75*

Tortoiseshell and White, 75, 75
Van Bi-color, 71, *71*
lordosis, *34*

M

Maine Coon, *22*, 94–9, *94*, 106
Bi-color, 96
Black, 96
Black Smoke, 97
Blue, 96
Blue Smoke, 97
Blue Tabby, 98
Blue-cream, 96
Blue-cream and White, 96, *96*
Blue-cream-and-white, 96, *96*
Brown Mackerel Tabby, 98
Brown Tabby, 98
Calico, 96
Cameo Tabby, 99
Cream, 96
Cream Smoke, 97
Cream Tabby, 98
Green-eyed White, 96
Mackerel Tabby and White, 98
Red, 96
Red Smoke, 97
Red Tabby, 98
Shaded Red, 97, *97*
Shaded Silver, 97
Silver Tabby, 98, 99
Silver Torbie and White, 99
Tabby, 94
Tabby-and-white, 99
Tortie tabby, 99, *99*
Tortie Tabby-and-white, 99
Tortoiseshell, 96
White, 96
male cats, 32–3, *32*
Maltese Blue *see* Russian Blue
Manx, *14*, 136–9, *136*
Martelli's wildcat, *11*
maternity, 35–7, *35*, *36*
mating, *34*, 34, 40
meals, 49, 52–3, *52*, *53*
Miacis, 11
minerals, 53
mouth, 49
muscles, *17*

N

National Cat Club, 66
neutering, 37, *37*
Norsk Skaukatt see Norwegian Forst Cat
Norwegian Forest Cat, 106–9, *106*, *112*

Bi-color, 110
Black, 112
Black Smoke, 111, *111*
Blue, 112
Blue Silver Tabby, *113*
Blue Smoke, 111
Blue Tabby, 113
Blue-cream, 110
Blue-cream-and-white, 110
Brown Tabby, 113, *113*
Brown ticked Tabby, *113*
Calico, 110
Chinchilla, 111
Cream, 112
Cream Tabby, 113
Red, 112
Red Shaded Cameo, 111
Red Shell Cameo, 111
Red Silver Tabby and White, *113*
Red Smoke, 111
Red Tabby, 113
Red and White, *110*
Shaded Silver, 111
Silver Tabby, 113
Tortoiseshell, 110, *110*
White, 112, *112*
nose, 49
nutritional requirements, 53

O

Ocicat, 182–3, *182*
Black Silver, *183*
Blue Spotted, *183*
Chocolate Silver, *183*
onychectomy, 20
Orange, Cream, Fawn and Tortoiseshell Society, 62
Oriental, *22*, 238–48, *238*
Black, 240
Black Silver Spotted, *247*
Black Smoke, 248
Black Tabby, 244
Black Tortie, 243
Blue, 240, *240*
Blue Tabby, 244
Blue Tortie, 243
Caramel, 241
Caramel Spotted Tabby, *244*
Caramel Tabby, 246
Caramel Tortie, 243
Chestnut, 241
Chestnut Brown Foreign, 240
Chestnut Tabby, 244–5
Chocolate, 241
Chocolate Classic Tabby, *244*
Chocolate Silver Shaded, 248
Chocolate Spotted Tabby, *245*
Chocolate Tabby, 244–5
Chocolate Ticked, *245*
Chocolate Tortie, 243
Chocolate Tortie Silver Ticked, *247*
Cinnamon, 241, *241*

Cinnamon Spotted, *246*
Cinnamon tabby, 246
Cinnamon Ticked, *246*
Cinnamon Tortie, 243
Classic Tabby, 244
Cream, 242, *242*
Cream Tabby, 245
Ebony Tabby, 244
Fawn, 242
Fawn Tabby, 246
Foreign White, 240, *240*
Havana Brown, 240, *241*
Lavender Tabby, 245
Lavender-cream, 243
Lilac, 241, *241*
Lilac Tabby, 245
Lilac Tortie, 243
Mackerel Tabby, 244
Patched Tabby, 247
Red Self, 242, *242*
Red Tabby, 245
Shaded, 248
Siamese White, 240
Silver Tabby, 246
Smoke, 248
Spotted Tabby, 244
Ticked Tabby, 244
Tipped, 248
Tortie, 243, *243*
Tortie Tabby, 247
White, 240, *240*
Oriental breeds, 10, *10*, 17, 20, 21, 27, 52
see also Balinese; Colorpoint; Javanese; Oriental; Seychellois; Siamese
Oriental (Javanese), 114
origins, 11–15

P

panleukopaenia, 46
parasites, 46
Persian, 11, *11*, 14, 17, 20, 21, *21*, 22, 27
see also Longhairs, Persian
points system, 43
proteins, 53
Pseudaelurus, 11

R

Ragdoll, 100–104, *100*
Blue Bi-color, 103
Blue Colorpoint, 104, *104*
Blue Mitted, 102, *102*
Chocolate Bi-color, 103, *103*
Chocolate Mitted, 102
Lilac Colorpoint, 104, *104*
Lilac Mitted, 102
Seal Bi-color, 103, *103*

Seal Colorpoint, 104, *104*
Seal Mitted, 102, *102*
Rex cats, 17
see also Cornish Rex; Devon Rex
rhinotracheitis, 46
Ross, Charles H., 58, 63
Russian Blue, *15*, 174–5, *174*, *175*

S

scent marking, *27*
Scottish Fold, *40*, 140–41, *140*
scratching post, *47*, 50
self-righting reflex, *17*
Semi Longhaired *see* Angora; Birman; Javanese; Maine Coon; Norwegian Forest Cat; Ragdoll; Snowshoe; Turkish
sexual behaviour, 32–4, *32*, *33*, *34*
sexual differences, *32*
Seychellois, 249, *249*
Huitieme, 249
Neuvieme, 249
Septieme, 249
Shorthairs, *14*, *20*, 21, *21*, *22*
Colorpoint *see* Colorpoint Shorthair
grooming, 48
Shorthairs, American, 17, 146–53, *146*
Blue Patched tabby, 153
Blue Tabby, 149, *149*
Brown Patched Tabby, 153, *153*
Brown Tabby, 151
Brown Torbie, *152*
Cameo Tabby, 151, *151*
Classic Tabby, 148, 149, *150*
Cream Tabby, 151
Mackerel Tabby, 149, *150*
Marbled Tabby, 148
Patched Tabby or Torbie, 153
Red Tabby, 151, *151*
Silver Patched Tabby, 153
Silver Tabby, 148, *152*, 153
Spotted Tabby, 148
Shorthairs, American Wirehair, 154–5, *154*
Black and White, 155
Shorthairs, British, 17, 120–33, *120*, 148
Bi-color, 124–5
Black, 122, *122*
Black SMoke, 132
Black Tipped, 133
Blue, 122, 123, *123*
Blue Calcio, 127
Blue Cream Coloupoint, *133*
Blue Smoke, *30*, 132
Blue Spotted, *129*
Blue Tabby, 131, *131*
Blue and White Bi-color, 125
Blue-cream, 124, *124*

Blue-eyed White, 122, *122*
Brown Classic Tabby, *128*
Brown Spotted, *128*
Brown Tabby, 130
Chocolate Tortie, *126*
Classic Tabby, 128–9
Colorpointed, *132*
Cream, 123, *123*
Cream Colorpoint, *132*
Cream Tabby, 131
Cream and White Bi-color, *125*
Lilac, *124*
Lilac Cream Colorpoint, *133*
Lilac Tortie, *126*
Mackerel Tabby, *128*, 129
Orange-eyed White, 122
Red Colorpoint, *132*
Red Mackerel Tabby, *128*
Red Silver Tabby, *131*
Red Tabby, 130, *130*
Silver Spotted, *129*
Silver Tabby, 130, *130*
Spotted Tabby, 128, *129*
Tabby, 128–31
Torbie, *131*
Tortoiseshell, 126, *126*
Tortoiseshell-and-white, 127, *127*
White, 122
Shorthairs, chartreux, 134–5, *134*
Shorthairs, European, 17, 142–5, *142*
Bi-color, 145
Classic tabby, *145*
Mackerel Tabby, *145*
Smoke, 144
Solid, 144
Tabby Van, 145
Tabby varieties, 144
Tortie, 144, *145*
White, 144
Shorthairs, Exotic, 17, 156–61, *156*
Bi-color, 159
Black, 158
Blue, 158, *158*
Blue Calico, *160*
Blue Tabby Colorpoint, *159*
Blue and White, *159*
Blue-cream, 160
Blue-cream Smoke, *161*
Blue-cream and White, 160
Brown Tabby, *160*
Calico, 160
Chinchilla, 160
Chinchilla Golden, 160
Chocolate, 158
Classic Tabby, 159
Color Pointed, 161
Cream, 158, *158*
Lilac, 158
Mackerel Tabby, 159
Red, 158
Shaded Golden, 160
Shaded Silver, 160, *161*
Shaded Tortoiseshell, 161
Shell Tortoiseshell, 161
Silver Tabby, *161*
Smoke, 161
Spotted Tabby, 159

Tipped, 161
Tortie Tabby, 159
Tortoiseshell, 160
Van Bi-color, 159
Van Blue-cream and White, 159
Van Tri-color, 159
White, 158
Shorthairs, Foreign *see* Foreign Shorthairs
Shorthairs, Manx, 136–9, *136*
Blue Tortie and White, *139*
Cymric, 139
Red Spotted, *138*
Tortie Tabby and White, *138*
Tortoiseshell Cymric, *139*
Shorthairs, Oriental, 238–48
Shorthairs, Scottish Fold, 140, *140*
Black and White, *141*
Calico Fold, *141*
Longhaired variety, *141*
Patched Silver Tabby and White, *141*
showing, 42–3, *42*, *43*
Siamese, *15*, 17, *38*, 88, 174, 224–9, *224*
Blue Point, 224, 226, *437*
Blue Tabby Point, 228, *229*
Blue Torbie Point, 229
Blue Tortie Point, 228
Chocolate Point, 224, *227*, *227*
Chocolate Tabby Point, 228
Chocolate Torbie Point, 229
Chocolate Tortie Point, 228
Cream Point, *227*, 228
Cream Tabby Point, 229
Frost Tabby Point, 228
Frost Torbie Point, 229
Frost Tortie Point, 228
Lilac Point (Frost Point), *227*, 228
Red Point, 226, *226*
Red Tabby Point, 229, *229*
Seal Point, 224, 226, *226*
Seal Tabby Point, 228
Seal Torbie Point, 229
Seal Tortie Point, 227–8
sight, 18, *18*
Simpson, Frances, 63
Singapura, 207
Brown Ticked, *207*
skeleton, *17*
skin, *49*
sleeping, 28, *28*
smell, 18, *18*
Snowshoe, 105, *105*
solids
coat color, 23
Somali, 168–73, *168*
Blue, 170, *170*
Blue Silver, 172, *173*
Chocolate, 170–71, *171*
Chocolate Silver, 173
Fawn, 170, 171, *171*
Fawn Silver, 173
Lilac, 171
Lilac Silver, 173
Lilac Usual, 170, *170*
Red Silver, *172*
Silver, 170

Sorrel, 170, 171
Sorrel Silver, 173
Usual Silver, 172, *172*
spaying, *37*
Sphynx, *22*, 40, 196–7, *196*, *197*
Black and White, *197*
stud cats, 40

T
Tabbies
colors, *23*
markings, *23*
taste, 18
territorial marking, *27*
The International Cat Association (TICA), 45
TICA *see* The International Cat Association
Tiffanie, 206, *206*, 221
Brown Smoke, 206
tipping, *22*, *24*
toilet training, 36, *37*
Tonkinese, *25*, 208–13, *208*
Blue, 210, *212*
Blue Tortie, *213*
Champagne Mink, 210, *211*
Chocolate Tortie, *213*
Cream, *212*
Natural Mink, 210, *210*
Platinum Mink, 210, *211*
Platinum Mink Tortie, *213*
Pointed varieties, 210
Red, 210, *212*
Tortoiseshell colors, *25*
Turkish Van, 116–17, *116*
Auburn, *117*
Cream, *117*

U
UCF *see* United Cat Federation
United Cat Federation (UCF), 44

V
vaccination, 46, 49, 50, *51*
veterinarian, 50, *51*
vitamins, 53

W
washing, 29, *29*
weaning, 36, *37*
witches, 14, *14*

ACKNOWLEDGEMENTS

Quarto Publishing would like to thank all the owners who kindly allowed us to photograph their cats for inclusion in this book and Rose Forrester for her invaluable help in researching breed lists and approaching cat owners.

Additional photographs were supplied by: **Page 8** Nick Nicolson and Harry Rinker Jnr; **9** Solitaire Photographic; **11 l, c, t** archive; **11 r** Mansell Collection; **12** Ardea; **13 a** CM Dixon; **14 l** CM Dixon; **18 cl** Marc Henrie, Asc.; **21 b & 26 r** Solitaire Photographic; **27 cr** Marc Henrie, Asc.; **27 bl & 26 br** Solitaire Photographic; **28 al** Image Bank; **34 ar** Solitaire Photographic; **35 bl & 37** Marc Henrie, Asc.; **38, 42, 43** Solitaire Photographic; **50–51** Marc Henrie, Asc.; **53 ar** Bradley Viner; **54 ar** Solitaire Photographic; **148** TFH Publications, Inc.

Key: **a** above, **b** bottom, **c** centre, **l** left, **r** right, **t** top

All other photographs are the copyright of Quarto Publishing.